Queen Elizabeth's Englishings.

Early English Text Society.
Original Series, 113.

BERLIN: ASHER & CO., 13, UNTER DEN LINDEN.
NEW YORK: C. SCRIBNER & CO., LEYPOLDT & HOLT.
PHILADELPHIA: J. B. LIPPINCOTT & CO.

Queen Elizabeth's Englishings

OF

Boethius, *De Consolatione Philosophiae,* A.D. 1593,
Plutarch, *De Curiositate,*
Horace, *De Arte Poetica* (part), } A.D. 1598.

EDITED FROM THE UNIQUE MS, PARTLY IN THE QUEEN'S HAND,
IN THE PUBLIC RECORD OFFICE, LONDON

BY

MISS CAROLINE PEMBERTON.

WITH A FACSIMILE.

LONDON:
PUBLISHT FOR THE EARLY ENGLISH TEXT SOCIETY
BY KEGAN PAUL, TRENCH, TRÜBNER & CO.,
PATERNOSTER HOUSE, CHARING-CROSS ROAD.

OXFORD

Great Clarendon Street, Oxford OX2 6DP
United Kingdom

Oxford University Press is a department of the University of Oxford.
It furthers the University's objective of excellence in research, scholarship,
and education by publishing worldwide. Oxford is a registered trade mark of
Oxford University Press in the UK and in certain other countries

© The Early English Text Society 1900

The moral rights of the authors have been asserted

Database right Oxford University Press (maker)

First Edition published in 1900

All rights reserved. No part of this publication may be reproduced,
stored in a retrieval system, or transmitted, in any form or by any means,
without the prior permission in writing of Oxford University Press,
or as expressly permitted by law, or under terms agreed with the appropriate
reprographics rights organization. Enquiries concerning reproduction
outside the scope of the above should be sent to the Rights Department,
Oxford University Press, at the address above

You must not circulate this book in any other form
and you must impose this same condition on any acquirer

Published in the United States of America by Oxford University Press
198 Madison Avenue, New York, NY 10016, United States of America

British Library Cataloguing in Publication Data
Data available

Library of Congress Cataloging in Publication Data
Data available

Original Series, 113
ISBN 978-0-85-991865-7

EDITOR'S FOREWORDS.

NICOLAS in his *Progresses of Queen Elizabeth*, ed. 1823, vol. i., quotes the testimonies of Camden and Ascham to Elizabeth's learning, also Lambard's and North's in his *Plutarch*. Camden says she translated Sallust's *De Bello Jugurthino*, and in 1598 the greater part of Horace's *De Arte Poetica*, and a little treatise of Plutarch's *De Curiositate*. In vol. iii. p. 564, we read : " At Windsor she amused herself with translating Boethius's *De Consolatione*, 1593, as she had at Enfield done the like favour to Ochinus Sermon."

Two specimens of these translations, one from Seneca's Epistles, the other from Tully's, are printed in Harrington's *Nugæ Antiquæ*, vol. i. pp. 109—140, but these will not be found to bear out the hyperbolical praise of Sir Henry Savile, who affirms that " he hath seen some translations of Queen Elizabeth which far exceeded the originals." She translated from the French the "Meditations of the Queen of Navarre," also a Play of Euripides, and two Orations of Isocrates from Greek into Latin ; and wrote a Comment on Plato.

The Queen's Translation from the Greek of a Dialogue of Xenophon is printed at length in the Miscellaneous Correspondence of the *Gentleman's Magazine* for 1742, No. ii., with a *fac-simile* of an entire page.

In Bacon's Letters and Life by Spedding, Vol. i. 254-5, appears the following letter :

EARL OF ESSEX TO FRANCIS BACON, 24 AUG., 1593 :

" I told her [Q. Eliz.] that (= what, the attorneyship) I sought for you was not so much your good,—though it were a thing I would seek extremely and please myself in obtaining ; as for her honour, that those excellent translations of hers [1] might be known to them who could best judge of them."

[1] Alluding perhaps to some translations from Boethius, *De Consolatione*, with which she is said to have consoled herself after the news of the French king's apostasy.

In the British Museum is preserved a little MS. book of prayers in French, Italian, and Spanish, written in the Queen's own hand.

In the *History of the English People*, by J. R. Green, we read the following: "Elizabeth studied every morning the Greek Testament and followed this by the tragedies of Sophocles, or orations of Demosthenes, and could 'rub up her rusty Greek' at need to bandy pedantry with a Vice-Chancellor. But she was far from being a mere pedant. The new literature which was springing up around her found constant welcome in her court. She spoke Italian and French as fluently as her mother-tongue. She was familiar with Ariosto and Tasso. Even amidst the affectations and love of anagrams and puerilities which sullied her later years, she listened with delight to the *Faery Queen*, and found a smile for Master Spencer when he appeared in her presence." We have ample evidence still existing, to show that these accounts of Queen Elizabeth's classical attainments are trustworthy, for besides the translations which have already appeared in the *Gentleman's Magazine*, there may be seen in the Record Office in MS. her translations of the whole of the *Consolation of Philosophy*, of Plutarch's *De Curiositate*, and a fragment of Horace's *Ars Poetica*.

[1].With the translation of Boethius, on three separate sheets of letter paper, with label of contents at back, we find three accounts of the date of the translations, the year of Her Majesty's reign when it was made, and the time which it occupied in making. These accounts have probably been written by different persons at different times, for all three vary a little in their statements as to the miraculously short space of time in which Elizabeth performed the work, this varying between twenty-four and twenty-seven hours.

One of these flatterers even calculates that the Queen translated at the rate of one page of Boethius to every half-hour. In order to convince myself of the utter impossibility of such a feat, I copied as rapidly as possible one page of the specified length, which occupied me just half an hour; so with all due respect to the great genius of good Queen Bess, we can scarcely give her credit for being able to translate, not only prose but difficult poetry in the same time that an ordinary mortal could write it down. Here follow the three computations:

---

[1] A modern note in the MS. appears to refer to a translation of Boethius by Lidgate, printed by Tottel, 1554, folio, under the title of *A Treatise excellent and commodious, showing the Fall of Sundry most notable Princes*.

FOREWORDS.

I.

"The Computation of the dayes and houres in wch your Matie began and finished ye translation of Boëthius.

Your Matie began your translation of Boethius the tenth day of October, 1593, and ended it the fift of Nouember then next Immediatly following, which were fyue and twenty dayes in all.

Out of wch xxv. dayes are to be taken fowre Sondayes, three other hollydayes, and six dayes on which your Matie ryd abrode to take the ayre, And on those dayes did forbeare to translate, amounting togither to thirtene dayes,

Which xiij being deductid from xxv, remaynith then but twelue dayes.

And then accompting twoo houres only, bestowed euery day one w^t another in the translating. The computation fallith out, That in fowre and twenty houres, your Matie began and ended your translation.

> [1] Computation of the nomber of dayes and houres in wch your Matie began and ended the translation of Boëthius.
>   At Windsor.

II.

being at windsor in the xxxvth yeere of her Raigne,

The Queenes Matie began her translation of Boetius, vpon the xth of October, a° 1593, and ended it [2] vpon the eight of Nouember then next following, wch were xxx dayes.[3]

Of wch tyme, there are to be accomptpted [4] xiij [5] dayes, parte in Sondayes and holly dayes, and parte in her Maties ryding abrode, &c., taking the ayre, vpon wch her Matie did forbeare to translate.

So that xiij dayes being deducted [6] from xxx,[7] Remainyth xvij dayes, In wch her Matie finished her translation.

And in [8] those xvij dayes [9] her Matie did neuer exceed one houre & a halfe at a tyme in following her translation.[10]

Whereby it appeerith that in xxvj or xxvij houres,[11] her Matie perfourmed the wholle translation.

---

[1] At back of the paper.   [2] "about th" cancelled.   [3] "xxviij dayes" cancelled.
[4] "deducted" cancelled.   [5] Both "xj" and "xij" cancelled.
[6] "abated" cancelled.   [7] "xxviij" cancelled.   [8] "of" cancelled.
[9] "for the moste parte" cancelled.
[10] "not intend to her translation, aboue one houre and a halfe & som tyme not aboue an houre or little more" cancelled.
[11] "thirty houres, or rather in xxvj or houres," cancelled.

The nomber of leaves in my booke are 88. So that it must be that her Matie did translate v leaves at ech tyme, and iij leaves [1] ouer and aboue in the wholle tyme.

[2] 15. Nouembre. 1593.
A note of the dayes and hours in wch her Matie finished her translation of Boethius, *de consolatione Philosophiæ.*

III.[3]

The Queenes Matie being at Windsor in the xxxv^th yeere of her Raigne, vpon the xth of October, 1593, began her translation of *Boethius de consolatione Philosophiæ*, and ended it [4] vpon the eight of Nouember then next following, wch were xxx^ty dayes :

Of wch tyme there are to be accompted xiij dayes, parte in Sondayes and other holy dayes, and parte in her Maties ryding abrode, vpon wch her Matie did forbeare to translate,

So that xiij dayes being deducted from xxx^ty, Remaynith xvij dayes, In wch tyme her Matie finished her translation.

And in those xvij dayes, her Matie did not exceede one houre and a halfe at a tyme, in following her translating :

Wherby it apperith, that in xxvj houres or thaboute*s*, her Matie p*er*fou*r*med the wholle translation.

[5] Nouember 1593.
Note of ye tyme wherin her Matie began and ended her translation of Boethius.

Of the three translations before us that of Boethius is the one which will add most to the Queen's reputation as a scholar : it is tolerably exact and generally very literal. In a few places, as may be seen by reference to

---

[1] "vj leaves" cancelled.   [2] On back of letter.
[3] This is a fair copy of II., with slight variations. Both are in the same handwriting, doubtless that of the Queen's clerk or secretary. These papers are much more carefully written than when he wrote from dictation ; but there is at the end of the volume, a fair copy of a portion of the First Book, which removes any doubt there might be as to the identity of the handwriting. It was evidently intended that he should make a fair copy of the whole in his best style ; a project which was never carried out.   [4] "about the" cancelled.
[5] At back of the paper. In the margins of II. and III., "17. dayes" and "26. houres" are written opposite to the lines where those totals are given.

the footnotes, the Queen has mistaken the meaning of the Latin text. Most of the "Meters" are in her own hand, but she dictated the greater portion of the "Prose" to a clerk or secretary. The Queen's handwriting is not always very legible, and she has in many places so heavily corrected her text that it is difficult to make out her meaning. The Prose is also corrected in numerous passages, sometimes by the Queen herself. Owing to these circumstances, there are in some places readings which may be considered as doubtful or conjectural.

Mr. R. E. G. Kirk, who has collated proofs with the original MSS. in the Record Office, has sent the following very interesting information as to who the Queen's amanuensis was :

" The Queen dictated a large portion of *Boethius* to a clerk, but I felt sure that he was not an ordinary copyist, and therefore I endeavoured to find out who he was. I tried the handwritings of Sir John Herbert, Sir John Wolley, and Thomas Edmondes, Secretaries of the period, without success, and was about to give up in despair, when I accidentally saw two papers in a similar handwriting, and on looking at the *Calendar*, I found they were by Thomas Windebank, Clerk of the Signet in 1568, and Clerk of the Privy Seal in 1598. I then procured other volumes containing his letters, and found that he was certainly the Queen's amanuensis. I presume he was an ancestor of Sir Francis Windebank, Secretary of State to Charles I. In 1561-3 he attended Thomas Cecil, son of Sir William Cecil, in his travels in France and Germany, where the young gentleman seems to have got into many scrapes, and totally to have objected to " learning," to the disgust and anger of his father, between whom and Windebank there are numerous letters on the subject. The dates of Windebank's appointments, as given above, are taken from Thomas's *Historical Notes*. His counter-signatures to sign-manuals of Queen Elizabeth may be seen among the Cecil MSS. at Hatfield. There is a very curious letter from his wife, 2 June 1600, relating to some temporary estrangement between them ; a full abstract being given in the *State Papers Calendar*."

In exactitude of translation the three works appear to me to slide down in a descending scale in the order in which they appear, *Boethius* being indifferent, *Plutarch* bad, and *Horace* worse, being in many places absolutely unintelligible, probably because this was the most difficult of the three. Perhaps in the translation of *Horace* the Queen herself recognized the fact that she had undertaken a task above her powers, as she never completed the *Ars Poetica*, having translated only 178 of the 476 lines. *Plutarch* has evidently been translated from the original Greek, but both this and *Horace* have been left in the rough as they were at first written down, and no fair copy has been made.

The "Queen's English" appears to our modern ideas most defective, and her orthography to have been untrammelled by any rules whatever. The same word is seen on one page spelt in two or three different ways : *they, thee,* and *the* are all written *the ; to* and *too* are both *to ;* double *ee* is almost always *i ; it* is sometimes *hit ; sun* and *son* are both *son.* Capitals seem to be used quite indifferently, proper names being sometimes written without them and common words with them, occasionally a capital is even introduced into the middle of a word. *V* is always used as initial instead of *u* and sometimes also in the middle of a word, and there is a much more abundant use of *y* instead of *i* than at present, *if* being almost always written *yf.* It is also interesting to notice the remnants of French spelling in such words as *parfaict, accompt, coulor,* and many others.

Queen Elizabeth's translations are, as we have said, anything but exact, and she sometimes mistakes one Latin or Greek word for another in a way which is surprising in a person who was so well versed in these languages as she appears to have been. We cannot, nevertheless, but admire the intelligence and industry of a Queen, who, at the age of sixty, occupied as she must have been with state affairs and the multifarious other duties pertaining to her position, could yet find inclination to undertake such tasks and time to devote to them. Even the incentive of literary fame was wanting, for her translations, not being printed, were probably read only by the secretaries who copied some of them, so that it is evident that Elizabeth loved learning for its own sake.

Boethius, the author of the *Consolation of Philosophy,* was a noble Roman, who lived in the latter half of the fifth Century; he was well versed in the learning both of Rome and Athens, and filled the offices of Consul and Senator under Theodoric the Great. Falling however into disfavour with this despot, he was for many years imprisoned at Pavia, and finally, at the age of forty-five, put to a cruel death in prison. He translated some of Aristotle's works, and wrote a treatise on Music which was a standard work on the subject during the middle ages : his greatest creation however was the *Consolation of Philosophy,* written during the sad years of his imprisonment.

The *Consolation of Philosophy* was a very favourite book during the middle ages, it being read not only in Latin but also in various translations. It was first done into English by King Alfred, and he was followed by Chaucer, Caxton, Queen Elizabeth, and many other translators of minor note.

FOREWORDS.

The language of the *Consolation*, written in such a barbarous age, must, by the wonderful perfection of its style, excite universal admiration and surprise. It is mainly formed on the model of the best ancient authors of the golden age of literature, particularly Cicero in his philosophical writings, and not seldom reminds us of the manner of Seneca, or of the *Florida* of Apuleius. Boethius diverges chiefly from the style of Cicero in two points; first, by a more lucid setting forth of syllogisms, and by a more strictly logical sequence. We gain consequently in Boethius, in perspicacity, what we lose in rhetorical beauty, and this increased adoption of logical forms sometimes borders on the dryness and subtlety of Aristotle and the Scholastics.

The second point of divergence is in the strong poetic vein which not only runs through the sometimes exceedingly beautiful meters, but also in the pathetic tone of many of his prose pieces. There is no doubt that Boethius had a marvellous facility in expressing even his most intricate thoughts, which he did with perspicacity, and often with great power and beauty.

In a few of my footnotes, Elizabeth's translation of Boethius is compared with that of Chaucer made more than 200 years previously, and it is most interesting to note the changes which two centuries had wrought in our language. In order to give the reader a still better idea of these, I have placed a few lines of the two translations from the first Prose, side by side—

BOETHIUS, FIRST PROSE.	BOETHIUS, FIRST PROSE.
Q. Elizabeth.	*Chaucer.*
While of al this alone in silence I bethought me, and tearesful complaint in stiles office ment, ouer my hed to stand, a woman did apeare, of stately face, with flaming yees, of insight aboue the comun worth of men; of fresche coulor and unwon strength, thogh yet so old she wer, that of our age she seamed not to be one; her stature, suche as skarse could be desernd, for sume while she skanted her to	In þe mene while þat I stille recorded þise þinges wiþ my self, & markede my wepli compleynte wiþ office of poyntel. I saw stondyng aboue þe hey3t of my heued a woman of ful greet reuerence by semblaunt hir eyen brennyng & clere seing ouer þe comune my3t of men. wiþ a lijfly colo*ur* & wiþ swiche vigoure & strenkeþ þat it ne my3t not be emptid. Al were it so þat sche was ful of so greet age. þat men ne wolde not trowe in no manere þat sche were of oure elde. þe stature of hir was of a doutous iugement. for sum*t*yme sche constreyned & schronk

the comen stature of men, strait she semed, with croune of hed, the heauens to strike, and lifting vp the same hiar, the heauens them selues she enterd, begiling the sight of lookars on. Her wides, thé wer of smalist thrides, parfaict for fine workmanship and lasting substance, as, after by herself I knewe, was by her handes al wroght.	hir seluen lyche to þe comune mesure of men. & sumtyme it semed þat sche touched þe heuene wiþ þe hey3te of hir heued. and when sche hef hir heued heyer sche perced þe selue heuene. so þat þe sy3t of men lokyng was in ydel. Hir cloþes weren maked of ry3t delye þredes and subtil crafte of perdurable matere. þe wyche cloþes sche hadde wouen wiþ hir owen hondes: as I knew wel aftir by hir selfe.

It may be observed that Chaucer's translation is much longer than that of the Queen, and that the chief differences between the two translations are in the orthography, which undoubtedly also implies a change in pronunciation. Some of the obsolete words used by Chaucer have in the Queen's rendering given place to others which still survive, such as: *delyé, smalist, perdurable, lasting, elde, age.* On the other hand we find, contrary to expectation, the modern words in Chaucer's translation and the obsolete ones in that of Elizabeth, such as: *clothes* (*wides*), *shrunk* (*skanted*); which proves that the ancient word and the modern one were used indifferently for several centuries. The old plural *n* in *eyen* has changed into *s, yees,* and many of the old weak conjugations are supplanted by the more modern strong ones, *hef, heaued.*

"DE CURIOSITATE."

This is one of the many small *Scripta Moralia* which Plutarch, Procurator of Greece under the Emperor Adrian, has given us, besides his world-famed βίοι παράλληλοι (Comparative Lives).

In *De Curiositate* as well as in his other writings, Plutarch proves himself to be a true stoic philosopher, to possess first-rate moral principles and great fear of God. As a writer, he displays much erudition, of which he earnestly endeavours to make the most, but this he does with little taste, and is consequently often exaggerated and pedantic. His religious views sometimes remind us, like those of Seneca, of Christian teaching, but here there is always one important omission, viz. the commendation of charity or neighbourly love; of this Christian virtue, the stoic, so virtuous in his own estimation, knows absolutely nothing.

"ARS POETICA."

It would be as useless as to attempt to increase the volume of the sea by pouring water into it, as to add any comment to this most celebrated treatise of Horace. It has been published in the original and in translations more than a hundred times in England alone, and among the editors and commentators we find the names of bishops and lords.

Garfield, late President of the U.S.A., for the sake of recreation in his leisure hours, compiled a list of all the editions of Horace's writings which have appeared, one-third of these being English : the translation of a part of *Ars Poetica* by our Queen not being then in print was omitted.

Enclosed with the translation of Horace is the following.

Her Ma^{ty} being at Windesor in the 35th yeere of her Raigne began her translation of Boetius vpon the *10th* of October, *1593*, and ended it vpon the fyft of November then next ymediatly following, wch are fiue & twenty dayes.

Out of w^{ch} *25* daies are to be taken 4 sundayes, three other holy dayes, & sixe daies on wch her M^{ty} ryd abrode to take the ayre, & on those daies forbore to translate, in all *13* dayes, so as there remayneth then but twelue dayes.

And then accompting two howers onely bestowed every day one wth an other in the translating, the computacoñ falleth out that in *24* howers her Ma^{ty} began and ended the translacoñ.

Her Ma^{ty} likewise translated a peece of Salust de Bello Jugurthino, but in what yeere of her Raigne I finde not.

Item her M^{ty} translated a peece of Horace de Arte poetica about November, 1598.

Item her M^{ty} translated a treatise of curiosity written by Plutark, & put it into English miter, she begun it the third of Novem: 1598 & ended it the *9th* of the same moneth.

Note that she writt all these translations w^t her owne hand.

J. G. 17/3/83.

The Editorship of Q. Elizabeth's translations was at first undertaken by Walford D. Selby, but he dying just as he had begun the work, I was requested to take it up.

The comments on the writings of Boethius and Plutarch are by Dr. J. Schenk of Meran, Tyrol, who has also assisted me with the notes on the Latin and Greek text.

C. PEMBERTON.

NOTE ON Q. ELIZABETH'S USE OF *I* FOR OUR LONG *E*.

By F. J. FURNIVALL.

IN my Forewords to the *Life of St. Katharine of Alexandria*, I showed from John Hart that in Shakspere's time, in 1569 (and in 1551), our sound of long *i* in *time* was freely used. But looking at the proofs of Queen Elizabeth's englishings in the present volume, I saw that she—in many words, at least—kept the older sound of *i*, that of our present long *ē*. The list following contains most of her spellings of our *ē* as *i*.

1. The words with both *i* and *e* :—

brede 141/17 ; *breeding* 130/6 ; yet *bride* 122/22, 25, 45 ; 127/37 ; 134/14, 18 ; 141/17 ; *brid* 124/26
beleue 130/5 ; yet *beliue* (crede) 26/15 ; 39/2 ; 112/4
cleare 14/33 ; 61/29 ; 121/8 ; 142/51 ; *cleere* 105/1 ; yet *clire* 72/2 ; *clirely* 57/2 ; *clires* 65/10 ; *clirest* 19/21 ; 61/26 ; 65/9 ; *clirrist* 19/9
ded (deed) 137/1 ; 49/6 ; *dede* 121/17 ; 129/18 ; 133/2 ; 139/201 ; yet *dide* 133/26
feteles (feetless) 133/29 ; yet *fite* (*bedsfite*) 3/40
gredy 16/11 ; *gridy* 24/11 ; 34/25 ; 39/6 ; 41/8 ; 126/10 ; 128/28, 31 ; *gridely* (greedily) 108/12
greny (greeny) 116/7 ; 145/130 ; yet *griny* 1/7 ; 19/8 ; 56/3
greve 125/27 ; yet *grives* 124/12
hede (heed) 138/7 ; yet *hideful* 137/24 ; *hideles* 128/6 ; *hidely* (heedfully) 130/18
kepe 69/8 ; yet *kipe* 97/22 ; 134/26 ; *kipar* (keeper) 46/9 ; 47/15 ; *kipes* 109/27 ; 134/21
kept 109/29 ; yet *kipt* 41/9
metest 143/94 ; yet *mit* (vb. meet) 128/5
seke (seek) 131/8 ; yet *sike* 144/180 ; 146/181, 184 ; *sikes* 129/10
vnnedeles 134/18 ; yet *vnnideful* 132/8

2. The words with *i* (= *e*) only :—

besiche 72/28
besiged 84/19
betwine 72/28
chifest 74/57 ; 125/6 ; 142/43
chire (cheer) 7/4
dipe (deep) 136/41
(eyes—ees 135/19—*see* yees)
fild (field) 4/4 ; 44/1 ; 129/20 ; 142/22 ; fildz 16/10
file (feel) 136/39
flise (fleece, *vallera*) 33/8
Grikis (Greeks) 143/63
hirars (hearers) 139/3
hiresay (hearsay) 145/132
ivel (evil) 127/31 ; 129/35 ; 130/16 ; 131/7 ; 133/16, 32, 37 ; 135/7 ; 138/25 ; 140/8
iven (even) 127/28 ; 130/28 ; 140/9
myter (metre) 1, 4, &c.
nid (need) 129/9
nide (need) 8/4 ; 123/11 ; 137/17 ; 138/19
nidful 129/7
nides (needs) 122/42 ; 127/27
nire (near) 65/8 ; 143/78
pices (pieces) 3/20
plised (pleasd) 72/13 (cf. pleading 130/9)
shild (shield) 8/17
shipe (sheep) 130/14
sithing (seething) 36/13
skrigd (screecht) 138/19
slipes (*somnos*) 33/10 ; 144/118
slipith (sleepeth) 128/11
spiche (speech) 124/26 ; 142/57
spike (speak, vb.) 138/19
swit (sweet) 2/13 ; 47/25 ; swite 3/33
wides (weeds, clothes) 3/11, 15

yea (eye) 135/14 ; (yea—verily—136/1)
yee (eye) 123/5 ; 125/34
yees (eyes) 2/3, 16 ; 3/23, 38 ; 5/2, 14, 15 ; 6/3 ; 74/56 ; 113/30 ; 123/7 : 135/2, 10 ; 136/33
yeles (eyeless) 100/11

NOTE ON Q. ELIZABETH'S USE OF 'I' FOR OUR LONG 'E'. xvii

For *ea*, see ease 136/3; ease 136/44; easy 134/7; read 134/10. *Friends*, I suppose the Queen pronounst with our long *e*: frendz 141/7; friendz 127/34; 134/15; 137/11; 139/5 (Compare *kept*, *kipt* above). Whether she gave the same $\bar{e}$ sound to her other *i* words, I don't pretend to say; though, from 'gridy desire' 39/61; 'like the clirrist' 119/91; 'clirest light' 19/21, and like instances, I suppose she did. A few of these *i* words follow:—

affrights 16/10; 30/10
assigneth 16/16
begiling 3/10; begiled 16/5
bide 132/33; bidz (bides) 2/10
crime 14/35; crimes 6/7
denies 2/16
desiar 24/16; desire 39/6; 57/7
desire 24/16; 39/6
dispised 3/14
deprived 3/30
deuidest 13/17
drie 36/12; dried 5/15
espies 36/9
exile 6/6
fertile 4/16
finde 28/9
fires 7/8; 34/3
flying 39/10
gidar 14/27; gidest 14/45; giding 14/25
gileful 2/17; 57/1
hiar (higher) 2/9; hie *adj.*? 7/10; hiest 3/18; 6/6; 13/22; 30/8
hide *vb.* 56/5
hied 2/9
I 3/36; 6/1, 3, 5, &c.; 57/3 &c.

indites 1/3; inditing 3/23
insight 2/4
ire 7/14
life 2/18, 20; 7/1; 40/23
light 4/2, 5, 19; 19/3; 24/4
like 19/9; 22/4; 34/7
liue 112/2
lire (? liar) 19/23
mankind 24/7
mighty 21/3
mild 4/14
mildding 26/5
mind 4/1, 19; 19/29; mynd 3/43; 5/4; 6/2; 39/11
myne 36/5
night 5/1, 6
pine 33/12
prising 57/5
pride 34/6
quiet 7/1; 30/20
retire 39/8
rife 57/6
righmes (rymes) 1/1
ripe *vb.* 97/26
ripest 4/17
rising 13/11
shine 3/17
sight 3/37; 19/13
silence 2/1

Sirenes 3/33
skie 19/2; skies 4/4; 13/4; 24/3; 30/22
sliding 26/16
slite (slight) 142/35
smile 30/22
spitful 22/6
stile 2/2
strike 5/10; 7/9
striving 97/2
ties 14/41
time 2/10; 5/1; 34/23; times 16/16
tirant 7/12; 36/3
titelz 40/11
trie 22/7
unlike 6/31
uprise 13/12
vice 31/23
violence 9/29
violent 3/19
violets 16/8
whi 4/12; 5/7; 7/11
while 2/7
whitty (whitey) 26/4
wight 2/14
wipe 5/13
wries 3/15
write 1/3

Dr. Otto Jespersen will, I hope, treat the whole subject when he edits Hart's *Orthographie* for us.

In the spelling of Windebank, the Queen's scribe, I have not noted anything peculiar.

CONTENTS.

	PAGE
EDITOR'S FOREWORDS	vii
NOTE ON Q. ELIZABETH'S USE OF *I* FOR LONG *E*	xvi
TRANSLATIONS OF BOETHIUS'S *PHILOSOPHIÆ CONSOLATIONIS* :—	
BOOK I.	1
BOOK II.	20
BOOK III.	43
BOOK IV.	75
BOOK V.	102
PLUTARCH'S *DE CURIOSITATE*	121
HORACE'S *ARS POETICA* (A FRAGMENT)	142
GLOSSARY	161

I.
Boethius.
DE CONSOLATIONE PHILOSOPHIÆ.
(ENGLISHT BY QUEEN ELIZABETH A.D. 1593.)
[*Public Record Office. Domestic Elizabeth* 289.]

THE FYRST BOOKE.[1]
I. MYTER.[2]

Righmes that[3] *my groing studie ons perfourmed,*   Boethius de-
In teares, alas! cumpeld, woful staues begin.   plores his mis-
My muses torne, behold what write I shuld indites,   following elegy.
Wher tru woful uerse my face with dole bedews.   4
Thes at lest no terror might constrain,
    that felowes to our mone our way they shuld refrain.
The glory ons of happy griny[4] *Youthe,*
    Now, fates of grounting Age, my comfort all.   8

---

[1] This translation of Boethius is continuously in the Queen's own handwriting as far as the eleventh line of *Prose* 3 of the First Book; from this point, with the exception of the opening lines of *Prose* 4, a few lines of *Proses* 6 and 8 of the Second Book, and *Prose* 9 of the Third Book, the prose was dictated by the Queen, but almost all the *Metres* are in her hand only. The punctuation is not according to the Queen, but to the Latin edition.

[2] The Queen's somewhat halting *verses* (!) will be more readily understood by comparison with the original Latin *metres* of Boethius, which are given in this and subsequent footnotes.   [3] Over *Verse ons* struck through.

[4] *Sic*, for "greeny." The Queen, it will be noticed, frequently uses *i* for double *e*—. *e. g.* "switest" 2/13, "wides=weeds, clothes" 3/2, "fite=feet" 3/40, "chire= cheer" 7/41, etc.

METRUM I.
Carmina qui quondam studio florente peregi,
    Flebilis, heu, maestos cogor inire modos.
Ecce mihi lacerae dictant scribenda camenae,
    Et ueris elegi fletibus ora rigant.   4
Has saltim nullus potuit peruincere terror,
    Ne nostrum comites prosequerentur iter.
Gloria felicis quondam uiridisque iuuentae!
    Solantur maesti nunc mea fata senis.   8

Q. ELIZABETH'S ENGLISHING OF BOETHIUS'S [BK. I.

Laments his immature old age.

    Vnlookt for Age hied by mishaps is come,
      And Sorow bidz his time to add withal.
    Vnseasond hore heares vpon my hed ar powrd,
      And loosed skin in feable body shakes.   12

Death turns a deaf ear to the wretched.

    Blessed dethe, that in switest yeres refraines,
      but, oft calld, comes to the woful wights.
    O with how defe eare she from wretched wries,
      And wailing yees, cruel! to shut denies.   16

While fortune shone on him Death came near, but now, in adversity, life is protracted.

    While gileful fortune with vading goodz did shine,
      My life wel ny the doleful houre bereued;
    Whan her fals looke a cloude hath changed,
      My wretched life thankles abode protractz.   20
    Why me so oft, my frendz! haue you happy cald?
    Who fauleth downe in stedy step yet neuer stode.

I. PROSE.

Philosophy appears to Boethius.

    While of al this alone in silence I bethought me, and tearesful complaint in stiles office[1] ment, ouer my hed to

Her description.

stand a woman did apeare of stately face, with flaming yees, of insight aboue the comun worth of men; of fresche coulor and unwon strengh, thogh yet so old she wer, that of our age she seamed not be one; her stature suche as skarse could be desernd. For sume while she skanted her to the comen stature of men, strait she semed with croune of hed the heauens to strike, and lifting vp the same hiar, the heauens

---

[1] *Styli officio,* rendered by Chaucer—"with office of poyntel."

    Venit enim properata malis inopina senectus,
      Et dolor aetatem iussit inesse suam.
    Intempestiui funduntur uertice cani,
      Et tremit effeto corpore laxa cutis.   12
    Mors hominum felix, quae se nec dulcibus annis
      Inserit, et maestis saepe uocata uenit.
    Eheu, quam surda miseros auertitur aure,
      Et flentes oculos claudere sacua negat!   16
    Dum leuibus male fida bonis fortuna faueret,
      Paene caput tristis merserat hora meum.
    Nunc, quia fallacem mutauit nubila uultum,
      Protrahit ingratas impia uita moras.   20
    Quid me felicem totiens iactastis amici?
      Qui cecidit, stabili non erat ille gradu.

them selues she enterd, begiling¹ the sight of lookars on. Her wides thé² wer of smalist thrides, parfaict for fine workmanship and lasting substance, as, after by her selfe I knewe, was by her handes al wroght. Whose forme, as to smoky imagis is³ wont, a certain dimnis of dispisid antiquitie ouerwhelmed. Of thes wides in the loweste skirtz Π, in the vpper side a Θ, was reade, al woven. And betwine bothe lettars, ladarwise, certain steps wer marked, by wiche from lowest to hiest element ascent ther was. Yet that selfe garment the handz of violent men had torne, and pices suche as get thé could, away tha stole. Her right hand held a booke, the left a sceptar. Who, whan she spied poetz musis standing⁴ by my bed, and to my teares inditing wordes, somewhat moued, inflamed with gloting yees: "Who sufferd," quoth she, "thes stagis harlotz aproche this sik man? wiche not only wold not ease his sorow with no remedies, but with swit venom nourris them. Thes thé be that with baren affections thornes destroies the ful eares of reasons fruitt, and mens mynds with disease invres, not fries. But if of vane man, as vulgar wontz, your alurements had deprived me, with les grefe had I borne hit. For by suche our worke had got no harme. But this man haue you touched, whom Stoike⁵ and Academique study broght out. Get you away, Sirenes swite; til ende be seen, to my musis leve him for cure and helthe." To this the checked rabel, with looke downe cast with wo, with blusche confessing shame, doleful out of doores thé went. But I, whose sisght,⁶ drowned in teares, was dimed, could not knowe what she was, of so imperius rule, and settelling my yees on ground, what she wold more do, in silence, I attended. Than she, drawing nar, on my bedsfite sat doune, and, vewing my looke of hevy woe and with my dole to the erthe throwne downe, in versis thes of my mynds pane complaineth thus.

Her clothes were finely worked, but dim from age

On the lowest skirt was the letter Π, and in the upper side Θ.

Her garment was torn. In her right hand she held a book, in the left a sceptre.

Philosophy asks who allowed the Muses to approach Boethius, as they would only increase his sorrow with their sweet venom.

Had their allurements deprived her of some profane person, she had grieved less, but they have touched one brought up in Eleatic and Academic studies. She dismisses the Syrens.

Boethius fails to recognize Philosophy.

who complains of the disorder of his mind in these verses.

---

¹ Originally "and begiled"; corrected in a blacker ink.
² *They* and *thee* are both in this translation written "the"; I distinguish therefore between them by "thé" for *they* and "thè" for *thee*.
³ Written over *was* struck out.   ⁴ Written over *sitting* struck out.
⁵ The Queen has, instead of *Eleaticis*, which all the MSS. give, read "Stoicis."
⁶ *Sic*.

II. MYTER.

Earthly cares, which he formerly dissipated by the study of astronomy, now darken the mind of Boethius.

O, in how hedlong depth the drowned mind is dimme!
and Losing Light, her owne, to others darkenis¹ drawne,²
as oft as driuen with erthely flawes the harmful care upward
    grows.
Wons this man fre in open fild used the skies to vew,   4
of Rose³ son the Light beheld,
of frosty mone the planetes saw;
And what star elz runs her wonted cours,
    bending by many Circles, this man had wone   8
by number to knowe them all,
Yea, Causis eache whens roring windz the seas perturbz :
acquainted with the spirit that rolles the stedy world,
And whi the star that falz to the Hisperias waters   12

He is no longer able to investigate the problem of the change of seasons, and his whole thoughts are now mournfully bent on his earthly sufferings.

from his reddy roote,⁴ dothe raise her self,
Who that gives the springes mild houres ther temper,
that with rosy floures the erthe be deckt?
Who made the fertile Autumne at fullist of the yere,   16
Abound with Grape al Solne⁵ with ripest fruits?
he, wonted to serche and find sondry causes of hiden nature,
downe lies of mindz Light bereued,
With brused Nek by overheuy Chaines.   20
A bowed Lowe, Looke! by waight bearing,
driven, alas! the Sely erthe behold.

---

¹ The text has "*externas tenebras*," translated "others darkenes," perhaps an error for "outer."
² *drawne* is doubtful. This line was originally—"And losing her light strives to run in others darkenis."   ³ *ly* struck out.
⁴ *spring* struck out. The Queen has here translated *ortus* by "root," whereas the correct meaning is "east" or "sunrise."   ⁵ swoln.

METRUM II.

Heu quam praecipiti mersa profundo
Mens hebet, et propria luce relicta
Tendit in externas ire tenebras,
Terrenis quotiens flatibus aucta   4
Crescit in inmensum noxia cura.
Hic quondam caelo liber aperto
Suetus in aetherios ire meatus
Cernebat rosei lumina solis,   8
Visebat gelidae sidera lunae;
Et quaecumque uagos stella recursus
Exercet uarios flexa per orbes,
Conprensam numeris uictor habebat.   12
Quin etiam causas unde sonora
Flamina sollicitent acquora ponti,
Quis uoluat stabilem spiritus orbem
Vel cur hesperias sidus in undas   16
Casurum rutilo surgat ab ortu,
Quid ueris placidas temperet horas,
Vt terram roseis floribus ornet!
Quis dedit ut pleno fertilis anno   20
Autumnus grauidis influat uuis?
Rimari solitus atque latentis
Naturae uarias reddere causas;
Nunc iacet effeto lumine mentis,   24
Et pressus grauibus colla catenis
Decliuemque gerens pondere uultum,
Cogitur, heu! stolidam cernere terram.

II. PROSE.

"But fittar time," q*uoth* she, "for medecin than Com-plaint." Than fixing on me her stedy yees: "Art thou the same," q*uoth* she, "who ons nourriched wit*h* my milke, fed[1]
4 .wit*h* our foode art growen to stre*n*gh of manly mynd? On whom we bestowed suche weapons as, if thou hadst not Cast away, had saved thè wit*h* invi*n*cible strengh. Dost thou me knowe? whi art thou doum? is hit shame or wo*n*dar makes
8 thè Silent[2]?" But Wha*n* she spied me not only stiL, but Woordles and dum, on my brest gently Layd her hand: Said, "ther is no danger, he is entered in a Lethargi, a Co*m*men diseace of mynd distract. He hath a litel forgotten
12 himself, easily his memory wyl retorne, Wha*n* first he hathe remembard me. And that he may, a litel Let us wipe his yees overdimd wit*h* Cloude of erthely things." Thus speaking, my yees flowing wit*h* teares, folding her garment she dried.[3]

Philosophy awakes Boethius out of his lethargy, so that he at last recognizes her.

III. MYTER.

Than Night overblowen, the darkenis,
   and formar strengh vnto my yees retornd.
*As, wha*n* the heavens astound with hedlong wind,*
   and Pale, amidst the Cloudy mistes,   4
The Son is hid, and in the heavens aperes no stars,
   from hy the night òn erthe is spred:
The same if boreas sent from his tracien den,
   dothe strike, and Opens the hiden day,   8
Shines out, and with his soudan Light Φebus shaken,
   Withe his beams strikes al Lokars On.

The return of Boethius to consciousness is compared with the breaking forth of the sun from the clouds.

---

[1] *Fed* for *nourissed* struck out.
[2] The Q. has here omitted to translate: *mallem pudore, sed te ut uides stupor opressit.*
[3] *Dried* for *wiped* struck out.

METRUM III.

Tunc me discussa liquerunt nocte tenebrae
   Luminibusque prior rediit uigor.
Vt, cum praecipiti glomerantur nubila coro
   Nimbosisque polus stetit imbribus,   4
Sol latet ac nondum caelo uenientibus astris,
   Desuper in terram nox funditur:
Hanc si threicio boreas emissus ab antro
   Verberet, et clausum reseret diem,   8
Emicat, et subito uibratus lumine Phoebus,
   Mirantes oculos radiis ferit.

III. Prose.

Boethius warns Philosophy to be careful not to subject herself to persecution.

No otherwise mistz of my wo dissolued to heauen I reached,[1] and raised my mynd to knowe my Curars face. Than whan on hir I rolled my yees and Loke I fixed, my nurs I saw, in whose retired Romes[2] in my Youthe I dweLt. "And how," q*uoth* I, "art thou Come to the Solitarenis of our exile, O, pedague[3] of al Vertus, fallen fro*m* the hiest step, Shalt thou w*ith* me be tormen*t*ed to w*ith* falz Crimes?"

Philosophy answers, that it is her duty to stand by the innocent Boethius.

"Shal I," q*uoth* she, "O, skolar myne! thè Lene, and not to ease thy burdain wiche for my sake[4] thou berest, in easing thy Labor w*ith* felowing of thi paine? Hit il becumes Φιλοσοφie to Leue alone an innocentz way, Shal I dread my none[5] blame,[6] and as if any nouuelty had hapt, shal I feare? Ar you now to[7] knowe how amonge wicked folkes wisedom is assailed w*ith* many dangers? Haue we not wrestled with Iollies rashnes among the elder sorte afore our[8] Platoes age, and made therewith great battaile? yea, he aliue, his master Socrates vniustely claymed the victory[9] of deathe when I was by: whose inheritance, when after the vulgar Epicurian and Stoick and all the rest, each man for his part, ment to bereaue me, sundred, as in parte of their pray, my garment, though I resisted and exclaymed. For being the workmanship of myne own hande, they plucking some ragges from it, supposing they had all departed from me. Among which,

That from the earliest times she has been accustomed to persecution.

for that some prints of my garment appeared, folly supposing they were my familiars, abused some of them with error of the vayne multitude. Though thou haste not knowen Anaxagoras flight, nor Socrates Venim, nor Zenos torment, because they are strange, yet Cauni, Senecæ, Sorani, thou[10] maist knowe, for they are not cowards[11] nor of vnhonored memory: whom nothing els to their bane brought, but that instructed with our conditions, they seamed vnlike the

---

[1] *Hausi coclum* is here wrongly translated by: "heauen I reached."
[2] The Queen has translated *lares* by "retired rooms." *Philosophiam* is omitted.
[3] *maistres* struck out.
[4] *mei nominis invidia* is in the translation shortened to: "for my sake."
[5] mine own.   [6] Now begins Clerk's hand.
[7] *Now first you shall* struck out.   [8] *olde* struck out.
[9] *victoriam promeruit* incorrectly translated "claimed the victory."
[10] *y* struck out.   [11] *Pervetustus* is translated by "cowards," instead of "very old."

32 wickeds endeuors. Thou oughtest not therefore to wonder, if in the sea of lyffe we be tossed with many a tempest rising, whose purpose is this chiefest, to dislike the wickedest.[1] Whose army, though it be great, ought to be despis[ed], as
36 whom no Guide rules, but hurled rashely with a dimme error. Which, if once setting battayle against vs, shuld fortune preuayle, our guide will drawe our troupes to castle, while they be busy to rauyne Vnproffitable baggage, and we from
40 hye shall skorne them while they spoile that is vyle, sure from the furious tumulte, and saffe in such a trenche, whether these foolish raueners may neuer attayne."

Philosophy also shows, that ignorance has never been able to obtain the victory over philosophy, but only over sophists, who give themselves out as philosophers.

IV. MYTER.

Who so[2] quiet in setled Life,
   proude fate kepes vnder fote,
And stable defending[3] eache fortune
   His chire vnwonne preserues: 4
him shal no rage nor Seas threates,
   from depthe that hurles her fome,
Nor wood Vesevus with holy pittz,
   that burstz out his smoky fires,   8
Nor way of flaming Sulφar,[4] wont to strike
   the towers hie, can moue.
Whi so muche Can wretched men
   at fiers tirants wondar, forsles, furious?   12
Hope thou naugh ne feare,
   Disarme thou may the powreLes Ire:

The wise man does not fear the raging elements, and therefore he should not fear the might of tyrants.

---

[1] End of this sentence, "*quibus hoc maxime propositum est pessimis displicere,*" badly translated.   [2] "who so" is in line with "And" in line 3.
[3] "z" written instead of "ing" struck out.
[4] "fulmen" (lightning) is translated by "Sulphar."

METRUM IV.

Quisquis composito serenus aeuo
Fatum sub pedibus dedit superbum
Fortunamque tuens utramque rectus
Inuictum potuit tenere uultum: 4
Non illum rabies minaeque ponti
Versum funditus excitantis aestum,
Nec ruptis quotiens uagus caminis

Torquet fumificos Veseuus ignes,   8
Aut celsas soliti ferire turres
Ardentis uia fulminis mouebit.
Quid tantum miseri feros tyrannos
Mirantur sine uiribus furentes?   12
Nec speres aliquid nec extimescas,
Exarmaueris impotentis iram:

> but who so quaking feares or wische,
> Not being stable, and in his strengh,[1]
> Downe falz his shild, and changing place,
> Huges the chaine by wiche he is drawen.

IV. PROSE.

Boethius, challenged by Philosophy, sets forth the wrong which he has suffered,

Knowest thou al this, and yet hast forgotten thè? art thou the Ass to the Lute? heare and remembar If thou Looke.[2] For thy Curars ayde, discover thy wound. Than I gathering my mynd to his ful strengh,[3] haue I yet nide of warning? hathe not the sowernis of Cruel fortune Ouertopt me by her self alone? doth not the vew of this place thè moue? Is not this the shop, wiche surist seat in all my inward romes for thè I chose? me which[4] by me oft sytting, of science diuine & humain matters thou disputedst?[5] was this thy habite? was this thy Looke? when with thè I serched natures secretes? when to me with ruler thou discribedst the starrès wayes, & framedst our woorkes & wholle trade of lyfe after the trade of celestiall order.

and asks, if this is the reward for following her precepts.

Shall we receaue such rewardes for obeyeng thè? When thou thy self this sentence paste of Platos mouth:[6] "that happy were those common welthes, if eyther wisdom studiers ruld them, or their Rulers wisdom[7] imbraced." Thou by the self same mans mouth didst teache that this was the necessariest cause, for wyse men to rule the common wellth, leste that the raynes therof, left to the wicked & harmfull citizens, might breede the plague & harme to good. This autoritie I following, which in thy secret leysure thou taughtest me, made me wish to tourne for Action of comon Rule. God & thy self doo witnes beare,

His only reason for desiring power was, to do good to others.

which he inspirde to wyse mens myndes, that no care brought me to magistrate Rule, but common care for all good men. Whence greate & vnappeased discorde with wicked folkes I

---

[1] The Queen has probably read *iuris* (right) for *vires* (strength).
[2] Incorrect translation of: "Sentisne, inquit, haec, atque-animo inlabuntur tuo? an ΟΝΟϹ ΛΥΡΑϹ? Quid fles, quid lacrimis manas? ΕΞΑΥΔΑ, ΜΗ ΚΕΥΘΕ ΝΟΩΙ."
[3] *colligere* left out in the translation.   [4] So far the Queen's hand.
[5] *despisest* struck out.   [6] *sanxisti* left out in the translation.   [7] *studi* struck out.

At quisquis trepidus pauet uel optat,   Abiecit clipeum locoque motus
Quod non sit stabilis suique iuris,   16   Nectit qua ualeat trahi catenam.

PR. IV.]   *DE CONSOLATIONE PHILOSOPHIÆ.*   9

  had, And that freedom that conscience libertie gaue me for to Boethius re-
28 saue right, I preserved, dispising the mighties offence. How counts his deserts in the
  oft have I crossed Conigastus, vsing violence to eche mans protection of the innocent.
  weke fortune? How many tymes haue I overthrowne Tri-
  guyl[a], In court cheefe officer, from his begon & almost ended
32 iniurye? How oft haue I protected poore[1] men, whom the
  vnpunished auarice of Barberous,[2] with infinite slanders vexed,
  throwing my autoritie against their perills! Never could
  any man drawe me from Law to Iniury. I sorowed for the
36 provinces misfortunes, wrackt by private ravins and publick
  taxes, no lesse than they that suffered them. Whan Cam-
  pania province seemed afflicted through want in tyme of And his disin-
  greatest famyne, & such as could not be exprest, when buying terested exertions in the cause
40 & selling was forbyd,[3] I began a quarrell against the pretorian of justice.
  Ruler, for cause of common good. I straue with him, the King
  knowing it, & wan it that no sale were made. Paulin the
  consul, whose goodes the palatine dog with hope & ambition
44 had deuourde, from the gapers Jawes[4] I drew. I opposde
  myself to the hate of Ciprian[5] the bakbyter, that the payne
  of the preiudical accusation[6] might not fall to the share of
  Albinus the consul. Have not I, suppose you, sharpned
48 quarrels against me ynough? and ought to have ben defended
  among the rest, euin them that for loue of Justice among the
  Courtiers might haue saued me, by which I should be safer;
  By what accusers am I now stricken? of whom Basilius, What sort of
52 fallen from princes seruice, is driven to slaunder of our name, men the accusers of Boethius are.
  for dettes sake. When by Kinges Judgement a censure was
  giuen for banishment, for Opilion & Gaudensius, for their
  Iniuries & many wronges, And when they denyeng to
56 obeye, saued them selues with defence of holy Sanctuary, &
  that the King knowing, proclaymde that without they departed from Ravenna towne at the prescribed daye, they
  should be driven out with their forheades marked. What
60 might be thought to crosse[7] such seuiritie? but yet in that

---

[1] *wretched* struck out.
[2] Here *barbarous*, adjective, appears to be mistaken for a proper name.
[3] *Coemptio* incorrectly translated. [4] The L. text has: "*hiantium faucibus.*"
[5] *Leithian* struck out. [6] *penaltie* struck out.
[7] The Latin word is *astrui* (add to).

daye, themsellves deferring the slaunder, touched me. What tho? hath our science deseruid this? or their foreruñing condemnacōn made their accusers Just? So fortune was nothing ashamde, if not [of] thaccused innocency, yet of thaccusers basenes?[1] But what is our faulte? will ye seeke the principall? we are sayde to wish the Senates surety. The waye[2] you desire, a sclaunderer, lest he might delay his Lessons[3] by which he might make me guilty of treason, we are accused to have letted him. What then think you, ô pedagogue myne? shall we deny the facte, that shame the we might not? but I wolde, & neuer to will, will leave. shall we confesse it? but shall the worke of hindering the sclaunderer, ceasse.[4] Shall I call it a faulte, to wish the surety of that state? He himself, by his own decrees against me, hath made this vnlawfull; but folie, that lyes euer against her self, the worth of thinges can neuer change. Nether Lawfull is it for me by Socrates Rule, to hyde trouth or graunte a lye. But this what it is, to yours & wyse folkes iudgement I leave the censure, whose manner of matter & trouth, that posterite may knowe, to my silent memory haue comitted. for as for false supposed lettres in which I am accusde to hope for Romayne libertie, what bootes it speake? whose fraude had lyen all open if I might have vsde my accusers confession, which in all matters beares greatest swaye: for what left liberty may be hoped for? that wold god there were any! I had aunswered then as Canius did, who accused by Caius Cesar, Germanicus sonne, to be guilty of the coniuration against him: "Yf I had knowen, thou hadste not knowen." In which matter, sorow hath not so duld my senses, to complayn of wicked men for dooing mischefe against vertue, but rather much wonder how they could hope performe it. For to will the worst, perchaunce might be our faulte, but to haue powre against Innocency, for ech wretch to doo what he conceaues, god being Looker on, seemes monstrouse. Whence ther is a question not with out cause, of thy familiar: "Yf there be a god," quoth he, "whence

---

[1] *wickednes* struck out.   [2] *reason* and *meanes* struck out.
[3] *Documenta* incorrectly translated by "lessons." Chaucer has "letters."
[4] *leave* struck out.

coms the euill? The good from whence, yf he be not?" But
it may be lawfull ynough for wicked men, that thursted the
blud of all the senate & all good men, to seeke our wrak,
whom they haue seene defend the good & saue the Senate.
100 But did we deserue the lyke of the fathers or no? You *and points out how he had defended the Senate at his own risk.*
remember, I suppose, for what I sayde or did present, you
directed me; You call to mynde, quoth I, At Verona,
when the King, greedy of common fall, did stryve to bring the
104 treason layde to Albinus, to the Senates order, how I defended
then the innocency of all the Senat with most assurance of my
owne danger. You know all this that true it is I tell, & that
no boste I make of any my prayse. for thassurance of a
108 graunting [1] conscience diminishith it self in a sorte, as oft as
bosting receauith rewarde of fame. But you see what end *Proofs that the Judges were not impartial.*
my Innocency hath. for true vertues rewarde we suffer false
factes payne. for whose manifest confession of wicked facte,
112 euer made all Judges so agree in seueritie, that eyther the
faulte of humaine witt, or thincertayne state of fortune, may
not leave out [2] somewhat? Yf we had bene sayd to haue
burned the sacred houses, to haue slayne the preestes with
116 wicked sworde, & bred destruction of all good men, the
sentence had punished present confessing & convicted. Now
allmost fyve hundred thousand paces of,[3] though farre of &
vnwearyed,[4] we are condemnde to death & exile, for our
120 ready indeuors for the Senates good: O[5] woorthy men, for
such a faulte none of them shall be convinced. the value[6] of
whose guiltynes, they themselues haue seene that brought it:
which to dym with mixture of som wickednes, they haue false
124 belyed me, to haue stayned my conscience with sacrilege for *Boethius' defence of himself, in pointing out his intimate acquaintance with philosophy, his domestic life, and his excellent friends and relations.*
Ambition sake. And thou thy self grafted in me, all desyre
of mortall thinges, from seate of my mynde hast pluckt, for
vnder thy sight ther was no place for sacrilege faulte, for in
128 to my eares thou didst instill, & to my thoughtes this pytho-

---

[1] *an honest* struck out.
[2] *Summittere* incorrectly translated by "leave out." Chaucer has "submit."
[3] *fyfty thousand myles of* struck out.
[4] The Queen has here read *indefessi*, "unwearied," for *indefensi*, "unprotected." Chaucer has "without defence."   [5] *that we* struck out.
[6] *worth* struck out. The meaning of "*O meritos de simili crimine neminem posse conuinci,*" is badly rendered.

gorian worde, Obey thy God. neyther did it becom me to seeke the help of vilest spirites, whom thou hadst framed to such an excellency, that lyk to god thou madest them.[1] Agayne, the Innocent closet of my house, resorte of honest frendes, my holy lawes fath^r Symmacus, And for his deedes reuerenced, defendes vs from all suspicion of this cryme.

<small>The reputation of being a philosopher injures B.</small>

But O mishap, They beleeuid all this cryme, & for this synne we were confyned, for that we were indewed with thy lesson, & framed of thy condition: So bootes it not ynough, that thy reuerence should protecte me, but that withall thou shouldest be vexed with my offence. But this is greatest heape to our mishap, that the valuing of most, regardes more fortunes event, than causes merit, And Judgith that best prouided, that felicitie recomendith. which makes, that true waight[2] first leaveth the vnhappy man.[3] What now the rumors be, how variable, & increasing their Judgmentes, to remember, it greeves me. This only can I saye, that the last

<small>The multitude judges the innocent and guilty only according as they are prosperous or the reverse.</small>

burden of fortune is, that whilest faultes be layde to the wretchedest charge, they are beleeuid to deserue that is layde to their charge. And my self bereued of all my goodes, spoyld of my dignities, spotted in my fame, for benefitt, receaue punishment. Me thinkes I see the wicked shops[4] of vilest men flowing with Joye & mirth. And euery wickedst man overlayeng me[5] with new fraudes of accusation. I see the good lye down prostrate for feare of my fall, Ech wicked

<small>Finally B. describes the triumph of the wicked and the downfall of the righteous.</small>

man bolde vnpunishd to faulte, To doo the which thorow rewardes[6] be styrred, but Innocent folkes not only of surety, but of defence depriued. Wherefore thus may I exclaime:

---

[1] From "whom" to "them" wrongly referred to the spirits instead of to B. Chaucer has "I þat þou hast ordeyned or set in syche excellence þat [þou] makedest me lyke to god."   [2] *waying* struck out.

[3] Meaning of this sentence "*Quo fit, ut existimatio bona prima omnium deserat infelices*," very indistinct.   [4] *officina*. Chaucer has "couines."

[5] Instead of *me* Chaucer has "goode folke."   [6] *they* struck out.

V. Myter.

O framar of starry Circle,
   who lening to the lasting[1] *grounstone,*[2]   Boethius prays the Godhead to introduce into the life of man the same strict order which they hold in the rest of the universe.
withe whorling blast hevens turnest,
   and Law Compelst the skies to beare;   4
Now that with ful horne,
   meting all her brothers flames
the Lessar stars the mone dimmes,
   Now darke and pale her horne,   8
Nar to Son Loseth her Light.
And she that at beginning of night,
Hesperus [her] frosen rising makes,
   And Lucifar palled by Φebus vpriseth   12
Againe her wonted raines exchangeth.
   thou, by the Cold of Lefe falne shade
straightist thy Light with shortar abode: Commends the regularity in the movements of the heavenly bodies, and the succession of the seasons.
   Thou whan the fervent sommar comes,   16
Easy nights houres deuidest.
   Thy power tempers the changing year,
that what Leues boreas blastz bereues,
Gentil Sefirus brings as fast: 20
Sedes that the Northe star doth behold,
at hiest blade the dok star burnith vp.
Naught loused from auncient Law
Leues the worke of her owne place.   24

[1] *whirled* struck out.
[2] Probably "groundstone." Here the Queen has read *solum*, ground, instead of *solium*, throne.

METRUM V.

O stelliferi conditor orbis	*Phoebi pallens lucifer ortu.*
Qui perpetuo nixus solio	*Tu frondifluae frigorè brumae*
Rapido caelum turbine uersas	*Stringis lucem breuiore mora:*
Legemque pati sidera cogis, 4	*Tu, cum feruida uenerit aestas,* 16
Vt nunc pleno lucida cornu	*Agiles noctis diuidis horas.*
Fratris totis obuia flammis	*Tua uis uarium temperat annum,*
Condat stellas luna minores,	*Vt quas boreae spiritus aufert,*
Nunc obscuro pallida cornu 8	*Reuehat mites zephyrus frondes:* 20
Phoebo propior lumina perdat.	*Quaeque arcturus semina uidit*
Et qui primae tempore noctis	*Sirius altas urat segetes.*
Agit algentes hesperos ortus,	*Nihil antiqua lege solutum*
Solitas iterum mutat habenas 12	*Linquit propriae stationis opus.* 24

> He compares this order with the great disorder and injustice in worldly matters, caused by Fortuna.

Al giding with assured end,
Mans workes alone thou dost dispice.
O gidar by right desart from meane to kipe.¹
for why so many slipar² fortune   28
turnes doth make? oppressing fautles
dew paine for wicked mete,
but in hy Seatz the wicked factz³ alide,   31
And wicked stamps on holy necks with uniust turne.
And Cleare vertu dimmed
with thick blackenis Lurketh,
And iust man the wickeds crime doth beare.
fals othe in fraude doth the annoy.⁴   36
who whan thé can vse ther forse,
whom many vulgar feare
the mightiest kings thé⁵ can subdue.⁶

> And concludes with a prayer that the power of Fortuna may cease.

O now behold of wretched erthe,   40
thou who so ties the bondz of all.
Vs men regard of thy great worke not the vilest part,
how tost we be with fortunes waues.⁷
O weldar apeace the Roring floudes,   44
And with what boundz the great heauen thou gidest the
    stable erthe do stedy.

---

¹ No meaning. Chaucer has: "O þou gouernour gouernyng alle þinges by certeyne ende. why refusest þou oonly to gouerne þe werkes of men by dewe manere."
² Chaucer has "slidyng."   ³ factz. Chaucer has "maneres."
⁴ Two negations not translated.   ⁵ A little "y" added at end, probably put in later.
⁶ Lines 38 and 39 not translated.   ⁷ Looks like waies.

Omnia certo fine gubernans			Nil periuria, nil nocet ipsis	
Hominum solos respuis actus			Fraus mendaci compta colore.	
Merito rector cohibere modo.			Sed cum libuit uiribus uti,	
Nam cur tantas lubrica uersat	28		Quos innumeri metuunt populi	40
Fortuna uices? premit insontes			Summos gaudent subdere reges.	
Demta sceleri noxia poena,			O iam miseras respice terras	
At peruersi resident celso			Quisquis rerum foedera nectis.	
Mores solio sanctaque calcant	32		Operis tanti pars non uilis	44
Iniusta uice colla nocentes.			Homines quatimur fortunae sale.	
Latet obscuris condita uirtus			Rapidos rector comprime fluctus,	
Clara tenebris iustusque tulit			Et quo caelum regis immensum	
Crimen iniqui.	36		Firma stabiles foedere terras.	48

V. PROSE.

This when with contynuall wo I had burst out, seeing her with mylde countenance nothing mooued with my mones: 'when thè,"quoth she,"sad & wayling I sawe, straight a wretch 4 & exule,¹ I knew thè. but,² how farre of thy banishment was, but that thou toldste, I knew not. but thou, how farre from countrey art not expulst, but strayed, yet if thou³ hadst it rather be thought expulst, thou thy self hastè throwne it. 8 for that for other was neuer lawfull than thè, to doo. for if thou remember from what countrey thou cammest, not guyded as Athens was, by rule of multitude, but one King & Ruler, that Joyeth more in subiectes nomber than their expulse: 12 with whose raynes to be guyded & Justice obeyde, is greatest libertie. Art thou ignorant of the auncientest law of thy Citie, which commaundz that no man may be banisht from it, Whoso choosith there to build a seate?⁵ for who so in her 16 trench & suerty is conteynde, no feare shall haue, nor exul deserues⁶ to be. but who so leaues to will her habitation, wantes allso deseruith;⁷ wherfore thy Looke, not this place, so much moouith me, nor doo I desyre my shops walles 20 adornid with yuory or glasse, rather than the seate of the mynde, In which I placed not bookes, but that that giues them price, sentences of myne owne woorkes.⁸ Thou haste rehersed truth of thy desert for common good, but little hast 24 thou told of nombers greate thou hast receaued.⁹ Thou hast remembred thinges knowen to all, obiected against thè, eyther for good or falshode. Of mischefz or fraudes of thy slaunderers rightly thou haste straightly touched, that they might 28 the better & farder be knowen with prayse of vulgare folk. Vehemently hast thou invayde against the Senates Iniustice. Of our complaynt haste moned, & bewaylde the wrack¹⁰ of

Philosophy reproaches B. with having forgotten that a wise man never can be banished from his true fatherland.

She tells him that he has recounted the injuries but not the benefits which he has received.

---

¹ *exile* struck out. ² *haste* struck out.
³ *woldest choosest rather to be* struck out.
⁴ "*potius ipse te pepulisti*"; "it" unnecessary.
⁵ *that choosith to build ther see* struck out. ⁶ *dreades* struck out.
⁷ The Latin is: "*Pariter desinit etiam mereri.*" Chaucer has: "he forleteþ also to deserue to ben Citezein of þilke Citee." ⁸ "Quondam" left out.
⁹ From "but" the sense is wrong; "*sed pro multitudine gestorum tibi pauca divisti.*" Chaucer has: "but after þe multitude of þi goode dedys. þou hast seid fewe." ¹⁰ *losse* struck out.

estymations Loste.¹ The last thy wo agaynst fortune invayed, complayning that she equalled not desertes rewarde. 32
In end of thy raging muse,² requirste a graunte that the same peace wh*i*ch ruleth the heauen, might so rule thearth. But for that a greate heape of affections ouerwhelme thè, & sorow, ire, wo, diuersly distractes thè, such as thy mynde is now, as 36 yet thy remedies be no greater. Wherfore easyer lett vs vse a while, that such as by growing paynes in swelling hath bene hardenid, that they may beare more sharp receites, with a soft touch be doulced." 40

B. is as yet too much confused by his own thoughts and feelings, and must therefore gradually and by gentle means be brought to a just recognition of his situation.

VI. MYTER.

As each season brings forth the natural productions proper to it, and not that of the other seasons,

*Whan heuy Cancer sm*ᵉ³
by Φebus beames inflames,
than he that Lent plentyes sead
to forowes that denied them,   4
bigiled by Ceres faithe
*Let h*i*m seake the Acorne tre.*
the decked wode seak not
whan thou violetz gather,   8
whan with the Northy blastz
Ther⁴ roring fildz affrightz,
Nor Seake not thou with gredy hand
The springy Palmes⁵ to weld: 12
Grapes if thou wische inJoy,
In Autumne bacchus rather
hys giftes bestowes.
Times God assigneth fit   16

so have also the mental attributes an exact order which is unalterable.

---

¹ *Lost opinion* struck out.   ² *wood moode* struck out.
³ Sic; *smitten?*   ⁴ Perhaps meant for *The*.
⁵ *Palmites*, which we find in the Latin, has never the signification of "palms." Chaucer has: "stalkes of þe vine."

METRUM VI.

Cum Phoebi radiis graue
Cancri sidus inaestuat,
Tum qui larga negantibus
Sulcis semina credidit,   4
Elusus Cereris fide
Quernas pergat ad arbores.
Numquam purpureum nemus
Lecturus uiolas petas,   8

Cum saeuis aquilonibus
Stridens campus inhorruit,
Nec quaeras auida manu
Vernos stringere palmites: 12
Vuis si libeat frui,
Autumno potius sua
Bacchus munera contulit.
Signat tempora propriis   16

for eche mans office best,
Nor the¹ tournes that he apoints
Suffers to be mixte.
So what so Leues by racheLous way the Certain
    rule,   20
Joyful ende shal neuer hit.

VI. Prose.

First then suffre me with questions few thy mynde state to touche, & it to prooue, that better may I know of thy cure the way? "Ask me," quoth I, "according to thy will, what thou woldest my aunsweres be." Then she : "thinkes thou that this world is wheeled by rash & happing chaunce? or dost suppose that Reasons rule is in it?" "I can no way think," quoth I, "that with so rash chaunce, so certain thinges are moued, but I know that God yᵉ maker hit guides, nor euer shall com day that from truth of this opinion shall draw me." "Is it so?" quoth she, "A little afore this thou hast tolde & hast bemonde that men were so furr from godes care depriued; for with the rest thou art nothing moued, but that with reason they were led. Good Lord, I wonder much, why placed in so right a mynde thou canst be sick! But let vs serch a little hyar : I wote not what, somewhat lackes I trowe. But tell me, for that thou doutst not the world by god be rulde, seest thou by what raynes it is guided?" "Scarce doo I know," said I, "the meaning of the question, ne² yet can I aunswer thy demandes, was I³ ignorant that somewhat lackt? by which lik cliff of Ramper shrinking,⁴ the woes disease into the mynde is crepte." "But tell me, dost thou remember, what is the end of all, And whither tended the intent of all nature?" "I have hard it aunswered, but my memory dampt sorow hath made." "But whom dost thou know, whence all

Philosophy enquires how far the delusion of B. is carried; and finds that he has an imperfect acquaintance with his own being, and an absolute ignorance of the aim and object of creation.

---

¹ *the* for "by," and *as* for "that," both struck out.   ² *nor* erased.
³ *not* erased.   ⁴ *as the roote of a tree* struck out.
A blank space is left here. The L. text is : *velut hiante valli robore*, which Chaucer translates : "So as the strengþe of þe valeys schynyng is open."

Aptans officiis deus,   17   *Sic, quod praecipiti uia,*   20
Nec, quas ipse coercuit,   *Certum deserit ordinem,*
Misceri patitur uices.   *Laetos non habet exitus.*

She hopes however to save him, because he acknowledges God to be the great first cause and guider of the universe.

proceedes?" "I know," quoth I, "And God is he," I aunswere. "How can it be then, that, begynning knowen, the end thereof thou knowest not? But this is the fashon of troubles, & such is theyr wont,[1] that mooue they may a man from his place, but ouerthrowe or wholly pluck vp,[2] they can not. But this wold I haue the aunswer, Remembrest thou thy self a man?" "What els," quoth I, "should I not remember that?" "Canst thou tell me, what man is then?" "Dost thou ask me this, whither that I know that I am a reasonable creature & mortall? I know it, & that to be I must confesse." Then she: "knowest thou not thy self ought els?" "Nothing." "But I know," quoth she, "that the greatest cause of thy disease, is to have left to know what thou art. wherfore eyther fully have I founde the reason of thy sicknes, or a waye to reconcile thè home agayne.[3] for being confounded through thy obliuion, thou hast bewaylde thy self an exul & spoyled of thine owne goodes.

She asks him whether he supposes that the events of fortune run without a guide.

For being ignorant of thy end, thou hast supposde mighty & happy the wicked folkes & lewde, & forgetting by what brydle the world is guided, The eventus[4] of fortune thou supposest with out a guide to run: Great causes not only to disease, but to ruine to. But thanked be thy hoste, that nature hath not yet wholly destroyde thè. We haue the greatful foode for thy helth, thy true opinion of the worldes Rule, whom thou belieuest not subiect to chaunce, but Ruled by diuine Reason. Feare nought therfore. Allready from this little sparke thy vitall heate is sprong. but because the tyme is not yet for stronger

Philosophy tries to remove the tendency which the human mind has to cast off the truth and take a false view of things.

remedyes, & that the nature of the myndes is such, that when they haue cast away the true, are indued with false opinion, by which a springing darknes of woe confoundes that true sight, I will assay a while therfore with lenitiues, & meane fomentations to skant them, that darknes of deceauing affection remoouid, the shyne of true light mayst obtayne."

---

[1] Transl. of "*ea valentia est*" is missing here. [2] *out* is erased.
[3] Quite an incorrect transl. of "*Aditum reconciliandae sospitalis inueni.*" Chaucer has: "þe entre of recoueryng of þin hele."
[4] This word is defaced; it looks like *aventus*.

VII. Myter.

Dim Cloudes	Oft is staid	As the stars do not shine when obscured by clouds,
Skie Close	by Slaked	
Light none	stone of Rock.	
Can afourd. 4	thou, if thou wilt 20	
If Roling Seas	in Clirest Light	
boustius Sowth	trothe behold,	
Mixe his fome,	by straight lin	
Griny ons 8	hit in the pathe: 24	
Like the Clirristz	Chase Joyes,	
days the water	repulse feare,	
straight moude	thrust out hope,	
sturd vp al foule 12	Wo not retaine. 28	
the Sight gainsais.	Cloudy is the mind	so in order to recognize truth, must man banish all emotions from his mind.
Running streame	With snafle bound,	
that poures	Wher they raigne.[1]	
from hiest hilz 16		

heere endith ye first booke.

[1] So far Elizabeth's hand, then Clerk's hand.

Metrum VII.

Nubibus atris	Mox resoluto	Cernere uerum,
Condita nullum	Sordida caeno 12	Tramite recto
Fundere possunt	Visibus obstat.	Carpere callem: 24
Sidera lumen. 4	Quique uagatur	Gaudia pelle,
Si mare uoluens	Montibus altis	Pelle timorem,
Turbidus auster	Defluus amnis, 16	Spemque fugato,
Misceat aestum,	Saepe resistit	Nec dolor adsit. 28
Vitrea dudum 8	Rupe soluti	Nubila mens est
Parque serenis	Obice saxi.	Vinctaque frenis,
Vnda diebus	Tu quoque si uis 20	Haec ubi regnant.
	Lumine claro	

THE SECOND BOOKE.

I. Prose.

Philosophy begins to comfort the distressed person.

After this, a while she pawsde, and when my heede by my modest silence she markt, thus she began: "If alltogither thy cause of greefe & state I know, thou pynest with the affection & want of former fortune. She so much changyth the state of thy mynde, as thou ymaginest ouerthrowes hit. I

She supposes a reverse of fortune to be the cause of his affliction,

vnderstand the many shaped¹ deceites of her wonder, and so farre exercisith a flattering familiaritie with them she myndes deceaue, till she confound with intollerable woe, whom without hope she hath left. Whose nature, conditions, & desert, if thou remember, thou shalt know that thou hast nether had nor lost by her any thing ought worth; but, as I suppose, I shall not neede to labour much to call these thinges to thy memory. For thou art wont when she was present & flattered the, to invay against her with manly woordes in chassing her from our doores,² with thy sentence invaydst her. But euery souden change neuer haps without a greate streame of the mynde. So doth it bifal,³ that thou a while hast parted from thy ease. But tyme it is for thee to drawe & taste som sweeter thing and pleasant, which passing to the inward partes may make a way for behoofuller draughtes. Let per-

and begins to console him by means of Rhetorik, which is here designated by Boethius a music slave of philosophy.

suasion of sweete Rhetorik assist the, which then goith in rightest path only, when she leaves not our precepts; and with this musick the guest of our home sowndes now easyer, now weightyer notes. What is it, therfore, O man, that hath⁴ throwne the down to wo & wayle? Thou hast seene, I beleue, som new vnwonted thing. Thou, yf thou thinkest that toward the fortune be changed, art deceaud. This was euer her manner, this was her nature. She hath euer kept

---

¹ Interlined over *sharp*, struck out.
² The Queen has here found in the original *aditu* with (i), and has taken it to be *adyto*, door.   ³ Interlined in the Queen's own hand, over *hap* struck out.
⁴ Corrected from *hast* by the Queen.

toward the rather her own constancy in her mutabilitie. Such one was she, whan she beguild thè, & did deceaue with allurementes of false felicitie. Thou hast vnderstode now,
32 the doutfull face of the blynde Goddesse, which though she hyde her self to others, hath made her self to thè manifest. Yf thou allow her vse her fashon, complayne not therof; yf thou hatest[1] her treason, skorne her & cast her of, that so
36 falsely beguylde thè; for she that now is cause of thy woe, the self same ought be of thy quyett. She hath left thè, whom no man can be sure that will not leave him. Canst thou beleeue flyeng felicitie precious, and can thy present
40 luck be deere? never faythfull in abode, and when she partes bringes nought but woe: And yf nether she can be kepte with iudgement, and whan she flyes, makes them wretched, what ought els meanith her flight than a show of a comming
44 calamitie? For alone it suffisith not to beholde what afore our eyes is sett, wisdom the end of all measures. for her mutabilitie in bothe, nether makes her fortunes threates feard, nor her beguylinges wished.[2] Lastly, thou must
48 paciently beare what so befalles in fortunes Courte, whan once to her yoke thy neck thou bowest; but if thou wilt prescribe her lawe, to byde or parte, whom thou hast freely chosen thy gouuernesse, shoulst thou not be iniurious, and
52 sharp thy luck with thy impatience, which change thou canst not? Yf thou woldst throwe the sayles to wynde, not whither will wolde, but whither the blast doth dryve, so furr thou goest: Yf thou doo lend the forrowes seede, thou
56 must beare with deere yeeres and barren: yf to fortunes guide thou hast betaken thè, thou must obey thy Dames conditions. Woldst thou stryve to staye the course of a turning wheele? But thou of all mortall men the foolisht, if hap
60 byde, it leavith to be chaunce."

[1] Interlined by the Queen, over *hast* struck out.
[2] The *ched* interlined in the Queen's hand.

I. MYTER.

Fortune uplifts the lowly, and abases the lofty; she knows no pity, and boasts that she has in a single hour made the same person unhappy, and then happy again.

This whan her proud hand changeth cours,
    And Euripus foming like is throwne.
Whilom she fierce kings cruel destroies,
    and lowe looke of won man deceitful raiseth.   4
She hereth not the wretche nor hedeth not his teares,
    Willingly skornes the sighs that spitful she made.
Thus playeth she, and so her strength doth trie,
    A wondar great to hers she shewes;   8
If any man you view, one houre
    both thralz him and extolz.[1]

II. PROSE.

A few woordes wold I pleade with thee on fortunes syde. Mark thou then whither she call thè not in plea. "Why me, ô man! guilty dost thou make of daily quarrells? What *Fortune herself takes up the word, and defends herself against the complainant.* wrong doo I thee? What goodes from thee haue I drawne? 4 Pleade thou against me afore any Judge for the possession of thy goodes & dignities. And if thou showest that any mortall man haue propertie of any of them that thou pretendst thyne owne, that thou ask, willingly I will yelde. 8 When Nature brought thè out of thy motheres womb, naked of all & needy, I vp tooke thè, and nourisht thè with my substance, & that that breedes now thy rage; with speedy[2] *She has taken from him nothing that was not her own.* fauour carefully I bred thè, and did indue with plenty & 12 glory of all such thinges as were my owne. Now is it tyme, now may I, if I list, draw back my hand: yeld[3] thankes for

---

[1] Chaucer has: "Yif þat a wy3t is seyn weleful and overþrowe in an houre."
[2] The Queen appears here to have read *favore prompto* instead of *favore prona*.
[3] The Queen must have read *habe gratiam*, which really has a better meaning than *habes gratiam*.

METRUM I.

Haec cum superba uerterit uices dextra,
Exaestuantis more fertur Euripi,
Dudum tremendos saeua proterit reges
Humilemque uicti subleuat fallax uultum.   4
Non illa miseros audit aut curat fletus,
Vltroque gemitus, dura, quos fecit, ridet.
Sic illa ludit, sic suas probat uires
Magnumque suis monstrat ostentum; si quis   8
Visatur una stratus ac felix hora.

vsing not thyne owne. Thou hast no lawe for quarrell, as if
16 thyne owne lost thou hadst. Why sighest thou than? With
no violence haue we vsed thè. goodes, honour, & all such
lyke, of right myne own. My maydes knowes their Lady,
with me they com, & whan I parte, giue place. Boldly I
20 affirme, if thyne they were that lost[1] thou complaynst at all,
thou hast not lost them. Am I[2] alone forbyd my right to
vse? To heauens is lawfull to bring thee pleasant dayes, & Constant change
is the nature of
24 the earthe's face with floures and frute, Som tyme with cloudes Fortuna.
and coldes confound. The Sea may with quyet calme be
pleased, now terrible by waues & tempest. the vnsaciable desyre
of men, shall it bynd vs to constancy furr from our condition?
28 This is our powre, this contynuall plan we make. The wheele
by turning Rolle we whirle, and Joye the lowest change with
hyest, and hyest makes the same to matehe. Com vp & yo^u
will, but on that condition, that ye counte it not iniury to
32 descend whan the fashon of my dalyance requires it. Wert Examples of
change of
thou ignorant of my conditions? Knewest thou not Cresus, fortune:
king of Lydia, a little before fearfull to Cyrus, straight way Crœsus and
wretched man bequeathed to flamy heate, defended from Perseus.
36 heauen by a mist sent downe? Dost thou not remember
how Paul shed many an honest teare for the calamitie of
Perseus king, whom he tooke? What does Tragedies
clamour more bewayle, than a man turning happy Raigne by
40 blynde fortune's stroke? Hast thou[3] not learnt that there
lay in Jupiters thressholl twoe barrells fyld one with yll, the
other of good? What yf thou suckest vp more largely of the The vicissitudes
caused by For-
better part? What yf I left thè not all alone? What if tuna are a com-
44 this my right mutabilitie haue bred thè cause to hope for tragedy.
better? But be not thou amasde, that sett in the common
raigne of all other, to lyve by thine owne lawe desirest."[4]

---

[1] Imitation of the Latin construction *Quae amissa conqueceris*.
[2] In the translation sometimes 1st per. sing., sometimes 1st per. pl. is used.
[3] After "thou" *adulescentem* is omitted.
[4] Incorrect; a better rendering is: "Yet that thou dost not make thyself unhappy,
& desirest to make a law for thyself while thou livest under the old common
sovereignty."

II. MYTER.

Mankind is insatiable, and content with nothing.

If sandz such store by raging flawes
   as stured sea turnes vp,
Or skies, bidect with mighty stars
   The heuens al that lightz,   4
And suche welthe bestowes,
   Nor plenty with fullist horne withdrawes her hand,
Mankind yet ceaseth not
   With wailing mones bewail him.   8
thogh God his vowes willingly receue
   The liberal dolar of golds plenty,

If Copia were to shake out of her horn blessings as innumerable as the sand of the sea or the stars of heaven, mankind would still be dissatisfied.

And gridy folke with honors great indues,
   Naught to haue got they seame: 12
But egar rauining, deuouring what they had,
   Stretcheth the Chawes for more.
What raignes can drawe bak
   hedlong desiar to stable end,   16
Whan thirst of getting inflames
   The flowing man with largist gifts?[1]
No man thinkes him riche
   Who quaking mones beleues a beggar.   20

III. PROSE.

Yf fortune for her self had spoken thus to thè, thou hadst no cause to grudge agaynst her, but if ought ther be wherby thy quarrell by law thou canst defend, tell it thou must; place to speake we giue. "Than fayre thes be in show," quoth I, "florist over[2] Retorik and musik, with the honny of

---

[1] Meaning not evident.   [2] *Florist over* interlined in the Queen's hand.

METRUM II.

Si quantas rapidis flatibus incitus
   Pontus uersat harenas
Aut quot stelliferis edita noctibus
   Caelo sidera fulgent,   4
Tantas fundat opes nec retrahat manum
   Pleno copia cornu,
Humanum miseras haud ideo genus
   Cesset flere querellas.   8
Quamuis uota libens excipiat deus
   Multi prodigus auri

Et claris auidos ornet honoribus,
   Nil iam parta uidentur: 12
Sed quaesita uorans saeua rapacitas
   Alios pandit hiatus.
Quae iam praecipitem frena cupidinem
   Certo fine retentent,   16
Largus cum potius muneribus fluens
   Sitis ardescit habendi?
Numquam diues agit qui trepidus gemens
   Sese credit egentem?   20

ther sweetnes; they only delite whan they be hard. but deeper sense of yll the wretched hath. Wherfore, when these haue
8 don, to sounde our eares, ingraffed wo our mynde oppressith." And she: "So it is," sayd she, "for these be not yet remedyes for thy disease, but serues for bellowes¹ against the cure of thy resisting sorowe. for when I see thine, I
12 shall apply such remedyes as shall pearce deeper.² But leste thou shouldst suppose thy self a wretch, Hast thou forgotten the tyme³ & meane of thy felicitie? I leave vntolde how desolate of parentes, the care of greatest men fosterd thè,
16 & chosen to affinitie of the cities Rulers, And that kynde that is of kyndred the neerest; first thou wert deere afore thou wert next. Who wold not haue famed thè most happy with so greate honour of father in lawe, of wyfes modestie, and
20 seasonable obtayning of a man childe? I ouerpasse (for so I will common thinges) dignities receauid in youth denyed to elder folkes: it pleasith me, That this is happed⁴ to the singuler heape of thy felicitie. yf any frute of mortall thinges
24 may beare a waight of blessednes, can the memory of such a daye be scrapte out by any waight of growing harmes? When thou hast seene twoo Consuls at once, thy children, accompanyed to⁵ with nomber of the fathers, & peeples Joye, when
28 they sitting in the Court as Curules,⁶ thou the Orator of kinges prayse, deseruest thou not⁷ glory of wit & eloquence, when amidst them both thou satisfidest the expectation of consuls with all the rowte, with a liberall tryomph?⁸ Thou
32 flatteredst fortune, as I suppose, while she stroked thè, and cherisht as her darling. Thou tokest away the rewarde that to priuate man she neuer lent afore. Will yoᵘ now spurne at her? hathe she with a heavy⁹ eye now strayned thè. Yf

Philosophy reminds Boethius that he has received more joys than sorrows,

and is therefore not justified in complaining of Fortune.

Enumeration of the benefits which he has received and the distinctions which have been conferred on him and his family.

---

¹ *Sic.* Translation of *fomenta*.
² Incorrect translation of "*Nam, quae in profundum sese penetrent, cum tempestiuum fuerit, ammouebo.*"   ³ Latin text and Chaucer have "number" instead of "tyme."
⁴ Correct reading: "It pleaseth me, that I have happed to the," etc.: *vide* Chaucer.
⁵ *To* interlined in the Queen's hand.
⁶ *Curules* is here erroneously taken to be an office, not a seat: *vide* Chaucer.
⁷ Here is no question, "*tu regiae laudis orator, ingenii gloriam facundiaeque meruisti.*" Chaucer has it correctly: "þou rethorien or pronouncere of kynges preysinges . deseruedest glorie of wit and of eloquence."
⁸ Here the Queen with "liberall tryomph" has better translated than Chaucer; for *triumphali largitione* signifies distribution of a largesse, which Chaucer does not express.   ⁹ The Queen has translated *liuenti* by *heavy* instead of *envious*.

If Boethius did not esteem himself fortunate in having once been in possession of so many blessings he should not now think himself unfortunate because he has lost them.	thou doo waye*n* the no*m*ber and trade of plesant & wofull, 36 thou canst not yet deny thy self happy : yf therfore thou thinkst not thy self fortunate for seeming Joyes by past, no cause why thou thy self a wretch suppose : for passe they doo that wofull now be thought. Camst thou now first into the 40 stage of lyfe, of a souden, & stranger? Supposest thou any co*n*stancy to be in humayne matters, whan speedy houre a man himself vndoes? for tho rare credit of abode owght happing chaunce to have, yet the last daye of lyfe may serue 44 for fortune that remaynes. What meanest thou to speake? Wilt thou leave her dyeng, or she thee flyeng?"

III. MYTER.

As the external face of nature is subject to constant change,	In poole[1] whan Φe*b*us *w*ith *reddy waine* *the light to spred begins,* *The star dimed with flames opprissing,* *Pales her whitty lookes.* 4 *Whan wood with Si*φ*irus mildding blast* *blusheth with the springing Roses,* *And cloudy Sowthe his blustering blastes ;* *Away from stauke[2] the beauty goes.* 8 *Some time with calmy fayre, the se* *Void of waues doth run,*
so we cannot expect the life of man to be exempt from vicissitudes.	*Oft boistrus tempestz the North* *With foming Seas turnes up.* 12 *If rarely stedy be the worldz forme,* *If turnes so many hit makes,* *Beliue slippar mens Luckes,* *trust that sliding be ther goodz!* 16 *Certain, and in Eternal Law is writ,* *"Sure standeth naugh is made."*

[1] "poole" probably pole, Latin *polo*.   [2] Chaucer has more correctly "þornes."

METRUM III.

Cum polo Phoebus roseis quadrigis
  Lucem spargere coeperit,
Pallet albentes hebetata uultus
  Flam̃*mis stella prementibus.*   4
Cum nemus flatu zephyri tepentis
  Vernis inrubuit rosis,
Spiret insanum nebulosus auster :
  Iam spinis abeat decus.   8
Saepe tranquillo radiat sereno

  Immotis mare fluctibus,
Saepe feruentes aquilo procellas
  Verso concitat aequore.   12
Rara si constat sua forma mundo,
  Si tantas uariat uices,
Crede fortunis hominum caducis,
  Bonis crede fugacibus !   16
Constat aeterna positumque lege est,
  Vt constet genitum nihil.

IV. Prose.

Than I: "truth hast thou told me, ô of all vertue the *Philosophy comforts B. first, by bringing to his recollection all the good which yet remains to him;* nursse; nor can I blame the speedy *course* of my prosperitie. But this is it, that co*n*sidering, most vexith me, that in all
4 fortunes adue*r*sitie I finde this most miserable, to haue bene happy." "That thou," q*uoth* she, "beares payne for false opinion, that Rightly thou oughtest not on matters them*s*ellves impose. for if the vayne name of chauncing felicitie mooue thè,
8 Repete w*it*h me w*it*h how many & greate thou aboundest. Yf the preciousest of all thou didst possesse iu fortunes Censure,¹ that to thy self² vnharmd or broken be kepte, canst thou when best thinges be retaynde, complayne by right, of
12 yll hap? Safe doth remayne Symmachus thy father in lawe, of all mankynde most worth, And that w*it*h price of lyfe thou careles should not³ buye, that man made of wisdom and vertue, *that he still has his best friend Symmachus and his excellent wife and children.* sure of his own, mones for thy wrong*es*. Thy wyfe of modest
16 wit, excelling for her shamfastnes, & that all her guift*es* in short I may include,⁴ her father lyuith, I saye, & keepith thy spirit, though hatyng lyfe, from w*hi*ch dep*r*iued, my self will graunte skanten thy felicitie, And for lack of thè, w*it*h
20 teares & woe pynith.⁵ What shall I speake of thy children Consuls, whose fathers & grandfathers witt appeerith as their yo*u*ng yeeres permitt. Whan then the cheefest care for mortall men is lyfe to keepe, ô happy thou, yf know thou
24 couldst thy good, to whom such thing*es* do hap, as no man doubt*es* the deerest thinges⁶ in lyfe. Drye vp therfore thy teares. Fortune hath not yet hated all men, nether hath to greeuous a tempest oue*r*whelmed thè, for Ankers holde re-
28 maynes, w*hi*ch nether suffers p*re*sent co*m*fort nor co*m*ming *Secondly, by pointing out the necessary imperfections of happiness.* hope to leave thè." "And let the*m* holde," q*uoth* I, "fast still, I pray. for they enduring, howsoeue*r* the world goes, out we shall wade. But you see," q*uoth* I, "how much

---

¹ "Censure" incorrect translation of *censu*.
² *diuinitus* left out; Chaucer has: "by þe grace of god."
³ The negation not according to the Latin text.
⁴ At the beginning of this sentence *viuit* is not translated, and at the end *patri similis*.
⁵ Meaning of this sentence, "*quoque uno felicitatem minui tuam uel ipsa concesserim, tui desiderio lacrimis ac dolore tabescit*," very doubtfully rendered. Chaucer has: "*and* is al maat *and* ouer-comen by wepyng *and* sorwe for desire of þe. ¶ In þe whiche þing only I mot graunten þat þi welefulnesse is amenused."
⁶ *thinges* interlined by the Queen.

One man is very rich, but of base descent, another has nobility of birth, but no possessions.

honour we have lost." Then she : " we will help thè, yf thou be not weary of all thy lott. But I can not abyde such your delytes as depriued of som of thy felicitie, wayling & carefull thou complaynst. for what man is of stayde felicitie, that quarrels not with som degre of his estate ? Carefull is the condition of mans goodes, which eyther neuer all happs, or euer bydes. This man hath honour,¹ but his blotted blud shames him. This man nobilitie makes famous, but inclosed with neede, rather vnknowen he choosith : An other man having² both, the sole³ lyfe bewayles : An other for

Another is unhappy because he has no children.

mariage happy, childles keeps his goodes for an others heire. Som Joye with children, with teares bemoanes the faultes of sonne or daughter. no man therfore easely agrees with his fortunes state. generall to all, that the vntryed knowes not, thexpert abhorrith. Add to withall that ech man hath a most delicate sense of his own felicitie, and without all hap to his beck, throwen down he is, with any vnwontid⁴ aduersitie, though in leste matters. Such tryfles they be that drawes from happyest men the top of bliss. How many be there, supposest thou, that wold think them neerest heauen, if skraps of thy fortune hap to ther⁵ share ? This place which thou thy bannishment callst,⁶ is the inhabitantes countrey. so nothing is wretched, but when it is thought so, & blessed is all luck that haps with sufferers ease. What man is so happy that hath giuen hand to impatience, that wisshith not his fortune changed ? The sweetnes of mans lyfe, with how many bytternesses is it mixt ! which if they seemid to the enioyer delitefull when he wolde, it is

All human prosperity is unsatisfactory because it is not lasting.

gon, therfore he may not keepe it. The blessednes of mortall goodes plainly is miserable, that nether perpetually duryth with the contented, nor wholly delites the afflicted. Why do ye mortall men seeke outwardly your felicitie within yo⁰ ?⁷ Error and blyndnes confoundes yo⁰. I will shew thè shortly the thressholl⁸ of thy felicitie. Is there to thè ought more

---

¹ The Latin *census* here means money, not honour. ² Or halving ?
³ What the Queen has here translated "sole" is in Latin *caelips*, celibate.
⁴ *Minimis* not translated.
⁵ *ther* interlined in the Queen's hand over *thy* struck out.
⁶ The *st* final added by the Queen.   ⁷ " Why do ye mortall men seeke outwardly your felicitie, when it is within you ? "   ⁸ Translation of Latin *cardo*, hinge.

precious than thy selfe?" "nothing," quoth I. "Then if thou be wise, thou shalt possesse that nether thou canst lose, nor fortune take away. And that thou mayste knowe felicitie not to stand in happing chaunces, considir it this. Yf happynes be the greatest good of nature lyuing by reason, nor hit[1] the greatest good that may be taken away, the cause hit[1] doth excede that may not so, It is manifest, that fortunes change can not attayn to the getting[2] of bliss. Besydes, whom falling felicitie caryes, eyther knowith her,[3] or seeth her mutabilitie. Yf he be ignorant, what happy luck can blynde felicitie haue? Yf he know it, he must needes feare to lose that he is sure can not be kepte. His contynuall feare then, depriuith his happynes. or if he haue lost, will he not care for it? for hit should be a slender good that a man wold[4] easely lose. And because thou art the same that art persuaded, and holdes it sure by many demonstrations, mens myndes not to be mortall, and when it is playne, that chauncing felicitie with bodies death is finished, no man can doubte, Can this bring felicitie, but rather all mortall folkes in misery by[5] deathes end is brought. Yf many we knowe to haue sought the frute of blessednes, not only by death, but by woes & tormentes, for that[6] how can the present lyfe make them happy, whom miserable tyme passed could not?"

Nothing is more precious than self, of which we cannot be deprived.

Finally Philosophy proves to Boethius that even the attainment of the highest pinnacle of human bliss cannot make him happy.

IV. MYTER.

Who lasting wyl
 Wary settel seat,[7]
And stable not of Roring
 Eurus blastz ben won, 4

Praise of a happy medium.

---

[1] *hit* interlined by the Queen over *it* erased.
[2] *getting* interlined by the Queen over *obtayning* erased.
[3] *her* interlined in the Queen's hand.
[4] *wold* interlined by the Queen over *will* struck out.
[5] *by* interlined by the Queen.
[6] *for that* probably intended to be omitted.
[7] The Queen wrote first: "Who warely a lasting seat wil settel," but erased it.

IV. METRUM.

Quisquis uolet perennem   *Stabilisque nec sonori*
 Cautus ponere sedem,   *Sterni flatibus euri,*   4

To attain which we must not build our hopes too high, but on a firm foundation.

>   And careth skorne
>   the waues of thretning Sea,
>   Shuns soking Sandes,
>   and top of hiest mount.   8
>   One the froward Southe
>   With all his affrightz,
>   The other lovsed refuse
>   A hanging waight to beare.   12
>   fleing perillous lot
>   Of pleasantz Seat,
>   On lowe stone remember
>   thy house sure to place.   16
>   Thogh wynd blowe
>   Myxing waters to botom,
>   Thou happy plast in strengh
>   Of quietz Rampar,   20
>   Happy shalt liue
>   And smile at Skies
>   Wrathe.

V. Prose.

The vanity of Fortune's gifts is demonstrated in a variety of ways.

"But because the fomentations of my reason haue entred in the, I suppose I must vse som stronger remedies. Go to. Yf now the giftes of fortune be not fleeting & changeable, what is ther that eyther thou canst make thyne, or if thou seest & perceuist, wilt not dispise? Are riches eyther thyne, or by their nature pretious? what is the golde therof? but heape of gathered pence? and such as shynes more with their spending than with their heapes. Hatefull men doth Auarice mocke, but bountie noble. And if it can not byde by a man that is giuen to an other, Than monny is most pretious, when turnd to others by liberall vse, hath lost the

---

Et fluctibus minantem		Sortem sedis amoenae	
Curat spernere pontum,		Humili domum memento	
Montis cacumen alti,		Certus figere saxo.	16
Bibulas uitet harenas.	8	Quamuis tonet ruinis	
Illud proteruus auster		Miscens aequora uentus,	
Totis uiribus urget,		Tu conditus quieti	
Hae pendulum solutae		Felix robore ualli,	
Pondus ferre recusant.	12	Duces serenus aeuum	20
Fugiens periculosam		Ridens aetheris iras.	

12 possession. The same, if but with one abyde, from how *Every one cannot possess these gifts, they are given to one and taken away from another.*
many it be pluckt, the rest it leaves full needy. The fame[1]
therof fills many mens eares, but Riches not distributed may
not[2] passe to many : which when it is don, they must make
16 poore whom they leave. O skant & needy riches, which
all to haue is not lawfull for many, & com not to any one
without they begger of the rest. Doo Jewels luster drawe
thyne eyes? Yf any beauty they haue, it is the stones light,
20 not mens; which I muse why men so admire. for what is
there that wantes a spirit and lymmes partage,[3] that Justly
may seeme fayre to the myndes and Reasons nature?[4] which
tho as Creators goodes & his diuisions,[5] may draw som later
24 beauty, placed vnder your worth, no way deserue your wonder.
Doo sick mens palenes please you?[6] What els? for it is a *Any excellence which they may have, belongs to themselues and not to their possessors*
fayre portion of a goodly woork. So somtymes we delite in
face of smothest sea: So doo we vew the heauen, the starres,
28 sonne & moone. Doo any of these touch thè? Darest
thou boste at any of their lusters? Shalt thou be paynted
out for the florishing springes sake? or shall thy plenty
increase to sommer frutes? Why art thou drawne with
32 vayne Joyes? Why dost thou cherish others goodes for
thyne? Fortune shall neuer make those thyne, that nature
hath made other folkes. The earthes frutes doutles be due to
best nourishment. Yf thou wilt fill the neede that Nature
36 Requires, thou needest not seeke fortunes plenty. for with few
or little nature is contented. Whose ynough if thou wilt
make to much, that noyfull & vnpleasant to taste will
make. But now, Thou thinkest it beautifull to shyne with
40 diuers garmentes, whose show yf it please the eye, eyther *These gifts sometimes only bring trouble in their train.*
they will wonder at nature of the substance, or the witt of
the Craftes man. But shall the long trayne of many servantes
happyn thè, who if they be of vile condition, it is an yll

---

[1] *Fame* is not a good translation of "vox." Chaucer has "voys."
[2] A negation too much.
[3] *partage* translates "compage," union. Chaucer has "ioynture."
[4] Chaucer has: "by ry3t my3t semen a faire creature to hym þat haþ a soule of resoun." The correct reading of the Latin text is: "what might justly appear beautiful to an intelligent human being."
[5] "distinction" is better than "divisions."
[6] Quite a wrong transl. of "*an vos agrorum pulchritudo delectat.*" Chaucer has: "And þe beaute of feeldes deliteþ it nat mychel vnto 3ow."

burden for the house, & most foe to his Lord: but if good they be, how canst thou sett other mens vertue among thy goodes? by which all, It is playne seene, that those thou reckenst for thy goodes, are none of thyne: In which, if ther be no beauty got, what is it that thou waylest for losse, or Joyest to haue? If by nature they be fayre, what carest thou? for such thinges of themselves separated from thy substance should haue pleased. for precious they be not to haue com among thy ryches; but because they were precious, thou chosedst rather place them among them. Why, lack you fortunes exclamation?[1] I beleeue you seeke to beate away beggery with plenty. But this happes awry, for ye had neede of many helps to preserue the variety of deere goodes. And this is true, that they neede many, that possesse muche. And agayne they lack leste, that mesure their own abundance by natures necessitie, not Ambitions greedynes. But is it so? Is ther [no][2] proper good ingraft in you of your own, that you should seeke it in outward & meane[3] matters? Is the world so changed, that the diuine Creature for Reason sake should no otherwise florish, but that it neede possession of dom[4] ware? And all other thinges contented be with their owne, but we[5] lyke god of mynde, shall we[5] take the ornamentes of excellent nature from basse thinges? nor shall not vnderstand how much therby we Iniure our Creatour. He wold haue vs exceede all earthly thinges, but you throwe your worth among basest stuff. For if euery mans possession seemes more deere that it is his owne, when the meanest thinges your own you judge, to them you yeld y[ou] with your prising, which not without desert happs. For this is the state of humayn nature, that then it exceedes all other, whan it self it knowes, but is made baser than very beastes, if to know it self it leave. For naturall it is for other beastes not know themsellves, In man it is a vice. How farre stretchith your errour,[6] which doo supposte to be deckt with other mens ornamentes?[7] For yf of outward thinges

---

[1] The correct transl. is: "Why do you desire such a noisy happiness?"
[2] Torn off.
[3] Latin *sepositis*, not correctly translated by "meane." Chaucer has "subgit."
[4] "dumb"; *inanimatae*, Latin.   [5] *Vos* is here incorrectly translated "we."
[6] Written over *arrowe*.   [7] Here "*At id fieri nequit*" is missing.

What faithful fruth containe
Hath lost by straying Lust
that weene the Longe taste
to Loade by ???? Acorne
that knewe not bacons gifts
Wth molten hony mixed
Nor ????? Sheep Hide
Wth tirino Vinsons Die
Sonne Slepes Gave the ????
their ???? Vunionystri???
Shand ???? Gave the best ???
???? depth of Sea ??? far ??? ???
Hot Words Choller too fier
Made Strangers find new Shores,
The ??? Manhicks St???
Hot bloudshid by Cruell hate
had fearfull weapos stoure
What first envy to this Shade
any areises ???
What Cruel wounds he Saw
and no K Word for blonde,
Wold God again our foringe time
to Wotid mans-to ???
but Gredy getting Loun Gureris
Sorast ??? Flema it her Hands

any lyke¹ be had, those be praysde from whence they cam: but if ought ther be hid or vnknowen, bydes in his own spot.² But I deny that is good, that harmes the hauer. Doo I saye vntruth? No, wilt thou saye. And riches oft haue harmed their owners, whan ech wicked man (and therfore greedier of others goodes) hath thought him only woorthyest, that hath obtayn[d] golde or Jewells.³ Thou that the speare and sword carefully hast feared, if wandering empty man, of lyfe the path hadst enterd, afore a theefe woldest sing, O beautifull hap of mortall goodes, which when thou hast taken, sure⁴ hath left thè!"

Too much prosperity is injurious to the wicked.

V. MYTER.

Happy to muche the formar Age
With faithful fild content,
Not Lost by sluggy Lust,
that wontz the Long fastz   4
To Louse by son-got Acorne.
that knew not Baccus giftz
With molten hony mixed
Nor Serike shining flise⁵   8
With tirius venom⁶ die.⁷
Sound slipes Gaue the grasse⁸
ther drink the running streme
Shades gaue the hiest pine.   12
The depth of sea they fadomd not
Nor wares chosen from fur

Lament over the loss of the Golden Age,

when mankind was content with a more simple life.

---

¹ Probably "light" (L. *luceat*).
² Whole sentence very unintelligible, "*illud uero his tectum atque uclatum in sua nihilo minus foeditate perdurat.*" Chaucer has: "But naþeles þe þing þat is couered *and* wrapped vndir þat dwelleþ in his filþe." ³ *jewells* incorrect.
⁴ Badly translated, from "*securus esse desistis.*" ⁵ fleece.
⁶ *ueneno* is better translated with juice. Chaucer has also "venym." ⁷ dye.
⁸ *herba* is better translated with herbs, as food is evidently meant. Chaucer has also mistaken the sense: "þei slepen holesom slepes vpon þe gras."

V. METRUM.

Felix nimium prior aetas
Contenta fidelibus aruis,
Nec inerti perdita luxu,
Facili quae sera solebat   4
Ieiunia soluere glande.
Non bacchica munera norant
Liquido confundere melle,
Nec lucida uellera Serum   8
Tyrio miscere ueneno.
Somnos dabat herba salubres
Potum quoque lubricus amnis
Vmbras altissima pinus.   12
Nondum maris alta secabat
Nec mercibus undique lectis

> *Made Stranger find new shores.*
> *Than wer Navies[1] Stil,*   16
> *Nor bloudshed by Cruel hate*
>   *Had fearful weapons[2] staned.*
> *What first fury to foes shuld*
>   *any armes rayse,*   20
> *Whan Cruel woundz he Saw*
>   *and no reward for bloude ?*
> *Wold God agane Our formar time*
>   *to wonted maners fel !*[3]   24
> *But Gridy getting Loue burnes*
>   *Sorar than Etna with her flames.*
> *O who the first man was*
>   *of hiden Gold the waight*   28
> *Or Gemmes that willing lurkt*
>   *The deare danger digd ?*

Marginalia: when peace reigned and wars were not. — An invocation to God for the return of the Golden Age.

VI. PROSE.

"What shal I dispute of Dignities and rule, wiche you, ignorant of true worthe and power, with the skies do mache? wiche happening to any wicked man, what Etnas fire with brusting flames, or what deluge suche ruine makes! 4 Surely, as I thinke you remember, how Consulz rule, beginar of liberty, for ther pride our fathers soght to put downe, who for like faulte out of the citie the name of kings abolisshed. but if sometime, as seldom haps, honors in Good men be 8 bestowed, what elz in them doth please than vsars goodnis? So haps,[4] that honour is not giuen to vertue for her worth, but vertue esteemd by dignitie. But what is this, your craved and beautifull force? Do yo^u not see how earthly be 12

Marginalia: Philosophy shows, that for many reasons, high offices and dignities, and even possessions, have no value of their own.

---

[1] The Queen has read *classis*, navy, for *classicum*, trumpet.
[2] Here she has read *arma* for *arua*, field. Chaucer has it also incorrectly *armurers*.
[3] Of this sentence the sense is reversed.
[4] The translation of Prose VI is in the Queen's hand up to this point.

Noua litora uiderat hospes.			*Vtinam modo nostra redirent*	
Tunc classica saeua tacebant,		16	*In mores tempora priscos.*	24
Odiis neque fusus acerbis			*Sed saeuior ignibus Aetnae*	
Cruor horrida tinxerat arua.			*Feruens amor ardet habendi.*	
Quid enim furor hosticus ulla			*Heu primus quis fuit ille*	
Vellet prior arma mouere,		20	*Auri qui pondera tecti*	28
Cum uulnera saeua uiderent,			*Gemmasque latere uolentes*	
Nec praemia sanguinis ulla ?			*Pretiosa pericula fodit ?*	

the bestes that yoⁿ Rule?¹ for euin among the myse, yf ye *and only obtain this from the*
see any one chalinging rule or gouuernment aboue the rest, *person and character of their*
what a laughter doo ye mooue! But what if ye haue respect *possessors,*
16 to the body? what can be weaker than man, whom somtyme
the byt of a flye, somtyme the passage² into any secret parte
may destroye? How farre ought any man stretch the Rule
but on the body alone and his circumstances, I meane fortune
20 her self? will you euer guide ought with free mynde? & *If a man has firmness of*
will ye remooue the same sticking to her self by good reason, *character it is impossible to*
from the state of her own quiet?³ Whan a tyrant thought *deprive him of*
to afflicte a poore⁴ man with his tormentes to confesse the *liberty.*
24 knowers of a conspiracy against him, his tongue he byt &
threw away, throwing it to the face of the wicked tyrant: So
the torture that he supposde to make stuff for his cruelty, a
wise man made for his vertue. for what is it that any man
28 can doo to an other, that to be don to himself can he not
beare? Bucidides, we heare, was wont his guestes to kyll,
slayne himself by Hercules his host. Regulus cast many
prisoners into yrons in the Punik warr, but straight himself
32 sett handes on victorerers chaynes.⁵ Dost thou think his
powre ought, what himself may, can not lett that an other
should doo him? Besides, if euin in Souueraynties &
powres, there should be any j naturall & proper good, neuer
36 should they hap to wicked. for contrarieties seld consorte. *Riches and*
Nature denyes that disagreins⁶ be Joyned. Wherfore when *dignities do not*
playn it is that many⁷ men beare greate office, this is sure, *make their possessors rich and*
that of their nature they be not good, wiche stick to wickedst *honourable in same way that*
40 folke. The greatest worth that fortunes guiftes woorthyest can *music makes those that have a*
giue, be such as in abondant sorte to wicked folkes do hap.⁸ *knowledge of it musical.*

---

¹ Here a part of the sense of the Latin text is omitted: "*nonne o terrena animalia consideratis, quibus qui praesidere uideamini.*"   ² *hidden* paþ written over *passage*.
³ Meaning doubtful: "*num mentem firma sibi ratione cohaerentem de statu propriae quietis amouebis.*" Chaucer has: "Mayst þou remuen fro þe estat of hys propre reste . a þouȝt þat is cleuyng to gider in hym self by stedfast resoun."
⁴ The Queen appears to have read *miserum* for *liberum*. Chaucer has "freeman."
⁵ Meaning not well given: "*sed mox ipse uictorum catenis manus praebuit.*" Chaucer has: "but sone after he most ȝiue hys handes to ben bounden with þe cheynes of hem þat he had somtyme ouercomen."
⁶ This word interlined by the Queen over "contrarieties" erased.
⁷ Transl. of *pessimos* is left out.
⁸ After *hap* a whole sentence is omitted. "*De quibus illud etiam considerandum puto, quod nemo dubitat esse fortem, cui fortitudinem inesse conspexerit.*"

Who so quicknes hath, hit swift a man doth make. So musick the musicall, phisick the phisician, Retorik Rhetorician makith, for the nature of ech thing doth his propertie, nor is myxt with effect of contrarietie, And freely expells that is against it: nether can riches vnsaciable auarice refrayne, nor makes not free his own, whom vitious lust with vnbroke chaynes, holdes bound: And dignitie on wicked bestowde, not only makes them not worthy, but betrayes & discouers their indignitie. Why doth it hap so? You Joye somtyme to falsifie with other name, whose effect shames themselues. Wherfore nether those riches, nor same powre, nor lyke dignitie, can by right be called. Lastly, the same we may conclude of all fortune, that hath nothing in her as it is playne to be desyrde, not of naturall goodnes, who eyther neuer accompanyes the good, nor makes them good whom she is neerest."

<small>Fortune is not to be desired for her own sake.</small>

VI. MYTER.

<small>Nero is taken as an example;</small>

We knowe how many ruines made,
  Whan flamed Citie and fathers slain,
that tirant who ons brother kild
  Imbrued with mothers bloude,   4
With looke overvewed her body Cold
  No teares bedewes his face, but was
A domar¹ of dedded beautye.
  the same yet with Sceptar peple ruled,   8
Euin suche as Son espies at furdest west
  from the Orison Come,
Whom frosty seuen stars Ouerlookes,

<small>to show how little influence the highest dignity has over the mind of its bearer.</small>

  Whom wrothful North with drie heat   12
Affraies in sithing of the burning sandz.
  Could al his lofty power at lenghe

---

¹ Old English *domar*, judge, transl. of *censor* (critic).

VI. METRUM.

Nouimus quantas dederit ruinas
Vrbe flammata patribusque caesis,
Fratre qui quondam ferus interempto
Matris effuso maduit cruore   4
Corpus, et uisu gelidum pererrans
Ora non tinxit lacrimis, sed esse
Censor extincti potuit decoris.
Hic tamen sceptro populos regebat,   8
Quos uidet condens radios sub undas
Phoebus extremo ueniens ab ortu,
Quos premunt septem gelidi triones,
Quos notus sicco uiolentus aestu   12
Torret ardentes recoquens harenas.
Celsa num tandem ualuit potestas

*Turne the rage of franti*que *Nero ?*
*O grevous hap wha*n *wicked Sword* 16
*To cruel Veno*m *Joingnes.*

VII. PROSE.

Then I: "Thou thy self knowest that no ambition of mortall things did rule vs. We were not guided by the pride¹ of any mortall glory, but wish a ground in our
4 affayres, by which silent vertue should not growe olde."²
Then she: "This is that that noble myndes by nature, but not yet brought by perfection to the vttmost top of vertue, might intice, I meane Gloryes desyre & fame of best actes
8 for common welth: which how small it is and empty of all waight, consider this. As Astrologers demonstrations haue told yo*u*, all the Earthes circle is playne, gettes som meane to know these partes of the heauens face, that if it be
12 matched with the greatnes of the celestiall globe, It is supposde to haue no space, and it is of this little region of the world almost but the fourth portion, As thou hast learnd by Ptolomés graunte,³ which is inhabited by vs Creatures known.
16 From this fourth, if in thy mynde thou draw away as much as Sea and marish couers, and so much as wasted ground by drynes hath distended, the straytest roome is left for mans habitation. If⁴ in this so small a point of title⁵ we be
20 hedged in & inclosed, what think we so much of enlarging fame, & name promoting? For what large and magnifick thing hath glory bounde in so straight & small lymites?
Ad to this that, though but small it self, enuirond is with
24 habitation of many nations tongues and conditions, that in all trade of lyfe differs, To which not only no report of ech

Marginalia:
The nothingness of earthly glory is shown in many ways, and especially by its circumscribed limits.

Astronomers teach that the circumference of the earth is a mere nothing in comparison with that of the heavens.

How useless is it then to set so much value on earthly fame.

---

¹ *pride* interlined by the Queen over *ambition* erased.
² Correct transl. of the sentence: "In order that our abilities may be celebrated before we grow old."
³ *graunte*, Latin *probante*. Chaucer has: "Pt. þat prouith it."
⁴ Instead of 1 per. plural, 2 per. should be used in this sentence throughout.
⁵ perhaps *little*, or *tittle*.

Vertere ignaui rabiem Neronis ?
Heu grauem sortem, quoticns iniquus   16
Additur sacuo gladius uencno !

In the time of Cicero, as he himself says, the name of Rome was quite unknown beyond the Caucasus.

man, but not of Cities can com through hardnes of way & difference of speeche, and diuers traffik. In Marcus Tull*ius* tyme, as he himself in place hath sayde, the fame of Romayn Empire neu*er* past Caucasus mounte, & yet it was florishing, fearfull to the Parthians & to all peeple inhabiting such places. Dost thou not see then, how narrow & neere presst glory is, w*hi*ch to stretch out spred thou labourst? shall the glory of a Romayn go so furr, as whence neu*er* Romayn name hath past? What, for that the diuers natures of peeple & their orders disagree? so that, what amo*n*g som is prayse, among the rest sett for cryme. So haps that if any mans prayse delyte, to him the same doth neu*er* proffit to many

No one is content that his fame should not extend beyond the limits of his own Fatherland.

peeple sent. Is any man co*n*tent that amo*n*g his own his glory byde, & Immortalities fame be tyed in bound*es* of his own soyle?[1] But how many noble men in their tymes fayling obliui*on* of writers have[2] dasht? But what proffit*es* writing*es*? which w*ith* the office[3] a long & dark age suppressith? But doo yo*u* think immortality w*ith* thought of co*m*ming tyme?[4] Yf thou Joyne it w*ith* the infinit spaciousnes of eternitie, what hast thou to Joye of thy lasting name? For if the abode of one moment, w*ith* ten thousand yeeres be compared, for that both space is ending, It shall haue, tho a

The continuance of earthly glory is nothing in comparison with eternity, because the finite cannot be compared with the infinite.

little, som portio*n*. But this nomber of yeeres, how oft so eu*er* multiplyed, may not co*m*pare w*ith* the vnending lasting. Somtyme som outward[5] thing*es* ther be, compard amo*n*g themselues, haue ende; twixt infinite and ending[6] no co*m*parison may beare. So is it that the lasting of any longest tyme, if it be matcht w*ith* vnbounde eternitie, not small but none shall seeme.[7] For wit*h*out you be ignorant, how rightly to please popular eares & vayne rumors, & leauing care of conscience & vertue, ask rewarde of other mens frute,[8]

28

32

36

40

44

48

52

56

---

[1] No question: "every man ought to be content," etc.
[2] *haue* interlined by the Queen.
[3] Here *auctoribus* is translated "with the office," instead of "with the author."
[4] No question. "*Vos uero immortalitatem uobis propagare uidemini, cum futuri famam temporis cogitatis.*" Chaucer has: "ȝe men semen to geten ȝow a perdurablete whan ȝe þenke þat in tyme comyng ȝoure fame shal lasten."
[5] Latin text has *finitis* (finite), not "outward."
[6] *twixt infinite and ending* interlined in the Queen's hand.
[7] The final *me* added by the Queen.
[8] *frute*, a wrong transl. of *sermunculis* (tittle tattle).

see how in the myldnes of such an arrogancy, how pleasantly
a man may be begylde. For when one once had skornde a
man that clothed him not with Philosophy for true vertues
vse, but for proude gloryes sake, & saide he wold try him
whither he were a Philosopher that easely could beare in
patience iniuryes, he tooke vpon him to be suffring, &
taking the skorne as a raging man:[1] 'Dost thou at length
understand me a Philosopher?' Then nippingly he said:
'I should haue vnderstode it, if thou hadst bene silent.'
What meanes it, that cheefest men (for of them I speake)
that seeke thorowgh vertue glory, what hath death to doo
with them after the body is dissolued, at their end? For be
it that our Reason it self denyes vs to beleeue that all men
dye, then ther is no glory, when he is not, of whom she
speakes. But if the mynde it self with conscience good
dissolued from earthly gial,[2] all freed seekes heauen, wold
she not all earthly thinges despise, who heauen enioyeng.
Joyes earthly thinges to want?"

Allusion to the celebrated Latin saying: "Si tacuisses philosophus mansisses.

The man who has a pure conscience and aspires to heaven, despises earthly things.

VII. MYTER.

Who so with hedlong mynd glory
    alone beliues as Greatest thing,
And quarters of Largist heuens behold
    With straightid seat of erthe,   4
Wyl blusche that hit not filz
    The Short Compas of Gridy desire.
Why proude men do you Crake
    Your necks from mortal yoke retire?[3]   8
Thogh fame by people strange
    flying spred the tonges Open

Human renown is confined within a very limited space, and is invariably brought to an end by death.

---

[1] Transl. of *inquit* left out.
[2] *gial* interlined in the Queen's hand over *geayle* erased.
[3] Quite unintelligible. Chaucer has: "he shal be ashamed of þe encres of his name. þat may nat fulfille þe litel compas of þe erþe. O what coueiten proude folke to liften vpon hire nekkes in ydel and dedely ȝok of þis worlde."

VII. METRUM.

Quicumque solam mente praecipiti petit
  Summumque credit gloriam,
Late patentes aetheris cernat plagas
  Artumque terrarum situm.   4
Breuem replere non valentis ambitum

Pudebit aucti nominis.
Quid o superbi colla mortali iugo
  Frustra leuare gestiunt?   8
Licet remotos fama per populos means
Diffusa linguas explicet,

Examples of the transitoriness of glory, Brutus, Fabricius, Cato.

And noble house by Great titelz shine :
  dethe hates the hiest glory,   12
Intangels Low and hauty hed,
  And equalz Lest to most.
Wher now lies faithful Fabritius bones ?
  Wher Brutus or Currish[1] Cato ?   16
Smal Lasting fame signes
  A vaine name with fewest lettars.
But why do we knowe noble names,
  Do we not See them to consumed ?[2]   20
Ly you shal vnknowen at all
  Nor fame shal uttar Who.

Fame does not lengthen life.

If you Suppose that Life be Longar drawen
  For brethe of mortal fame,   24
Than the Second dethe Exspect.[3]

VIII. PROSE.

Evil fortune is more profitable for man than good, because it teaches him to know his friends.

"But lest you shuld suppose against fortune I make an Endles war, Ther is a time when she, the begiling one, somewhat wel of men desarues: Euen than when discouerd, herself she shewes, and maners hers detectz. Perchanche 4 yet thou wotz not what I say. Wondar hit is that I mynd tel, and mening skars with wordes may Expres. For men I suppose more get by aduerse than lucky fortune, for she euer with shewe of blis, with seming al false, deceues : and 8 euer true she is[4] in change, when vnstable she seemes. The one beguyles, the other instructes. This tyes the enioyers myndes with show of lyeng good, the other lovsith[5] them

---

[1] Transl. of *rigidus*. Chaucer has "stiern."
[2] Meaning not well rendered. Chaucer has: "it is nat ȝeuen to knowe hem þat ben dede and consumpt." [3] The previous Latin line not translated.
[4] The transl. of Prose VIII up to this point is in the Queen's hand.
[5] *loosith* altered to *lovsith* by the Queen.

Et magna titulis fulgeat claris domus ;
  Mors spernit altam gloriam,   12
Involuit humile pariter et celsum caput,
  Aequatque summis infima.
Vbi nunc fidelis ossa Fabricii manent,
  Quid Brutus aut rigidus Cato ?   16
Signat superstes fama tenuis pauculis
  Inane nomen litteris.

Sed quod decora nouimus uocabula,
  Num scire consumptos datur ?   20
Iacetis ergo prorsus ignorabiles
  Nec fama notos efficit.
Quod si putatis longius uitam trahi
  Mortalis aura nominis,   24
Cum sera uobis rapiet hoc etiam dies,
  Iam uos secunda mors manet.

12 with knowledge of frayle felicitie. This know therfore, for *One of the uses of aduersity is, that it teaches us to distinguish true from false friends.* wyndy, fleeting,[1] & ignorant of her self. The other sober, ready & wise by aduersities exercise. At last happy he that drawes the strayeng with deceite from greatest good, but
16 aduersitie of tymes retourning them to surest haps, as by a hooke[2] doth drawe. Thinkest thou this for lest good, that this Currish & fearfull fortune hath discouerd the mynde of thy faythfull frendz,[3] The other hath shewed the fellow
20 sure[4] lookes & doubtfull, in departing hath taken hers, & thyne hath left thè.[5] With how much woldest thou, in prosperous state haue bought this, when thou thoughtest it most? Leave to seeke lost goodes, The preciousest kynde of
24 ryches, frendes thou hast founde."

VIII. MYTER.

> That world with stable trust
> the changing seasons turnes,
> And diuers sedes stil holdes league,
> That Φebus the ruddy daye   4
> With Golden Car bringes furthe,
> that Mone may rule the night
> Wiche Hesperus broght,
> The gridy Sea her Streame   8
> In Certaine limites kipt,
> That Lawful be not to wide world
> to bancke her spatius boundz :

Praise of Love as the preserver of the whole terrestrial fabric.

The warring elements are kept within certain limits.

---

[1] *fleeting* (fluens) better translated with *weak.*
[2] *hoode* corrected to *hooke* by the Queen.
[3] The *z* in *frendz* added by the Queen.   [4] At first written *sure fellow.*
[5] Meaning of this sentence not well given : "*haec tibi certos sodalium uultus ambiguosque secreuit, discedens suos abstulit, tuos reliquit ?*" Chaucer has : "ek the dowtos visages of thy felawes // whan she departyd awey fro the / she took awey hyr frendes and lafte the thyne frendes."

VIII. METRUM.

Quod mundus stabili fide
Concordes uariat uices,
Quod pugnantia semina
Foedus perpetuum tenent,   4
Quod Phoebus roseum diem
Curru prouehit aureo,

Vt quas duxerit Hesperos
Phoebe noctibus imperet,   8
Vt fluctus auidum mare
Certo fine coerceat,
Ne terris liceat uagis
Latos tendere terminos :   12

These limits are kept by the influence of love.	Al this hole molde ties	12
	in ruling erthe and Sea	
	Loue ruling heuens.	
	Who if the raines he slake,	
	What so now by loue is linked	16
	Straict maketh war	
	And seakes to wracke that worke	
The power of love in social and family life.	Whiche linked faithe,	
	hit quiet motions moued.	20
	He in holy peace doth hold	
	the bounded peoples pact,	
	And Linkes sacred wedlok	
	With Chast Goodwyl,	24
	Who Lawes his owne	
	to true Associates giues.	
	O happy humain kind,	
An exhortation to man to allow his mind to be guided by heavenly love.	If loue your mindz	28
	The same that heuen doth rule	
	Mygh[t] gide.	

Heere endes ye second booke.

Hanc rerum seriem ligat,
Terras ac pelagus regens
Et caelo imperitans, amor.
Hic si frena remiserit,   16
Quidquid nunc amat inuicem
Bellum continuo geret,
Et quam nunc socia fide
Pulchris motibus incitant,   20
Certent soluere machinam.

Hic sancto populos quoque
Iunctos foedere continet,
Hic et coniugii sacrum   24
Castis nectit amoribus,
Hic fidis etiam sua
Dictat iura sodalibus.
O felix hominum genus,   28
Si uestros animos amor
Quo caelum regitur regat.

THE THIRD BOOKE.

I. Prose.

Thus ended she her song, when greedy[1] me & astond w*ith* lyfted eares, the doulcenes of her verse, perced. Wherfore a little after: "O cheefest comfort," q*uoth* I, "of wearyed 4 mynd*es*, how much hast thou reviued me, w*ith* waight of sentence, or pleasa*n*tnes of song. so as heerafter I shall think me not inferio*ur* to fortunes strok*es*. and so the remedyes that a little before thou saidst to sharp, not only doo I not feare, but 8 ernest to heare of I greedely beseech." Then she: "I perceauid," q*uoth* she, "when silently o*ur* word*es* w*ith* attentyue eare thou cacht, that this state of thy mynde eyther I lookt for, or that is truer, my self haue made: The rest that doth 12 remayne, be such that tasted, smart*es*, but inwardly *received*, sweetens. But for that thou namest thy self ernest to heare, w*ith* what desyres shouldest thou be inflamed, yf thou couldst know whither we meane to bring thè?" "Whither?" q*uoth* I; 16 "to true felicitie,[2] w*h*ich thy mynde dreames of, whose eyes being vsed to pictures,[3] it self can not beholde." Than I: "doo, I besech thè, and w*ith*out delay, shew what is the true one." "Willingly shall I doo it," q*uoth* she, "for thy sake, but cause 20 that thou doost better know the same in woord*es*, I shall[4] describe and seeke to inform thè that she knowen,[5] when eyes thou turnst to co*n*trary p*ar*te, the show of truest good, thou mayst knowe."

Boethius feels stronger, and desires from Philosophy the most powerful panacea which she promised him.

Philosophy accedes to his demand, and in conclusion promises to point him out the path to true happiness.

---

[1] Observe that the clerk spells "greedy" and "sweetens" with *ee* not *i* like the Queen.   [2] *Inquit* left out.
[3] Latin, "*occupato ad imagines visu.*" Chaucer: "occupied and distorbed by Imagynasyon of herthely thynges."   [4] Translation of *prius* (first) left out.
[5] Incorrect translation of "*ut ea perspecta.*" Chaucer has: that thou knowest.

I. MYTER.

<small>Several similitudes which are intended to show, that error must be cast on one side before truth can be recognized.</small>

Who frutfulst fild wyl sowe,
 first fried of fruit[1] must make his leas,
With Sithe must fern and busches cut,
 that Ceres may swel with new sede.   4
The flies[2] Labor swetar is,
 If strongar[3] tast be first eate.[4]
As Luciφar dothe the darkenis chase,
 A fayre day spurs the ruddy hors.   8
Thou Looking so on falsed Good
 Begin thy neck from yoke to pluck.
Therby thy mind may true obtaine.

II. PROSE.

<small>All human endeavours are directed towards the attainment of happiness.</small>

Than fixing her looke awhile, and as taken with straight conceite of mynde,[5] thus begyns: "All mortall care which labour of many studyes vsith, goes on in diuers pathes, and yet stryves to com to one end of bliss: But that is right 4 good which a man obtayning, no furder may desyre, which is of all the greatest good, & in it self contaynes them all, of which if any want, it can not be the moste, for outwardly were left somthing to be wisht. Playne then it is, that state of all 8 good thinges perfect in his gathering, is onely blisse. This,

<small>Nature has engrafted in our minds the desire for true good, but error seduces us to false.</small>

as we sayde, by diuers path all mortall men indeuors gett. For nature hath ingraft in mens mynd desyre of truest good, but strayeng errour to falshode doth seduce vs. Among 12 whom som, beleeuing hit greatest good nothing to want, stryve

[1] The Queen appears to have read *fructibus* for *fruticibus*.
[2] In the Latin we find *apes* (becs) not flies.   [3] The Latin word is *malus* (bad).
[4] The next two lines are missing. Chaucer has: "the sterres shynen more agreably whan the wynde Nothus letith his ploungy blastes."
[5] Inexact translation: "*et uelut in augustam suae mentis sedem recepta sic cocpit.*" Chaucer has: "and with drow hir ryȝt as it were in to the streite sete of hir thouȝt."

METRUM I.

Qui serere ingenuum uolet agrum,
Liberat arua prius fruticibus,
Falce rubos filicemque resecat,
Vt noua fruge grauis Ceres eat.   4
Dulcior est apium mage labor,
Si malus ora prius sapor edat.
Gratius astra nitent ubi notus

Desinit imbriferos dare sonos.   8
Lucifer ut tenebras pepulerit,
Pulchra dies roseos agit equos.
Tu quoque falsa tuens bona prius
Incipe colla iugo retrahere.   12
Vera dehinc animum subierint.

to be rych : som, supposing honour best, when gotten they *Various definitions of true happiness; some think to find it in honour and power.*
haue, seeke of their Citizens honour. Others ther be that
16 settels greatest good in hyest powre. such will or raigne
themselves, or stryve to cleaue to such as doo. But they that
suppose honour greatest good, they eyther with warre or
peaces worth hast to inlarge a glorious name. But many
20 good men measure the frute of good with joy & mirth, and
they think it happyest to wallow in delytes. Then be to,
that enterchange ech end & care with other, as they that
riches & delyte[1] for powres sake desyre, the other powre for
24 monnyes sake or glory doo desyre. In these & such lyke
humayne actes or desyres, intent abydes, as Nobilitie & *Others in the joys of family life.*
popular fame they seeme to get som show. wyfe & children
for plesure sake desyre, but partaking[2] of of[3] frendes (that
28 holyest is) not recken by fortune nor[4] force, The rest eyther
for powres sake or delyte be taken. It is playne that bodyes
good to hyer thinges be referd, whose strength & bygnes
it is that makes their woork commended. Beauty & agilitie[5]
32 their fame, hath their delyte,[6] to whom only bliss they ad,
for that that ech man thinkes aboue the rest exceede, that
greatest good he thinkes. And greatest we suppose[7] blisse
to be, which makes men think blessedst thing, that ech
36 man aboue the rest couetes. Before thyn eyes thou hast the
forme sett out of mans felicitie, Riches, honour, powre, glory,
and delyte, which last only the Epicure considering, hit
followes that the greatest good he thought, for that delyte
40 bringes all delytefull thing to mynde. But let me retourn
to mans study, whose mynde albeit with blynded memory, *Defence of the common definition of happiness against that of Epicurus and the Cynics.*
yet seekes the greatest good, but as dronken man knowes not
the path to bring him home. Doo they seeme to err that
44 nothing to neede desyres? for that nought can so well
obtayne happynes as flowing state of all good thinges, not
needing others, contented with it self. Be they deceaud that
hit supposith best, that worthyest is of Reuerente respecte?

---

[1] The Latin text has: "they that desire riches for power and delight's sake."
[2] This word is not found in the original.   [3] *Sic.*
[4] The Latin word is *sed* (but).
[5] Here the translation of "*salubritas voluptatem*" is wanting.
[6] These words from "agilitie" seem to be a repetition in the original.
[7] The Latin text has *definivimus*.

There are many different roads which lead to true happiness, but they all converge in one goal, goodness!

No sure, nether is that vyle to be despisde that the care of ech mans labour couettes to gett. Is not force to be nombred among good thinges? What then, is that weake and to be estemid feeble, that of all other thinges exceedes? Is not honour to be regarded? It can not be denyed, but that that is most worth, ought be most honord. For carefull & sorowfull, blisse we can not call, nor subiecte to care & woe we may not saye, when in lest thinges that is desyrd, that most delytes haue & enioye. And these be those which men wold obtayne, & for their cause desyre ryches, dignitie, Raygnes, glory, & delytes. for that by these they beleeue they may gett ynough, honour, powre, glory, and Joye. Good it is therfore that men by so many ways doo seeke; In which, what force of nature ther is, is[1] showed, that tho dyuers & sondry opinyons, yet in looving goodnes end, they all consent."

II. MYTER.

The power of nature is stronger than that of education and custom.

How many raines of Causis gideth
   nature powreful, by wiche the great
World with Lawes provident kepes
   and tijnge, Strains with vnlousing   4
Knot eche thing,[2] wel pleases with shirllest
   note expres with drawing strings.
Thogh Africke Lionnes faire
   giues beare and takes giuen food with paw[3]   8
And Cruel kipar feares the wonted stripes that bare:
   If bloud haue ons dyed ther Looke,[4]
Ther courage retournes to formar state

The lion is given as one example.

And with rorings lowde them selues remembring,   12

---

[1] Translation of *facile* left out.
[2] Ties single things together with an insoluble knot.
[3] The text has "feed from the hand."
[4] *horrida* is missed. Chaucer has: "yif þat hir horrible mouþes ben bibled."

METRUM II.

Quantas rerum flectat habenas	*Quamuis poeni pulchra leones*
Natura potens, quibus immensum	*Vincula gestent, manibusque datas* 8
Legibus orbem prouida seruet,	*Captent escas, metuantque trucem*
Stringatque, ligans inresoluto 4	*Soliti uerbera ferre magistrum;*
Singula nexu, placet arguto	*Si cruor horrida tinxerit ora,*
Fidibus lentis promere cantu.	*Resides olim redeunt animi,* 12

Slacks from tied knotz ther necks ;	The caged bird is another, which in spite of the sweetest food given him in a cage, desires liberty.
And furius first with Cruel tothe	
On kipar raging wrathe bestowes.	
The Chatting bird that sings on hiest bow, 16	
In holow den Shut is she:	
to this thogh Cups with hony lined	
And largest food with tendar loue	
beqiling Care of man bestowes, 20	
If yet skipping on the Eues [1]	
Spies pleasing shady wood,	
With fote she treds her skatterd meat,	
in Sorowing seakes the woodz alone, 24	Natural growth, if distorted by artificial means, returns to its original form as soon as this is removed.
And with swit vois the trees resountz.[2]	
the twig drawen ons with mighty fors	
Bowing plies her top:	
the same if bending hand do slack, 28	
The top vpright doth turne.	
The Son to Hesperius waters falz,	
But by Secret pathe againe	
His Cart turnes to Est. 32	
Eache thing Sekes owt his propre Cours	
and do reiois at retourne ther owen:	
Nor ordar giuen to any remains,	Another instance of the power of Nature is taken from the course of the sun.
onles he Joinge to end his first 36	
And so stedyes his holie round.	

[1] Most of the texts have *textum* (wicker) not *tectum* (roof).
[2] Whispers to the woods with a sweet voice.

Fremituque graui meminere sui:
Laxant nodis colla solutis
Primusque lacer dente cruento
Domitor rabidas imbuit iras.   16
Quae canit altis garrula ramis
Ales, caueae clauditur antro:
Huic licet inlita pocula melle
Largasque dapes dulci studio   20
Ludens hominum cura ministret,
Si tamen arto saliens texto
Nemorum gratas uiderit umbras,
Sparsas pedibus proterit escas,   24
Siluas tantum maesta requirit,
Siluas dulci uoce susurrat.
Validis quondam uiribus acta
Pronum flectit uirga cacumen: 28
Hanc si curuans dextra remisit,
Recto spectat uertice caelum.
Cadit hesperias Phœbus in undas,
Sed secreto tramite rursus   32
Currum solitos uertit ad ortus.
Repetunt proprios quaeque recursus
Redituque suo singula gaudent:
Nec manet ulli traditus ordo,   36
Nisi quod fini iunxerit ortum,
Stabilemque sui fecerit orbem.

III. Prose.

More convincing proofs that riches do not possess the power of conferring happiness.

"You allso o erthly wightes, though by single figure doo dreame of your own begynning. & that true end of blissednes perceaue, tho with no playne yet with som thought, vnderstand. And thither bringes you a naturall instinct to true goodnes, and increasing errour leades yo^u from the same. Consider therfore, whither men can obtayne their end desyrd, by those meanes that men suppose gettes happynes. For if eyther monny, honors, or such lyke can bring such thinges to whom nothing is lacking of, best, let vs then confesse that som men may be happy by their obteyning. For if neyther they can doo that they promise & wantes greatest good, is it not euident that they haue but a false show of blessidnes?

Philosophy asks Boethius, if, when he was so rich, he did not find many causes of unhappiness.

First therfore let me ask thè, that a little afore aboundedst in ryches, Among thy flowing heaps, did not conceyte of conceauid iniury amase thy mynde?" "I can not remember," quoth I, "that euer my mynde was so free but somwhat greeuid it." "Was it not because that was a waye that thou woldest not forgo, or was with thè that thou caredst not for?" I answered, "so it is." "Then thou desyredst the ones presence, and the others want?" I confesse. "Does any man neede than," quoth she, "that euery man wantes & needes?¹ He that lackes is not wholly content.² No, sure. When thou hadst welth ynough, hadst thou not this want?" "What els?" said I. "Then Riches can not make a man lack nothing, nor yet content himself. And this is that promise they seemed. This I suppose ought most be considered, that monny of his own nature hath nothing that he can not be spoyled of that possesses it." I confesse it. "Why shouldst thou not confesse yt. Whan a mightyer takes it away from the vnwilling. Whence come these Courtes complayntes?³ but that coyne is taken away from the losers by force or guyle?⁴ He shall

Riches must be unsatisfactory because their possessor may, at any moment, be deprived of them.

haue neede therfore of outward help by which his monny he may keepe. Who can this deny?⁵ He should not neede such help that possest of monny lose he wold not. This is doutles.⁶ The matter is fallen otherwise now, for such

---

¹ Translation of "*Eget, inquam,*" left out.
² "Suffisith not himself" struck out.   ³ Actions at law.
⁴ "*Ita est, inquam*" left out.   ⁵ *Inquam* left out.   ⁶ *Inquam* left out.

36 riches as were thought sufficient of them selves, are needy of others ayde. But what is the way to dryve away lack from ryches? for rych men can they not honger, Can they not thirst, nor can not somtyme the cold wynter hurt the
40 lymmes of the rich man? But yoᵘ will say, they haue ynough, thurst & colde to dryue away. But by this meanes yoᵘ may saye the lack of rich men may be comforted, neuer take away. For if she euer gape & serch for som
44 thing els, tho fild with ryches ynough, it must be that ther somthing remaynes that it should be filld withall. I neede not tell you that Nature with lest, & Auarice with nothing is contented. Wherfore if nether Riches can take away their
48 lack, & they make their own neede, why should we think them sufficient?

The greatest amount of wealth is insufficient to insure happiness.

III. MYTER.

Thogh riche man with flowing golden golfe
Couetous hepes not rechis that Suffice
His neck adornes with geme of Reddis Sea
With hundred oxe the fruitful fildz doth til: 4
Yet Eating Care leues not him quicke,
Nor ded the fliting good accompagnies.

Riches do not ward off cares and do not follow us after death.

IV. PROSE.

" But thou wilt say dignities makes honorable, reuerenced to whom they hap. Haue the[n] dignities this force? that they can ingraff in vsers myndes vertue, & expulse vice. Nay,
4 they are wont, not to chace iniquitie but to adorn it; so as we disdayne¹ somtyme that they should hap to wickedst men: wherfore Catullus, tho Nonius sate as Curule, calld him Lump of flesh. Dost thou see how great a shame ² som-
8 tyme dignity receuith? Which indignitie should not be so euident, if honour should not show it. You allso, could you

Arguments to prove that also it is not in the nature of high dignities to confer happiness.

---

¹ "disdayne" transl. of *indignemur*. ² Transl. of *malis* is left out.

METRUM III.

Quamuis fluente diues auri gurgite
 Non expleturas cogat auaras opes,
 Oneretque bacis colla rubri litoris,

Ruraque centeno scindat opima boue: 4
 Nec cura mordax deserit superstitem,
 Defunctumque leues non comitantur opes.

Q. ELIZ.

The holders of high offices are not on that account reverenced, if they themselves are unworthy.

haue bene brought by so many perils to accompany Decoratus in office, when in him you sawe a mynde of a wicked Ruffin,[1] and slanderer tongue? For we can not for honors sake iudge them worthy Reuerence whom we suppose vnworthy of their dignities. But if thou sawest a wyse man, couldst thou not[2] think him wourthy of reuerence euin for that wisdom he enioyes? Yes surely, for ther is a peculiar dignitie for vertue, which alltogither[3] is bestowde on them to whom she haps. Which because they cannot euer haue popular honors, they may not enioy the beauty of their worth: wherin this is to be noted, that if it[4] be the lesse worth, that it[4] is dispised of many, when they can not make them reuerenced,

Wicked men bring the dignities with which they are invested into contempt.

thorow the contempt that many makes it,[5] Then honour makes many wicked; but yet not without punishment; for wicked men giues this good[6] turn to dignitie, that they spot them with their own infection. And that thou mayst know that true honour can not hap by these shaded dignities, gather it this: Yf a man haue oft tymes bene Consul, & fortune to com to barbarous Nations, shall there honour make him be esteemd? Yf this be a naturall gyft to all dignities, whither euer they go, they should vse the self office, As the fyre in ech Country neuer leaues to burne. But because not their own force but false humayne opinion hath bred it, straight they vanish, when to them they com that esteemes not such dignities. but thus much for foren Nations. Among them

The changes which time works in the nature of an office and the estimation in which it is held.

that made them, doo they euer last? The Prefectures office was once a greate powre, now a vayne name, and a combersom waight of Senators Censure.[7] He was wont be greate that cared for the peeples prouisions. No[w], what baser than that office? For as a little afore I said, That it had nothing in it self of his own proper valure, that takes or loses luster

12

16

20

24

28

32

36

40

---

[1] Transl. of Latin *scurrae*, jester.
[2] The negation should come before "worthy" instead of before "think," and therefore the answer should be "no" and not "yes."
[3] Transl. of *protinus*, quick.   [4] "It" incorrect in both places, should be "he."
[5] Incorrect translation of: *quos pluribus ostentat despectiores potius improbus dignitas facit*. Chaucer has: "than maketh dignities shrewes more dispised than preised."
[6] Here, "*parem vicem reddere*" is badly translated by "good turn:" it should be "like with like."
[7] *census* means here office. Chaucer has: "and the rente of the senatorie a gret charge."

by the vsers opinion. Yf then honors can not make men reuerenced, which are despisd by wicked mens infection, if by change of tyme they leave to be famous, yf by vulgar opinion despysd, what beauty haue they in them selves, or can giue others?

IV. MYTER.

Thogh the proude man with Tirivs shelles[1]   Nero is taken as
  be dekt, and shining stone,   an example of
hated yet of all liued Nero   the preceding
  for Cruel Lust.   4   argument.
But ons Thogh wicked he gaue
  Vnmete Curules to reuerent fathers.
Who yet happy thoght them
Whom wicketz Sort estemed?   8

V. PROSE.

"But kingdomes & kinges familieerities, can they not make a man happy?[2] What els? yf their felicitie euer last. But full be old examples & of present age, that kinges haue changed with misery their lott. O noble powres, which is not able to keepe them selves. Yf this Raigne of kinges be autour of felicytie, shall it not bring misery in part that lackes, and so diminish Luck? For tho mens dominions stretch furr, yet more peeple ther must needes be, vnacquaynted with kinges Raigne. For wher the making felicitie endith, there skanted is the force, & wretched makes. Thus must it needes follow that greatest portion of myserye kinges haue. The tyrant that proued the danger of his Lot, dissembled[3] his Raignes feare by sword hanging on his head. What then is powre? that can not chace bittes of Care, nor shun the stinges of feare? Will they haue to lyue secure, but may not, and

Of the vicissitudes and dangers of monarchy and of friendship with great men.

Of the first of which Damocles is given as an example.

---

[1] *ostro* means "purple" and not "shells."
[2] The Latin word is *potentem*, powerful.   [3] Latin text *simulavit*, simulate.

METRUM IV.

Quamuis se tyrio superbus ostro
  Comeret et niueis lapillis,
Inuisus tamen omnibus uigebat
  Luxuriae Nero saeuientis.   4
Sed quondam dabat improbus uerendis
  Patribus indecores curules.
Quis illos igitur putet beatos
  Quos miseri tribuunt honores?   8

yet boast of their force?[1] Dost thou suppose him mighty, whom thou seest can not what he wold, performe; dost thou think him strong that fills his sydes with garde[s], that whom he affrightes, himself doth feare? who, that he may seeme mighty, throwes himself to the handes of slaues? What shall I speake of kinges fauorites, when the kingdoms[2] themsellues I haue shewde full of such weaknes? whom ofttymes kinges force hath preseruid, som tymes opprest? Nero compeld Seneck his familiar & tutour to chose his own death. Antony threw to soldiours glaiues Papinian, long in Courte, of Credit. And both wold willingly giue vp their autoritie. Seneck offerd Nero all his goodes, & straue to return to his own ease. But while the waight it self thrust them downe, nether that he wold obtayned. What is this autoritie then? which the hauers feare, such as when thou woldst haue, art not safe, & seekest putt of, canst not shun? Shall thy frendes be helpers, whom not vertue but fortune gat the? But whom felicitie made a frend, misery makes an ennemy. What plague is there more of strength to harme,[3] than a familiar ennemy?

Of the second, Seneca and Papinian.

A warning against self-interested friends.

V. MYTER.

The attainment of great political power is undesirable.

He that Sekes mighty be,
 Cruel[4] myndz must tame,
Nor won with lust his neck
 filthy[5] raynes subdue.   4
Thogh India Soyle far of
 At thy Lawes do shake,
And uttermost island[6]
 serve the to,   8

---

[1] *Atqui uellent ipsi uixisse securi, sed ne queant: dehinc de potestate gloriantur.* Badly translated: no question.   [2] Literal translation of *regna*; kings are meant.
[3] "harme" iuterlined by the Queen for "hurt" struck out.
[4] *ferox* here translated cruel; means also proud, which is more appropriate.
[5] Vile would have been a better transl. of *foedis* than filthy.
[6] In the Latin text we have "*ultima Thyle.*"

METRUM V.

Qui se uolet esse potentem,
Animos domet ille feroces
Nec uicta libidine colla
Foedis summittat habenis.   4

Etenim licet indica longe
Tellus tua iura tremescat
Et seruiat ultima Thyle,

Yet is hit not thy powre
hiden Cares Expel,
Nor wretched mones
Expulse thou Canst not   12

VI. Prose.

"But glory how begyling, how fowle is she? Wherfore Of the vanity of glory and of a the Tragik poet wro*n*gfully exclaymes not: O Glory, glory, noble name. on thousa*n*des of men nought worth, a greate name thou haste bestowed. For many haue lost[1] greate renoune through vulgar false opinio*n*, than w*h*ich what can be worsse? for they that falsely be praised,[2] needes must they blush at their own laude.[3] W*h*ich if hit[4] may be got by desart, what may they allow the *con*science of a wise man, who mesurith not his good by popular fame, but *Con*science trouth? And if to stretch fur mens fame, seeme best, it followes then, to skant the same is worst. But since, as I haue afore tolde, it must The limits of fame are extremely circumscribed. nedes be that many Nations ther ar[5] to whom the fame of one man could neuer com, It followes then, that whom yo[u] thought most glorious, in the next climate of the earth seemes vnspoke*n* of. Among all this I suppose not popular fauo*ur* woorthy of memoriall, whom neyther Judgement bred,[6] nor steddy lastes. But now how vayne, how slippery[7] is noble name. Who sees it not? wh*i*ch if to honour yo*u* refer, an other man makes it. For nobilitie seemes to be a prayse proceeding of pare*n*tes desart. And if the speche therof make The only advantage of nobility is, that it sometimes inspires its possessors with the wish to emulate the glory of their ancestors. it knowen, they must be noble that be spoken of. Wherfore if thyne own thou haue not, an other mans lawde shall neuer make th*è* famous. And if ther be any good thing in nobilitie, this I think it only, that it breedes the hauers a co*n*straynte, that they may not degenerate from their au*n*cestors vertue.

---

[1] Latin *abstulerunt* means "obtained" not "lost."
[2] "be praised" interlined by the Queen for "betrayes" struck out.
[3] "laude" in the Queen's hand, over "prayses" struck out.
[4] "hit" in the Queen's hand for "they" struck out.
[5] "ar" in the Queen's hand.   [6] Bad transl. of "*iudicio provenit.*"
[7] "slippery" here translates *futtile*, which means contemptible.

Tamen atras pellere curas,
Miserasque fugare querelas   8
Non posse potentia non est.

VI. Myter.

Al humain kind on erthe
from like begininge Comes:
One father is of all,
One Only al doth gide. 4
He gaue to Son the beames
and hornes on mone bestowed,
He men to erthe did giue
and Signes to heauen: 8
He closed in Limmes Our Soules
fetched from hiest Seat.
A noble Sede therfor broght furth
all mortal folke. 12
What Crake you of your stock
Or forfathers Old?
If your first spring and Auther
God you view, 16
No man bastard be,
Vnles with vice the worst he fede
And Leueth so his birthe.

All men are children of God, and therefore equal in birth, and all of noble descent.

But the wicked may lose their birthright by vice.

VII. Prose.

"But what should I speake of the bodye's pleasure, whose greedie desyres be full of wo, and sacietie of repentance? What diseases, how intollerable paynes is wont as frute of wickednes, hap to the enioyers body. What pleasure soeuer 4 their motions haue, I know not. But who will remember his own delites, shall vnderstand what wofull end those pleasures haue; which if they could yeld men happy, ther is no cause why beastes should not be lyke, whose wholle delite 8

Bodily enjoyments, even marriage and children, often entail painful consequences.

Metrum VI.

Omne hominum genus in terris simili surgit ab ortu:
Vnus enim rerum pater est, unus cuncta ministrat.
Ille dedit Phoebo radios, dedit et cornua lunae,
Ille homines etiam terris dedit ut sidera caelo: 4
Hic clausit membris animos celsa sede petitos.
Mortales igitur cunctos edit nobile germen.
Quid genus et proauos strepitis? si primordia uestra
Auctoremque deum spectes, nullus degener extat, 8
Ni uitiis peiora fouens proprium deserat ortum.

hyes to satisfy their lust. Most laudable shuld be delite of wyfe & childe, but I know not how somtyme against nature it haps that children haue tormented them, whose state how
12 wearing it is, I neede not now tell thè, but knowst it well ynough, and nedest not now wayle it.[1] Which makes me allow Euripides opinion, who said, he was happy in mishap that lackt ofspring.

Which coincides with the opinion of Euripides, who said that the childless man was the most fortunate.

VII. MYTER.

Al deligh[t] hathe this with hit,
With stinge in Joyars hit
Like to the winged flies,
Whan hony thé haue made 4
Away thé go and with stikking
Bite,[2] the stinged hartes strikes.

The same argument as regards bodily enjoyments, with a parable of the bee.

VIII. PROSE.

"Doubte then ther is none, but that these to blesse, be crooked steps, nor thither can any man bring, whither[3] they promise leade him. How wrapt they be in euills,
4 shortly I can shew yo^u. For what, wilt thou snatch monny? Thou must take it from the hauer. Woldst thou shyne with dignities? Thou wilt pray the giuer; & thou that desyrst to aduaunce others in honour, with lowlynes of request, art dasht.
8 Dost thou desyre powre? to subjectes ambusshes thou shalt lye in danger. Dost thou seeke glory? Thou leauest to be sure, that art drawen by so sharp wayes. Pleasurable lyfe dost thou desyre? But who wold not despise & throwe away
12 the bodyes bondage so frayle & vile? But now, such as cares for bodyes strength, on how frayle & meane a possession doo they trust! Can yo^u in force exceede the Elephantes

Recapitulation of the arguments against the value of riches, of dignities, of pleasures, of power, and of beauty.

---

[1] because thou hast never experienced it, nor hast any anxiety about it now.
[2] "Bite" written first "bight." "Thé" refers to *voluptas*.
[3] "Whither" interlined by the Queen.

METRUM VII.

Habet omnis hoc uoluptas,   *Vbi grata mella fudit,*   4
Stimulis agit fruentes,   *Fugit et nimis tenaci*
Apiumque par uolantum,   *Ferit icta corda morsu.*

waight, or bulls strength? Shall yo⁽ᵘ⁾ forego the Tigres swiftnes? Looke thou on heauens compasse, stabilitie and speede, & leave to wonder at that is base. A marveill[1] in reason it were that Skye it selfe were better than he by whom it is guided.[2] Whose forme is so much the fayrer as it is caryed with soudain[3] & speedy change of Springes floures? Yf, as Aristotle sayes, men could vse Linxes[4] eyes, to peirce throw that they sawe, wold they not whan bowells all were seene, suppose that that fayre body whose covering Alcibiades spake of,[5] should fowlest seeme? Wherfore not thy nature but weaknes of vewars sight makes thè seeme fayre. Esteeme how much yo⁽ᵘ⁾ will of bodyes goodes, when this yo⁽ᵘ⁾ knowe, whatso yo⁽ᵘ⁾ wonder, a fyre of a Tercian may dissolue. Of which all, this in somme[6] yo⁽ᵘ⁾ may gather, that these which neyther can performe that they promise be good, nor when they are alltogither can be perfecte, These nether can add strength to bliss,[7] nor make them blest that haue them.

Quotation from Aristotle in support of the argument with regard to beauty.

VIII. MYTER.

People often take the wrong path to happiness.

O in how begiling[8] pathe
   men Ignorance Leades.
Seake not the Golde in griny tre
   nor Louke for precious stone on Grape,
Hide not on hily tops your baites,
   Your dische with fische to fil ;
And gotes if thou wylt take,
   The Tyrrhene Sea not Serche.[9]

---

[1] "Marveil" interlined by the Queen over "wonder" struck out.
[2] The meaning of the Latin text is: "The heavens themselves are not so much to be admired on account of their external glories, as on account of the high intelligence by which they are governed." [3] "Soudain" interlined by the Queen.
[4] The text has: "*Lynceus,*" the demi-god.
[5] Not "Alcibiades spake of," but his beauty is used as example.
[6] "Some," sum. [7] The text has here: "*quasi quidem calles.*"
[8] The text is: "*miseros.*"
[9] The original uses here four times the indicative, instead of the imperative.

METRUM VIII.

Eheu quae miseros tramite deuios
   Abducit ignorantia.
Non aurum in uiridi quaeritis arbore
   Nec uite gemmas carpitis,

Non altis laqueos montibus abditis,
   Vt pisce ditetis dapes,
Nec nobis capreas si libeat sequi,
   Tyrrhena captatis uada.

> For hid in the waues man knoes the Waters streame,[1]
> And what fiersist[2] riuer haue whittist pearle
>   Or wher the Reddys rubies[3]
> And shores also fild most with smallist[4] fische   12
>   Or haue most porpos[5] skales.
> But hiden for they know not
>   The Good thé Seake,
> Blindid Ignorant must thé bide,   16
>   to cerche byonde the Northen Pole,
> Drowned in the erthe thé rake.[6]
>   What hest shall I for dullardz make?[7]
> Euen this that whan with Carke the falz haue got,   20
> Truist than shalt knowe
>   the best.

The right one may be found in many simple pleasures.

IX. Prose.

"Hitherto hit sufficeth to shewe the forme of gileful felicitie, wiche if you Clirely beholde, the ordar than must be to shewe you the true." "Yea I se," quoth I, "that ynough
4 suffiseth not riches, nor Power kingdomes, nor honor dignities, nor glory the prising, nor Joy the pleasure." "Hast thou gathered the cause of this?" "Methinkes I see hit as by a rife slendarly,[8] but do desire plainliar of thè to knowe hit."
8 "Ready is the reason. Whan that wiche vnmixt and by nature vnparted is, that humaine error partz, and from the true and right to falz and wanting brings.[9] Dost thou suppose that

Philosophy reiterates in the following sentence all that has been said against false happiness.

---

[1] The text has: *recessus*.
[2] The Queen has mistaken *feracior* (fruitful) for *ferocior*.
[3] The text says "red purple."   [4] The text has: "*tener piscis.*"
[5] The text has: *echinis* (sea urchin).
[6] Difficult of comprehension. The sense of the original is: That people seek in the earth what is to be found beyond the stars. *Polum* here only means heavens.
[7] Transl. of next line "*Opes honores ambiant*," omitted.
[8] Chaucer has: "I se hem ryȝt as þouȝ it were þrouȝ a litel clifte."
[9] This "Prose" is in the Queen's hand up to this point.

Ipsos quin etiam fluctibus abditos
  Norunt recessus aequoris,
Quae gemmis niueis unda feracior
  Vel quae rubentis purpurae,   12
Nec non quae tenero pisce uel asperis
  Praestent echinis litora.
Sed quonam lateat quod cupiunt bonum,
  Nescire caeci sustinent,   16
Et quod stelliferum trans abiit polum,
  Tellure demersi petunt.
Quid dignum stolidis mentibus inprecer?
  Opes honores ambiant,   20
Et cum falsa graui mole parauerint,
  Tum uera cognoscent bona.

True happiness is single and indivisible.

nothing he wantes that powre needes?" "I think not so." "Truly thou hast sayde, for if ought be that is of weakist worth, must needly neede som others help." "So it is," said I. "Therfor the one & self same is nature of sufficiency & powre." "So it seemes." "But that ther is such thing, dost thou think it to be despised or wourthy all regarde?" "This is not to be doubted."[1] "Let vs ad to this sufficiency, powre, reuerence, that these three we may Judge one." "Let it be, for trouth we wyll confesse." "Dost thou think this any obscure matter or ignoble, or of more show than any other dignitie? But consider lest it be graunted that that needes not, is most of powre, & worthyest most honour, yet wanting estimation, which to it self it can not giue, And therfore may seeme in som parte to be lesse wourth. We can not but graunte that this is

People imagine however that they can divide it and possess themselves of a single part.

most reuerenced.[2] Then it followes, that we confesse a show of glory doth nothing differ from the other three." "Yt followes," quoth I. "Tham that that needes none other, that doth all of his own strength, that is beautifulst & most reuerenced: Is it not playne, that so is most pleasing to? I can not imagine,[3] how to such a man any sorow can happen, wherfore necessarily it must be confest, that he is full of Joye, if the forenamed remayne. And by all this it needfully follows, that theffecte of sufficiency, powre, honour, Reuerence, plesure, be diuers names, in substance nothing differs.[4] That that is then one & symple by nature, humayn synne dispersith; And in seeking to obtayne such thing as wantith partes, myndith the same to gett, And so nether gettes that portion that is none, nor that partie that desyres none." "How may this be so?" quoth I. "He that seekith riches by shun-

Therefore they gain neither one part nor the whole.

ning penury,[5] nothing carith for powre, he chosith rather to be meane & base, & withdrawes him from many naturall delytes, lest he lose the monny that he gat. But that waye, he hath not ynough, who leves to haue, & greeues in woe, whom neerenes ouerthrowes[6] & obscurenes hydes. He that only desyres to be able,[7] he throwes away riches, despisith

---

[1] *Inquam* left out. [2] *Inquam* left out.
[3] *Inquam* left out. [4] Here is missing the transl. of: "*Necesse est, inquam.*"
[5] *Inquit* left out. [6] Incorrect transl. of "*vilitas abicit.*"
[7] The Queen has misunderstood *posse*: it means here power.

plesures, nought esteems honour nor glory that powre wantith. *Happiness is not complete without the whole.*
but how many thinges these men lackes, thou seest. Somtyme
48 he lackes that necessary is, so as his want doth byte him, &
whan he can not throwe of this, that, that most he sought,
hability he wantes.¹ Thus may we reason of honour, glory,
& plesure. For if all these thinges weare ioynd togither,²
52 yf any one³ were had without the rest, he can not gett that
he requires." "What then?" quoth I. "Yf any man all this
can gett, shall he haue the greatest felicitie, shall he fynde her
in these that we haue shewed yoᵘ, promise more than they
56 giue?" "Not so," quoth I. "In such thinges as ech man
desyres to excell in, the true blesse is neuer to be found."⁴
"I confesse it," quoth I, "Than this nothing can be true."
"Thou hast," quoth she, "heere a forme of false felicitie &
60 the cause. Turn thy selfe now to the contrary syde of the *A dissertation on false felicity.*
mynde,⁵ for ther shal thou see strait way the true that I
promysd." "This euin to a blinde man is playne," quoth I,
"and to a litle afore thou showedst, In opening the faulse cause.
64 For els I am deceaued, that is the true & parfet felicitie that
makith man content, mighty, reuerenced, honord, & pleasant.
And that thou mayst know, I haue inwardly lookt which of
all these might trulyest all exceede. This I confesse to be true
68 bliss, that is without a doubte." "O scholler myne, happy art
thou for this opinion, yf thou wilt ad one. thing withall."
"Whats that?" quoth I. "Dost thou think that ought in
mortall & fleeting thinges can make such a state?" "No,"
72 quoth I, "That thou hast showde sufficiently, as nothing more
doth neede. For these thinges as pictures of true good, seeme *There is nothing on this earth which can afford true and perfect happiness.*
to giue som imperfet good to mortall men; but the true &
perfet, bring they can not.⁶ Because thou knowest now, what
76 be the true good, & what belyeth the true blisse, now it
followith, that thou mayst knowe whence thou mayst ask the

---

¹ Bad translation of "*potens esse desistat.*" Chaucer has: "he forleteþ to ben myȝty." ² In the text is: "*idem quod cetera sit,*" "the same as the others."
³ Transl. of *horum* (of these) omitted.
⁴ *In his igitur quae singula quaedam expetendorum praestare creduntur, beatitudo nullo modo vestiganda est.* Badly translated. Chaucer has: "ne sholden men nat by no weye seken blysfulnesse in swiche þinges as men wenen þat þei ne mowe ȝeuen but o þing senglely of al þat men seken."
⁵ A better translation would have been "Turn thy mind's eye to the other side."
⁶ "*Assentior inquam*" left out.

6

Appeal for Divine aid to help us to the discovery of true happiness.

true." "That is hit," q*uoth* I, "I haue long lookt for. But as Plato in his Time*e* wills,[1] that we should ask for divine help in meanest maters, what now thinkest thou to be don, wherby we may merite to fynde the seate of greatest good?" 80

"We must call," q*uoth* I, "to the father of all, who leauing out, no good founda*ti*on is neue*r* layde." "Rightly," said she, And thus began to sing: 84

IX. MYTER.

Praise of the Creator according to Platonic ideas.

O *thou in Lasting sort the world that rulest,*
Of erthe and heauen the framar! who time from first
Bidst go, and stable stedy all elz dost while,
Whom outward Causis forst not to forme 4
The worke of sliding substance, but [2] *shape*
of Greatest good that envy wantz, thou al
by hiest sample gides: the fairest thou,
The goodlist world that mindst, and of like mold hit made,[3] 8
bidding the perfaictz the Complete partz performe.

Setting forth of the order in the created universe.

In number thou Elementz ties, as ryming Cold
to melting flames be ioingned: Lest purest fire faile[4]
Or waights to drowned Land befall.[5] 12
Thou binding the Soules spirite that moues
Al that Concernes the triple nature

---

[1] *Inquit* left out. [2] *insita* (innate) left out.
[3] Chaucer has: "formedest þis worlde to þe likkenesse semblable of þat faire worlde in þi þou3t." [4] Latin *euolet* (fly up). Chaucer has "fleye heye."
[5] Chaucer has: "ne þat þe heuynesse ne drawe nat adoun ouer lowe þe erþes þat ben plounged in þe watres."

METRUM IX.

O qui perpetua mundum ratione gubernas,
Terrarum caelique sator, qui tempus ab aeuo
Ire iubes, stabilisque manens das cuncta moueri,
Quem non externae pepulerunt fingere causae, 4
Materiae fluitantis opus, uerum insita summi
Forma boni liuore carens, tu cuncta superno
Ducis ab exemplo: pulchrum pulcherrimus ipse
Mundum mente gerens similique in imagine formans, 8
Perfectasque iubens perfectum absoluere partes.
Tu numeris elementa ligas, ut frigora flammis
Arida conueniant liquidis; ne purior ignis
Euolet aut mersas deducant pondera terras. 12
Tu triplicis mediam naturae cuncta mouentem

and dost deuide them into agrying limmes.
Who Cut in Circles two the motion,   16   The same order may be observed in the laws by which the human kind is governed.
And brething to her selfe retournes
The dipe mind bisetz and alike heauin rules.
Thou with like Cause the Soules Conserues
And Liues that meanar be to swiftist wains   20
Thou fitting hiest Spirites
In heauen and erthe dost sowe,
Whom with a gentil Law to thè retourned
thou makest be broght to fire from whence it came.   24
Graunt that the mynd, O father! Clime to thy hiest Seat,[1]
And On thy vew the clirest Sigh[t] may Set.
Away Cast erthely Cloude and Waight of this mold
do thou with lustar then them Grace :   28   An invocation to the Creator.
Thou art the Cleare and quiet rest for best folke,
Thè to admire is first last helpe Gide
    Pathe and stedy Last.

X. PROSE.

"For that now thou hast seene the forme of imp*er*fett, &   If we admit the existence of im-
true good, Now I think to shew thè by what the p*er*fection of perfection, we
this felicitie is made. In w*hi*ch first this I think to be sarily admit that
4 inq*u*yrd of, whither any such good ther be, as thou hast which is God.
defynd a lyttle afore, among natures woorkes, leste a vayne
imagina*t*ion of thought deceaue us wyde from the truthe of
that we talke of. And to proue it so, It ca*n* not be denyed

---

[1] Transl. of "*Da fontem lustrare boni*" left out.

    Conectens animam per consona membra resoluis.
    Quae cum secta duos motum glomerauit in orbes,
    In semet reditura meat, mentemque profundam   16
    Circuit, et simili conuertit imagine caelum.
    Tu causis animas paribus uitasque minores
    Prouebis, et leuibus sublimes curribus aptans
    In caelum terramque seris quas lege benigna   20
    Ad te conuersas reduci facis igne reuerti.
    Da pater augustam menti conscendere sedem,
    Da fontem lustrare boni, da luce reperta
    In te conspicuos animi defigere uisus.   24
    Dissice terrenae nebulas et pondera molis,
    Atque tuo splendore mica : tu namque serenum
    Tu requies tranquilla piis, te cernere finis
    Principium uector dux semita terminus idem.   28

In God, goodness is one and the same with his substance.

that this is the fountayne of all good thinges. For all that we call imperfett, is shewed such by the definition¹ of perfection. So haps it, that if in any thing ther be imperfection, In the self same, somthing must needes be that can be perfett. For perfection taken away, we can not ymagyne what that is that is imperfect. For Nature tooke not her begynning of thinges diminished & worne,² but of hole & absolute, & so cam downe into thes barren & uttermost partes. And if, as a little before I told yo^u, there be imperfect felicitie of a frayle good, It can not be doubted but that ther is a solide & parfet one." " This is sure, and truly concluded."³ " But wher this dwellith," quoth she, " In this wise consider. The common conceite of mens myndes allowes, that God of all thinges the Ruler, is good hit self. For when nothing⁴ can be imagined better than himself, who can doute that that is the best, whom nothing can better? For so doth reason shew that God is⁵ good, that is won to confesse he is the perfect good. For without such he were, the Prince of all thinges he

The highest conception of good is also the highest conception of happiness.

could not be : for so much the rather doth he possess perfection, that he was the first & aboue⁶ all : for the perfetest doo show them sellves first afore the lesser sorte. and lest our reason should neuer have end, we must confesse that the greate God is indued with the wholle & perfett good. And we doo saye that true blisse consistes in perfection, we must then conclude, that true felicitie is in the greatest god." "I take it so," quoth I, " nether can any thing gayne say it." " But, I pray thè," quoth she, " Looke how prouuest thou that most holyly & without spot, that we say God is the full perfection of greatest good ? " " How shall I prooue this," said I ? " Presume not to think that the father of all thing[s] haue taken this great good with which he is fulfilld eyther of outward cause or naturall,

The nearer man approaches God the happier must he be.

in ymagining a diuers substance of him that hath the obtaynid felicitie. For if from outward cause thou supposest he has taken, thou mightest than think that better, than he that gaue. But most worthely we confess that he excellith

8

12

16

20

24

28

32

36

40

---

¹ The text has *inminutione*, diminution.
² The text has *inconsummatis*, imperfect.
³ Transl. of *inquam* omitted.   ⁴ Transl. of *melius* omitted.
⁵ Transl. of *vero* omitted.   ⁶ Latin text is : "*prius atque antiquius*."

all. Yf Nature haue done any thing in him, & in a diuers *Nothing can be better than its*
44 sorte, when we speake of God the guyder of all thinges, who *originator, therefore nothing in*
can imagine to haue Joynd all these diuersities?[1] Last of all, *Nature can be better than God*
that that differs from any thing, that cannot be the same *the creator of it.*
that is not hit. Wherfore that is contrary from the greatest
48 good that can not be hit selfe, which were sacrilege to think
of God, whom nothing can exceede. For nothing in Nature
can be better than her begynning. Wherfore that was the first
of all, in his own substance by a right argument I conclude the
52 greatest good." "Rightly," quoth I. "But it is graunted that
the greatest good is blesse." "So it is," quoth I. "Therfore,[2]
it needes must be graunted that God is blisse it selfe. Nether
can the foresaid reasons fayle me,[3] & by them I finde the con-
56 sequence true." "See," quoth she, "whither this be not more
truly prooued, for that twoo greatest goodes diuers in them
selues can neuer be. Therfore goodes that differs, One can
not be that the other is, for none of them can be perfect,
60 whan in both there lackes. Then that that is not perfecte, is
playne can not be the greatest good. By no meanes therfore
can they be greatest good that be dyuers. Wherfore we *Goodness and happiness are*
gather that bliss & God be the greatest good, which makes *one and the same.*
64 that the greate Diuinity is the greatest bliss." "Nothing can
be concluded," quoth I, "nor in it self more true, nor by
reaason more stable, nor for god wourthyer." "In these causes,[4]
as Geometricians be wont to doo, demonstrations propounded,
68 They bring in somthing which they call πορίσματα. So will I
give thè somthing as a breefe gathering. For since men be
blissed by getting of felicitie, & felicitie is Diuinitie, It concludes, that by getting of Diuinity men be blessed. For
72 as Just men be made by getting Justice, & wyse men by
wisdom, So men getting Diuinity, by lyke reason are made
lykest to God. So euery blessed man, is in a kinde a God, but
in nature one, in participation many may be. Most fayre *Felicity is Divinity, and*
76 & precious is this, which yo^u call your πόρισμα, or your *Divinity is most like to God.*
Collection.[5] And so much is it the fayrer, that naturall

---

[1] Bad translation of: *Quod si natura quidem inest, sed est ratione diuersum, cum de rerum principe loquamur deo, fingat qui potest ; quis haec diuersa coniunxerit.*
[2] Transl. of *inquit* omitted.   [3] Transl. of *inquam* omitted.
[4] Transl. of *inquit* left out.
[5] The Latin word is *corollarium*. Transl. of *inquam* left out.

<small>*Repetition of the preceding arguments.*</small> reason it self perswades yo^u thus to ioyne them." "What of that?" said I. "When blissidnes conteynes many thinges in hit,[1] whither be all the partes of this gatherd in one, as by varietie deuided, conioyned, or is ther som thing els, that fullfills the fulnes of bliss, & to this all the rest is referd." "I wold thes thinges were explained," quoth I, "as by a memoriall." "Dost thou not think blisfulnes good?"[2] "Yea the greatest," quoth I. "This all will graunte.[3] for it is the only sufficiency, the only powre, reuerence, beauty, delyte. What tho? all these good thinges, sufficiency, powre, all be but lyms of blissidnes. Be all thinges referd to good as to the Top?" "I know," quoth I, "what thou propoundest to seeke, but what thou determynest, to heare I desyre." "Take this division of this sorte. Yf all these were partes of blisse, then should they differ in themsellves. For this is the nature of partes, that deuided <small>*All good things are only parts, which joined together make up happiness*</small> they make a hole body, & all these thinges we haue shewed be one, Then they are not partes, or els bliss should seeme to be made of one parte, which can not be." "This doute I not,[4] but that that remayns I attend. For to the greatest, all the rest of goodes must needes be referd. For therfore sufficiency is desyrd, that good it is suppos̃d, & powre in like manner: so may we gesse of reuerence, honour, & delyte. For the somme of all desyred thing[s] is good. That neyther in hit self nor in his lyke retayns any blisse, that no man ought desyre. And contrary, those that by nature be not good, if they seme to be, as true good be desyrd. So is it, the greatest good, by right ought be beleeuid, the grownd[5] work & cause of all desyred. The cause for which we wish ought, that most we desyre, as yf for helthes sake to ryde we desyre, we seeke not more the styrre of the exercise, than the good effecte of our helth. When than all thinges be desyrd for greatest good, we desyre not those thinges more than good <small>*All worldly possessions are coveted for the happiness which they confer.*</small> it self. And that we graunt, that all thinges be desyrd to obtayne blisse, So we conclude she is only to be sought: wherby it playnly appeeres that one only is the substance of that is good & blisfull. I see no cause why any man

---

[1] Transl. of *inquit* omitted.
[2] Transl. of *inquit* left out.
[3] Transl. of *inquit* omitted.
[4] Transl. of *inquam* left out.
[5] The Latin word is *cardo*.

should doute heerof. And God we have showed to be the only & alone good.¹ So may we safely conclude that Godes substance is in that good & none other concluded."

X. Myter.

Al you togither come that taken be,
Whome begiling lust with wicked chanes hath bound,
dabeling ² the erthely myndz,
here rest of labor shal you haue,³   4
here Open Sanctuary for wretchis alone.
Not al that Tagus with her golden sandz
doth give, Or Hermus with her glitering ⁴ shore,
Or Indian dwelling nire to hottische Circle,   8
That griny stone with Chirst doth mixe,⁵
So Clires the Sight, nor more the blindid mindz
Returnes into ther shades.
What of al thes hathe pleased and delited,   12
  that erthe hathe kept in darkist Caue:
The lustar that doth gide the heauen and rule,
  the ruines darck of Soule forbidz:
This Light he who can decerne,⁶   16
Beauty suche in Φebus beames denies.

When freed from earthly defilements, the soul will find rest in the celestial regions.

Dwellers upon earth cannot discern the celestial light, which in brilliancy surpasses that of the sun.

XI. Prose.

"I graunt," quoth I: "for eche thing with strongest reason linked is."⁷ "How muche, woldz thou prise hit, if the tru

---

¹ The answer of Boethius, "*ita inquam*," left out.   ² Probably "dwelling."
³ Fifth line missing: "*Hic portus placida manens quiete.*"
⁴ "glitering." False transl. of *rutilante* (ruddy).
⁵ Inexact transl. Chaucer has: "þat medeleþ þe grene stones wiþ þe white."
⁶ *notare* better translated by "blame" than "decerne."
⁷ "*Tum illa, inquit*" left out.

METRUM X.

Huc omnes pariter uenite capti,
Quos ligat fallax roseis catenis
Terrenas habitans libido mentes,
Haec erit uobis requies laborum,   4
Hic portus placida manens quiete,
Hoc patens unum miseris asylum.
Non quidquid Tagus aureis harenis
Donat, aut Hermus rutilante ripa,   8
Aut Indus calido propinquus orbi

Candidis miscens uirides lapillos,
Inlustrent aciem, magisque caecos
In suas condunt animos tenebras.   12
Hoc quidquid placet excitatque mentes,
Infimis tellus aluit cauernis:
Splendor quo regitur uigetque caelum,
Vitat obscuras animae ruinas: 16
Hanc quisquis poterit notare lucem,
Candidos Phoebi radios negabit.

Q. ELIZ.

good thou couldst knowe." "At how infinite rate,[1] for so shuld I obtaine to knowe what God wer." "And this with truest reason I wyl expres,[1] if it be grauntid that afor was sayd." "Be it so."[2] "Haue not we showed,[1] that those things that be desyrd of many, therfore are not perfect & good, because they differ among themselves, So as where any want ther is of one thing to an other, than can no playne nor resolute good com? But then is good ther true, when they are gathered in one forme & performance, that what suffisith may haue powre, reverence, honour & delyte, for without all these be in one, a man hath nought that ought to be esteemd."

"This is euident," quoth I, "& no man neede to doubte therof, for those that, when they disagree, be not good, when they are one, must needes be so." "But are not all these things made good by getting of a true vnity?" "Yes, sure," said I. "But all that is good, dost thou suppose it good thorow the participating of that is so?" "Yes." "Then needes it must be that that is only good that is euer one. for the substance is the same of ech man, whose effectes naturally they haue." "I can not deny it."[3] "All that is so,[3] long must last & holde togither, as it is one, but must needes perish & decay, whan so it leaves to be;[4] as in beastes we see,[5] when they ingender, & be made of lyfe & body, then it is a Creature. But when this vnitie makes a separation, then they are deuided, perish & decay. This body allso when hit remayns in one forme & joyntes of lyms, then humayn shape is seene. But if distract or partid in twoo they be, then they leave their vnitie which made them be. In that sorte, all the rest shall be playne to the sercher, that euery thing shall last while it is one, but when it leaves that order, it perishith. When I haue considered many thinges I find no other thing."[6] "Ys ther," quoth I,[7] "any thing that naturally, leaving desyre of lyfe, wischith to com to ruine & an end?" "In beastes themsellves that haue som kynde of will to fly[8] or not, I fynde yf

---

[1] *Inquam*, and *inquit* (twice) omitted.   [2] In the Queen's hand to here.
[3] *Inquam* and *inquit* omitted.
[4] Answer of Boethius, "*Quonam modo*," left out.   [5] *inquit* left out.
[6] Transl. of *inquam* omitted.   [7] Here *inquit* is translated quoth I.
[8] The Queen has read *volandi* for *volendi*, but "to fly" is underlined, which may mean that those words are to be omitted. *Inquam* left out after "not."

men compell them not, they will not cast away their mynde of
lasting, and hye them to the way of destruction. For ech
best I finde studys safety to keepe, & shunnith death &
40 decay. I can not tell what I may say of herbes, of trees, of
rootes.[1] I may doute, And yet ther is no greate cause, when
we see the trees & herbes reviue[2] agayn in their fittist
place, that as much as [3] nature will permitt, they may not
44 soone dry & dye. Som in feldes, som on hills doo spring,
others marish beare, others stick to stone, som prosper on
barren sand, which if any man pluck vp to sett in other
place, they wither. So Nature giues to ech that him becoms,
48 & stryves that while they may remayne, they may not end.
What shall I say? that som we see of them, as hauing turnd
their top [4] to earth, draw nourishment to the roote, & by
their sap, spredes strength [5] & bark? What, yea! that that
52 is most soft, as were the marrow, is euer hyd in innermost
rynde,[6] without couerd by strength of som wood, but the vtter-
most bark against the heauens wether, as sufferer of harme,
is set a defendour? Now how greate is Natures diligence,
56 that all thinges be inlarged by most seede, which all, no
man is ignorant, not only for a tyme of remayning perpetually
stryues to remayn?[7] Those thinges that only haue life,[8]
doo they not euer by a naturall instinct[9] desyre their own?
60 Why does lightnes draw vp the flame, & waight, the earth
dounward drawes, but that all these agrees in their place &
in their own motion? And that agrees that euer is conserued:
as those thinges that discorde doth corrupte. Those thinges
64 that of Nature be hard, as stones, they stick most fast to their
own roote,[10] & so resist as easely they be not pluckt of.
The fleeting thinges as ayre & water, these easely be de-

Consequently, every being endeavours to preserve its unity by avoiding decay and death.

Nature gives to animals and plants what is suitable to each.

Such things as air and water are easily dispersed, but quickly return from whence they came.

---

[1] The text has "*inanimatis rebus*," here translated "rootes."
[2] The text has *innasci*.   [3] *carum* left out: "their nature will permit."
[4] Wrong transl. of "*quid quod omnes vclut in terras ore demerso trahunt alimenta radicibus ac per medullas robur corticemque diffundunt*. Chaucer has: "þat they drawen alle hyr norysshynges by hyr rootes / ryht as they hyr Mowthes I. plounged with in the erthes."
[5] *robur* means here wood, not strength.
[6] *rynd* in the text is "*interiore sede*," inside seat.
[7] This sentence is rendered quite unmeaning by the omission of several words.
[8] "Life" here is a translation of *animata*, instead of *inanimata*.
[9] The Latin text is: "*nonne quod suum est quaeque simili ratione desiderant?*"
[10] The Queen has mistaken *partibus* for *partubus*.

But fire cannot be separated.

p*ar*ted, but quickly return fro*m* whence they were drawe*n*. But fyre refusith all separa*t*ion. We doo not talk now of the volo*n*tary motions of the soule of man, but of the naturall intent by nature given. As o*ur* meate we take wit*h*out great study, & breth we drawe in o*ur* slomber when we know it not. For in very beastes, the desyre of co*n*tynuance, not of their lyves pleas*u*re, but of their natures begyning p*r*ocedith. For oft tymes o*ur* will imbracith death, cause compelling, w*h*ich nature dreades, & co*n*trarywise desyre of making o*ur* lyke, wherby co*n*tynuance doth endure, o*ur* wills som tymes keeps

The love of ourselves and desire of self-preservation is implanted in us by Nature.

vs fro*m* that nature desyres. Wherfore this loue of o*ur* selfes p*r*ocee*des* not of a Creatures notio*n*, but of a naturall intent. For Godes p*r*ouidence hath giue*n* to all thinges that be made the desyre of remayning, that as long they may, naturally they will byde. So neede*s* thou neuer doute that such thinge*s* as naturally desyre an abode will shun destructio*n*." "I co*n*fesse it," q*uoth* I, "for now I plainly see such thinge*s* as doutfull I found, that couete*s* euer to be one, that couete*s* to remayn : "¹ " & last this being taken awaye nothing can abyde.² An vnity

The aim of all beings is unity, and this is at the same time the acme of good.

therfore all desyre.³ And one we haue showed that is only good.⁴ Since therfore ech thing seekith the good, it is playne, that is only the good that of all is desyred." "Nothing," q*uoth* I, "can trulyer be thought. for eyther all thing shall co*m* to nought, and as wanting a head, wit*h*out a guide shall ruyne,⁵ or yf any thing ther be, to which all hastes, that shall be the somme of all best." "O scholler myne," q*uoth* she, "I ioye that I haue fixd⁶ in thy minde one m*a*rke of meane to truth, and heerby mayst thou see that a little before thou sayedst thou knewest not." "What is that?" q*uoth* I. "What was of all thing the end.⁷ For that is it that of all men is most sought, wiche by caus we suppose o*n*ly good is hit, therfore we co*n*fesse that to get is all owre end."⁸

68
72
76
80
84
88
92
96

---

¹ Transl. of *inquit* left out.
² The answer of Boethius, " *Verum est, inquam,*" left out.
³ Transl. of *inquit* omitted, and the answer of Boëthius, *consensi*, also.
⁴ "*ita quidem*" omitted.
⁵ The Latin text is: "*sine rectore fluitabunt.*" Chaucer has: "and floteryn with owte gouernour." ⁶ The Latin text is *fixisti*. ⁷ Transl of *inquit* left out.
⁸ This sentence has been much corrected by the Queen.

XI. Myter.

Who so the trueth with deapest mynd doth sirche	Exhortation to consider ourselves.
And sekes by no bywais awry to stray,	

Into him selfe returne the Light of newar mynd,
And Longe discours straining to a round,   4
And teache his mynd what so without he seke,
Layd up amonge his treasure Let him kepe.
Lately that wiche blacky Cloud hathe dimmed,
that Lightar shal thou shine Out.[1]   8
for not al Light from mynd hath drawen
the body carying a forgetful waight ;
Ther Stiks I trowe an inward Sead of trothe.
Wiche kindelz best by Learnings belowes.[2]   12
for axed why do you the right desire,
If Imstinct [3] in thy hart ther wer not ?
If Platoes Musis tales the trueth,
That Eache man lernes   16 Because everything that we can learn is really already within us.
Forgetting he remembars.

XII. Prose.

Than I: "I agree well to Plato, for twise thou hast remembred me of it. First, when memory I lost thorow bodyes syn, next, prest with sorowes burden." Then she: "yf the abouesaid

---

[1] Considerable deviation from the Latin text *lucebit*, etc.
[2] Chaucer has: "awaked and excited by the wynde and by the blastes of doctryne."
[3] The Latin text is *fomes*, tinder.

Metrum XI.

Quisquis profunda mente uestigat uerum,
Cupitque nullis ille deuiis falli,
In se reuoluat intimi lucem uisus
Longosque in orbem cogat inflectens motus,   4
Animumque doceat quidquid extra molitur
Suis retrusum possidere thesauris.
Dudum quod atra texit erroris nubes,
Lucebit ipso perspicacius Phoebo.   8
Non omne namque mente depulit lumen,
Obliuiosam corpus inuehens molem.
Haeret profecto semen introrsum ueri
Quod excitatur uentilante doctrina.   12
Nam cur rogati sponte recta censetis,
Ni mersus alto uiueret fomes corde ?
Quod si Platonis musa personat uerum,
Quod quisque discit immemor recordatur.   16

The Being who preserves the unity of the world is God.

thou hast regarded, thou wilt not be long ere thou remember that lately thou hast confest thou knewest not." "What's that?"[1] "thou meanest by what Raynes the world is guided," sayd she. "I remember it, & that my ignorance confessed shewes, Albeit I see what thou hast brought me, yit playnlier of thè to heare it I desyre." "A little before," quoth she, "Thou thoughtst ther was no doute but that the wourld by God was ruled." "Nether now nor euer will I doute it,[1] and

The universe could never have been formed out of such divers and contrary substances, unless it had been joined together by one masterhand.

what therfore be my reasons, in short I will tell yo^u. This world had neuer com togither into one forme of so diuers & contrarious partes, without one it were that so diuers thinges doth Joyne. And being so knytt, the diuersitie of their own natures among themselves disagreeing, should vncouple & breake them, without one it were that held that so he knytt. For so certain an order of nature should not contynue, nor should show so many diuers motions in their place, tyme, woork, space, & quality, without one it were alone that euer bydiñg himself, disposeth their mutable varietye. What euer this is, wherby the made remayns, & be wrought, by vsuall name of all men, God is calld." Then she: "Since this thou thinkst, I shall haue but little labour that thou, that comprehendst felicitie, as an inhabiter[2] should renew thy Countrey. But let vs looke on our own propositions. Haue we not set sufficiency in nomber of blisse, and so graunte that God it is?[3]

God alone governs the world.

And to rule the world he needith no other help.[4] For els, yf ought he needed, full sufficiency he had not." "That must needes be." "Then by him self all he disposes alone.[5] And God is he that only we haue showed to be the good.[6] By goodnes therfore all he doth dispose, for by himself he rulith all, whom we haue graunted the only good. And he is the key & helm wherby this worldes molde stable & vncorrupt is kepte." "I agree to this," quoth I, "and with a slender suspicion I sawe afore what yo^u wold saye." "I beleeue it well.[7] For euin now, as I think more heedely to looke, to truth thou hast turnd thyne eye, And that I say is playne now that thou

---

[1] Transl. of *inquam* omitted.
[2] The Queen has read *hospes* for *sospes*; "guest" is struck out.
[3] "*Ita quidem*" omitted.   [4] *Inquit* and *extrinsecus* omitted.
[5] "*negari, inquam, nequit*," left out.   [6] "*memini, inquam*," left out.
[7] Transl. of *inquit* left out.

wi*th* me may see." "Whats that?"[1] "When rightly we *God governs beneficently, and*
40 beleeue that God all Rules by goodnes order, & that all thing*es* *all things willingly obey Him.*
as I haue taught yo*u*, by naturall instinct hyes to the hiest
good, Can any man doute, but that willingly they are so
rulde, & turnes the*m*selfes to the beck of the disposer, as
44 Ruler of meetest & best agreeing?" "It must need*es* be,"
qu*oth* I, " for els it could not be a blessed raigne, yf it should
be the yoke of drawers back, not the favo*u*r of the obeyeng.
And so nothing can co*n*serve nature that stryves to gaynesay
48 his God.[2] But what if he went about it,[2] Can any thing euer
prevayle against him who*m* all men graunte by lawe of bliss,
the mightyest?" "It should nought prevayle," said I, "for *Nothing can prevail against God,*
ther is nothing that eyther can or may resist the greatest *because He is*
52 good."[3] "Then that is the top of felicitie, that stowtly rules *almighty and the highest form of*
& gently all disposith." "How much," quoth I, "these *good.*
thing*es* not only that are co*n*cluded by great Reason, but thy
word*es* themselves much more delyt*es* me, So as a man may be
56 ashamd of him self, that foolishly hath babled [4] so much."
" You haue hard er now," sayd she, " in fables how Gyant*es*
haue clamard to the hevens, but the*m* to as hit was meete,
the gentle force hath deposd. But will yo*u* haue me make a
60 co*m*parison? Perchance thorow such debate, som cleere sparkell
of trouth shall leape out. Thy Judgeme*n*t hath made thè
suppose that no ma*n* dout*es* but God is of all thing the
mightyest.[5] No man will doubte therof, w*i*thout he be mad.
64 and he that Rulith all, nothing ther is that doo he can not."
"Nothing," q*uoth* I. "can God do yll then?" "No," q*uoth*
I. "For yll is nothing, when he can not make it, that can *Evil has no substance, because it does*
do all."[5] "Do you dally with me," q*uoth* I, " & wrap me in *cause it does not proceed from*
68 vndooing laberinth of Reason, in which thou entrest in, whence *God.*
thou wentst out, & now goest out where thou camst in? So
hast thou not thus wrapt a Rondell [6] of dyuine sinceritie?
For a little afore begy*n*ning from bliss, thou saydst she was

---

[1] Transl. of *inquam* omitted.
[2] "*Nihil, inquam*" omitted, and "*ait*" in the next sentence.
[3] Answer of Philosophy, not continuation of Boethius, as it appears. "*Non, inquam, arbitror*" omitted.   [4] The Queen has read *blaterantem* for *lacerantem*.
[5] All this part of the translation is quite confused, *inquam* and *inquit* being transposed, and sometimes left out.
[6] Transl. of *orbem*: Chaucer has, "cercle or envirounynge."

greatest good, which only abode in the greatest God. Then thou saydst that God himself was the greatest good & blisse, of whom no man was made blessed, but he that was lyke to him, And that thou gauest for a reward. Then thou saydst that the shape of good was the substance of God & bliss, and so didst saye, that he alone was greatest good, which Naturally ech man desyrd; and didst dispute that God was he that ruld the vniuersalitie by the raynes of goodnes, & all things willingly did obey, And so ther was no euill in Nature. And didst show how all thinges, not by outward, but one from an other lynking beleefe, had ingraft prooues and their own."[1] Then she, "We doo not sporte, as godes gyftes the greatest doo require, that thing that of late we so much desyrd. For such is the shape of diuine substance that neyther it slyppith to outward cause, nor inwardly doth take for him self any thing without him.[2] But as Parmenides sayth: A lyke compasse in Roundnes ech Circle caryes.[3] Then if we haue so well compast, that we haue not gatherd our reasons out of the matter, but agreing with that that we haue treated, ther is no cause then why thou shouldst doute, when thou hast lernt by Plato, that all talke should agree as neere of kyn to matter that we speake of."

No man can be happy unless he is like God.

Quotations from Parmenides and Plato.

XII. MYTER.

The example of Orpheus is taken to show, that even after attaining to the light of truth, it may be lost by returning to darkness.

Blist, that may of Good
The fontaine Clire behold,
happy that Can Of waighty
Erthe the bondes to breake. 4
The Tracian profit wons
his wives funeralz wailing

---

[1] Meaning doubtful of: *sed ex altero fidem trahente insitis domesticisque probationibus explicabas.* Chaucer has, "þe whiche proeues drawen to hem self hir feiþ and hir accorde eueriche hem of oþer."

[2] *Ut neque in externa dilabatur nec in se externum aliquid ipsa suscipiat* is badly rendered.

[3] After "caryes" is omitted: "*rerum orbem mobilem rotat, dum se immobilem ipsa conseruat.*"

METRUM XII.

Felix qui potuit boni	*Terrae soluere uincula.* 4
Fontem uisere lucidum,	*Quondam funera coniugis*
Felix qui potuit grauis	*Vates thracicius gemens,*

DE CONSOLATIONE PHILOSOPHIÆ.

 Whan with sorows note
 The wauering trees he moued,   8   The effect of his music upon Nature and animals.
 And stedy rivers made,
 And hind caused Join
 Unfearing Sides to Lion fierce.
 Nor hare did feare the Looke   12
 Of Cruel dog so plised with Song,
 Whan ferventar desir the inward
 brest more burnt,
 Nor Could the notes that al subdued   16
 Pacefie ther Lord,   How he descended to the infernal regions.
 Of Ireful Godz Complaining
 The helly house went to.
 Ther faining verse   20
 Tuning to Sounding Stringe
 What he drew from springes
 The greatest of Mother Godz,
 What feable mone could Giue,   24
 What doubled Love afourd,
 by Wailes and hel doth stur
 And with dulce suite pardon
 Of darkenes Lorde besiche.   28   He craves pardon from the god of hell.
 Wondar doth the thre hedded
 Jailor amasid with unwonted verse,
 Revenging Goddes of faultes
 That wontid [1] Gilty feare   32

[1] The Latin text has *agitant*.

Postquam flebilibus modis
Siluas currere mobiles,   8
Amnes stare coegerat,
Iunxitque intrepidum latus
Saeuis cerua leonibus,
Nec uisum timuit lepos   12
Iam cantu placidum canem.
Cum flagrantior intima
Feruor pectoris ureret
Nec qui cuncta subegerant   16
Mulcerent dominum modi,
Inmites superos querens
Infernas adiit domos.

Illic blanda sonantibus   20
Chordis carmina temperans
Quidquid praecipuis deae
Matris fontibus hauserat,
Quod luctus dabat impotens,   24
Quod luctum geminans amor,
Deflet Taenara commouens,
Et dulci ueniam prece
Vmbrarum dominos rogat.   28
Stupet tergeminus nouo
Captus carmine ianitor,
Quae sontes agitant metu
Vltrices scelerum deae   32

Ixion ceased to revolve with his wheel, and the vulture to tear the liver of Tityus.	Sorowing with teares bedewed thé were. not Ixiones hed The whirling while did turne And lost with longue thirst Tantalus riuers skornes. The Vultur fild with notes, Tityus livor tared not. At last wailing Said the Juge Of Shady place " we yeld ; To man we giue his wife for feere, Won by his Song.	36 40
Eurydice restored on condition that Orpheus does not look back.	With this Law bound be the gift, While in the Tartar thou bidest, turne back thy looke thou must not." but who to Loue giues Law ? for greatest Law his Love he made. So night drawing to her ende, Eurydicen his Orφeus Sawe, Lost, and killed. this fable toucheth you Who so doth seak to gide	44 48 52
He looks back and loses her.	To hiest day his mynd. for who in hely [1] Shade Won man his yees doth bend, What so he chifest held In vewing hel hathe lost. Et Sic bene.[2]	56

[1] helly.   [2] This is added in the Queen's hand.

Iam maestae lacrimis madent. Non ixionium caput Velox praecipitat rota, Et longa site perditus Spernit flumina Tantalus. Vultur dum satur est modis, Non traxit Tityi iecur. Tandem " uincimur " arbiter Vmbrarum miserans ait : " Donamus comitem uiro Emptam carmine coniugem. Sed lex dona coercat, Ne, dum Tartara liqueret,	36 40 44	Fas sit lumina flectere." Quis legem det amantibus ? Maior lex amor est sibi. Heu noctis prope terminos Orpheus Eurydicen suam Vidit perdidit occidit. Vos haec fabula respicit Quicumque in superum diem Mentem ducere quaeritis. Nam qui tartareum in specus Victus lumina flexerit, Quidquid praecipuum trahit, Perdit, dum uidet inferos.	48 52 56

THE FOURTH BOOKE.

I. Prose.

Thus when Philosophy her stately looke & graue countenance keeping, In mylde & sweete sorte had song, Then I, not forgetting my late ingraven woe, burst out to tell som part
4 of my intent. " O," q*uoth* I, " Thou, the guide of true light, such thinges as thy talke hitherto hath vtterd, by diuine speculation & Reason thyne, are showed inuincible. And though the same of late my iniuryes sorowe forgate, yet altogither of
8 the*m* I was not ignorant. But this was the self & greatest cause of all my woe, that when the Righter of all thing is good, eyther at all euills can be, or vnpunished pas. That, how worthy wonder it is, co*n*sider I pray yo^u. But to this a
12 greater mater is added. For wickednes ruling & florishing, not only vertue wantes rewarde, but subiect to the feete of wicked men, is troden downe & suffers payne that wicked folkes deserue. W*hi*ch happening in a Raigne of him that all
16 knowes, all ma[y], and such a god that wills but only that is good, No man can but mervell and co*m*playne." " It should be worthy mervell," q*uoth* she, " And horrible more than any monster, if, as thou supposest, in a house guyded by such a
20 m*aster*, base vessells should be esteemd, & precious are despisd. But so it is not. For if such thinges be kepte w*hi*ch we of late concluded, & be kepte togither, he being the maker of whose kingdom we spake, thou shalt knowe that
24 euer good men be mighty, yll men slaues & weake. And how vice is neuer w*ith*out punishme*n*t, nor vertue w*ith*out rewarde. And how prosperitie to the good, yll luck to euill betydes. And such lyke, wh*i*ch may leaving quarrels, stre*n*gthen
28 thè w*ith* steddy soundnes. And for that thou haste scene the picture of true blisse, which I shewed thè, and haste knowen where hit is placed, passing all those thinges that necessary I think not, I will show thè the way that home to
32 thy house may bring thè, and stick fethers in thy mynde,

Philosophy promises to controvert the idea that bad men enjoy prosperity upon earth, while the good ones suffer.

Good men are ever mighty, and evil ones slaves and weak.

Vice is never without punishment nor virtue without reward.

7

wherby thou mayst sore up on hye, so as woe trode down, homedweller in thy country by my guyding path & Charyot mayst return."[1]

I. Myter.

Philosophy furnishes the mind with pinions,

For Spedy quilles haue I
  That fur aboue the Pole do reache,
Wiche whan my fliinge mind putz on,
  hating the erthe despice hit, 4
And hiar hies than erthes Globe,
  and Cloudes behind me See,
And pas aboue the fiars top,
  With swiftnis that the heavens heat 8
Until to Starry house hit comme
  With Φebus sorteth way,
And Soldiar made of shining Star
  Cold Saturne doth felowe, 12
Or wher the shewing night,
  The Circle Round doth make;
and whan got ynough she hathe,
  The owtmost Pole he leues, 16
And worthy made of hiest Light

by which it is enabled to soar above the stars to God,

Presseth the waight of spidy skie.
  he, Lord, holdz of kings the Septar
  and Raines of world doth gide, 20
And stable rules the Spidy Cours.[2]
  Of all the noble Juge.

---

[1] *Ut perturbatione depulsa sospes in patriam meo ductu, mea semita meis etiam uehiculis reuertaris.* [2] Here the Queen has read *cursum* for *currum*.

Metrum I.

Sunt etenim pinnae uolucres mihi
  Quae celsa conscendant poli,
Quas sibi cum uelox mens induit,
  Terras perosa despicit, 4
Aeris inmensi superat globum,
  Nubesque postergum uidet,
Quique agili motu calet aetheris,
  Transcendit ignis uerticem, 8
Donec in astriferas surgat domos
  Phoeboque coniungat uias,
Aut comitetur iter gelidi senis

Miles corusci sideris, 12
  Vel quocumque micans nox pingitur,
  Recurrat astri circulum;
Atque ubi iam exhausti fuerit satis,
  Polum relinquat extimum 16
Dorsaque uelocis premat aetheris
  Compos uerendi luminis,
Hic regum sceptrum dominus tenet
  Orbisque habenas temperat, 20
Et uolucrem currum stabilis regit
  Rerum coruscus arbiter.

> *Hither if the way bak do bring thè,*
>   *Wiche now forgetting thou requirest :*   24
> *" This," wilt thou Say, " my country is, I knowe ;*
>   *hens Came I, hire wyl I stay my step."*
> *And if of erthe hit please thè*
>   *the darkenes left to vewe,*   28
> *The grimme Lookis, that people dredeth so,*
>   *Of banissed Tirantz shalt behold.*[1]

where it will find its true home.

II. PROSE.

Than I : " O Lord,[2] how great thinges dost thou promis, nether doubt I but that performe thou canst hit, but stik not now at that thou hast begon." " First therfor, thou must knowe," quoth she, " that good men haue euer power, Iuel men lack euer strengh for good and yl, being so contrary, yf powreful be the first, the last doth shewe his Lack.[3] But that your[4] Opinion may haue more Credit, by ether pathe I wyl treade, and therby my propositions confirme. Two things ther be by wiche the effecte of eache mans doings apere, wyl and power, of wiche if ether lacke, nothing may be perfourmed. For wyl wanting, No man wyl go about that he wold not. and power fayle, vain is wyl. So hit folowes, that whan he wants that he wylz, no dout but power failes to get the desired." "That is plain,[5] and can not be denied." "And whom thou seest optone[6] that he wold, dost thou dout that he may not haue the power?[7] In that he prevailes, In that man is able, but weke must nides be, in that he may not.[8] Dost thou remember[8] that in our last arguments this was gathered that the intent of eache man's wyl, thogh diuersly distracted, is

It is endeavoured to prove, that good men are mighty, and bad ones weak, and the objections to this theory are shown.

If a man is wanting in power, will is of no avail.

---

[1] These two lines badly translated. Chaucer has : " þan shalt þou seen þat þise felonous tyrauntes þat þe wrecched poeple dredeþ now shule ben exiled from þilke faire contre."   [2] The text has the interjection *papae*.
[3] Bad transl. of : *si bonum potens esse constiterit, liquet inbecillitas male*. Transl. is omitted of : *et si fragilitas clarescat mali, boni firmitas nota est*.
[4] The text has *nostrae*.   [5] *inquam* missing.
[6] *Sic* ; optaine ?   [7] *minime*, answer of Boethius missing.
[8] The answer of Boethius, "*Fateor, inquam*," again missing, and *inquit* in the next sentence.

Huc te si reducem referat uia,
  Quam nunc requiris immemor ;   24
" Haec," dices, " memini, patria est mihi,
  Hinc ortus, hic sistam gradum."

Quod si terrarum placeat tibi
  Noctem relictam uisere,   28
Quos miseri toruos populi timent
  Cernes tyrannos exules.

Repetition of the axiom that bliss is the highest form of goodness. only to hie to blis?" "I remember hit was so shewed." "Dost thou cal to mynd that blis is the greatest good, and so whan that is soght al best is got?"[1] "I remember that well Inough," quoth I, "for that hold I fixd in mynde." "Therfore all good men & yll stryve to com to the best by diuers intentes!" "So it is. But most sure it is they are made good men by obtayning good."[2] "But is it sure that good men doo allwayes obtayne that they desyre?" "So it seems." "But if yll men might obtayne good, they could not be yll." "So it is." "When they both desyre good, but the one gettes it, the other not, It

If two men desire good and only one gets it, it is certain that good men are mighty, and evil ones weak. is certain that good men be mighty & yll weake."[3] "Who euer," quoth I, "doutes therof neyther can consider Natures property, nor sequele of Reason." "Then if twoo ther be[4] that by nature requires one thing, one of them naturally does that & performs, & the other no way can do it, nor can agree to what Nature will, & so to fullfill his intent doo but follow the fulfiller: which of them ij thinkest thou more of powre?" "Though I coniecture what yo^u wold, yet plainlyer I desyre to heare." "The motion of walking, yo^u can not deny but all men ha[ue],[5] nor does not doute that is not the feetes office?[6] Yf any man then that can go, & an other to whom the naturall propertie of the feete is wanting, stryving with his handes, stryves so to walke, which of these ij suppose yo^u more worth?" "Perform[7] the rest if that you will, for no man doutes but he is more of force that hath the vse of nature, than he that wantes it." "But the greatest good," said she,

Good men desire good from a natural duty of virtue, and evil men only from a scatterd desire. "that is set before yll & good, the good desyre by naturall duty of vertue, the other by a scatterd desyre, & stryue to get that which is no proper gift, to such as will obtayne the greatest good. Doest thou think the contrary?" "No," quoth I, "for that is playne that followes. For heerby may we gather that I graunted afore, good men to be mighty, & yll men weake." "Rightly hast thou discourst, And so, as phisicians ought to hope, that it is a signe of a helthy & Resisting Nature. But for that I see thè redyest to understand, I will

---
[1] The prose is in the Queen's writing up to this point.
[2] *certum* (answer of Boethius) joined to the next question of Philosophy.
[3] A question.   [4] *Inquit* left out.
[5] "*secundam naturam*" is missing, and Boethius' answer, "*minime, inquam*."
[6] "*Ne hoc quidem, inquam*," left out.   [7] *Inquam* missing.

heape vp many reasons. Beholde, how greate a weakenes is
56 there appears in vicious men that can not obtayne that to
which their naturall intent leades & well nye compells.
And what if they be left of the greate & almost invincible
help of his precedent nature? Consider how great a feblenes
60 holdes wicked men. For nether can they gett light & vayne
rewardes, which they can not obtayne, but fayles in the
Top of height, neither does good effect hap to the wretched,
euen the same that night & day they seeke. And yet in
64 self same thing we see the good mens strenghth excell. For
as a man that walkes to that place whence chefely he wold
com, being such as has no way beyond, woldst thou not
think him best footeman? so shoulst thou think him
68 mightyest that can comprehend[1] the end, beyond which no
furder is. Wherby it haps that who contrary is, the same be
wicked & weake of all strength. For why doo they follow
vice, leauing vertue behind them? For ignorance of good?
72 But what is more feeble than ignorance blyndnes? But they
know what follow they ought? But their lust doth ouer-
throw them: so doth intemperance the frayle men that in
vice be delited.[2] But wittingly & knowing do they leaue
76 that is good, and so bend them to vice? This waye, not only
without powre, but they leaue to be. For they that forsake
the common end of all thinges that be, they leaue themselues
to be. Which may seeme strange to men, that euill men
80 (that many be) we shall not say to be, but so the case
standth. For they that euill be, I deny them not to be yll,
but I deny that they be purely or simply. For as we call a
Carcas, a dead man, symply we can not call him man: so
84 vicious men we graunte them to be yll, but absolutely to be,
that can we not confesse. For ther is that, that keps & retaynes
Natures order: Ther is that fayles from that, & leaues that in
their Nature is grafted. But thou wilt say, yll men may doo,[3]
88 nether can I denye. But this powre to doo coms not of force,
but of weaknes. For they can doo yll, which they should
not doo, if they wold remayn in their creation of good.

A great weakness is always observable in wicked men.

The wicked follow vice, leauing virtue behind them.

What is more feeble than the blindness of ignorance?

As a dead body cannot be called a man, so vicious men have no existence.

[1] The text has *apprehendit*.
[2] The Queen has read *oblectari* instead of the correct *obluctari*.
[3] The Queen has missed the meaning of this sentence: "*sed possunt, inquies, mali*," "Evil men have great power."

7 ★

Which possibilitie to doo, In not dooing shewes they can doo nothing. For yf, as we haue gatherd afore, euill be nothing, when but only the yll they can doo, wicked men can doo nothing." "Thats playne." "And that you may understand what is the force of this powre, we haue defynd afore, that nothing is fuller of force than the greatest good.¹ But that can not the wicked doo.² But what man is that thinkes man can doo all?" "None but a mad man will so think." "And that the same can doo yll to?" "Wold God they could not," quoth I. "When then he is mightest that can do all good, & mightyest men in yll, can not such thinges obtayne, then is it playne, that they can lest doo that be wicked.³ And so it haps, that rightly we haue showed, all powre to consist in thinges to be obtaynd ; And all such referd to greatest good, as to the top of Natures best. But possibilitie of wicked acte can not be refered to good, desyrd therfore it ought not be, & all powre is to be desyrd : It followes therfore, possibilitie of euill men is no powre. By all which, the powre of good men plainly appeares, & makes vndouted the weaknes of wicked men, veryfyeing Platoes sentence, to be true, that only wise men can performe, that they desyre to doo. But wicked men vse only that they will, but what they most desyre can not obtayne. For they doo certain thinges, in which delyting they suppose they haue obtaynd the good that they desyre : but obtayne it they can not, for reproche⁴ neuer coms to blisse."

sidenotes: Evil is nought, and nothing is stronger than the greatest good. — The power of good men and the weakness of wicked men is verified by a saying of Plato.

II. MYTER.

Those who do not allow themselves to be deceived by outward appearances, see that

Thos wiche you se as kings
Sit in ye top of hiest seate,
Florishing with purple fayre,
Enuyrond with dredfull armes, 4

---

¹ Boethius' answer missing ; "*ita est inquam.*"
² Again *minime* missing, and *inquit*, in the questions of Philosophy.
³ Meaning not well given of : *Cum igitur bonorum tantummodo potens possit omnia, non uero queant omnia potentes etiam malorum, eosdem qui mala possunt, minus posse manifestum est.* ⁴ Wicked men are meant.

METRUM II.

Quos uides sedere celsos solii culmine reges
Purpura claros nitente, saeptos tristibus armis,

With ireful looke that thretes,
for hartz yre scant drawing brethe,
If any take from wicked men
Of false honor the couer,   8
Within shal se ther Lordz
Straightned giues to beares
hither Lust them drawes,[1]
hire ire ther myndz afflictz,   12
Who sturred raiseth stormes,
Sorow or the taken wers
Or Slippar hopes tourment.
Wherfor whan One hed   16
So many tirantz beares,
He doth not that he wold,
Prest with so wicked Lordz.[2]

<small>tyrants are mere slaves to their own bad passions.</small>

III. Prose.

"See you not in what a great slowe, wicked thinges be wrapt in, & with how great a light, godlynes shynith? by which tis playne, that neuer reward wantes to good, nor punishment to wicked folke. For it is no wrong that of thinges don, that be ech reward for which ech thing is don: as a Runner in a race has a guarland for which he ran, in rewarde. But we haue shewed how blisse is that self good, for which all thinges be don. Then it followes that the only good is sett as the vniuersall reward to men. And this from good men can not be deuided, for nether can he be iustly cald a good man by right, that wantith true good. Therfore good conditions can neuer want rewarde. For though euill men afflicte them, a wise mans garland shall not fall nor wither. For other

<small>A good man is rewarded by his own goodness, and a wicked man is punished by his own wickedness.</small>

---

[1] "*avidis corda venenis*" left out.
[2] The first copy of this meter is in the hand of another secretary, on folio 52; the second copy is in the Queen's own hand, out of place, on folio 57.

Ore toruo comminantes rabie cordis anhelos,
Detrahat si quis superbis vani tegmina cultus,   4
Tam uidebit intus artas dominos ferre catenas.
Hinc enim libido uersat auidis corda uenenis,
Hinc flagellat ira mentem fluctus turbida tollens,
Maeror aut captus fatigat, aut spes lubrica torquet.   8
Ergo cum caput tot unum cernas ferre tyrannos,
Non facit quod optat ipse, dominis pressus iniquis.

Godliness is all-sufficient, and a good man may attain Divine dignity.

mens wickednes can not pluck away the true honour from honest myndes. For yf he reioyce at ought received from outward meane, som other man or he that gaue it might take it awaye. But because Godlynes it self suffisith, then shall he want reward, when he leaves so to be. Lastly, since all rewarde is therfore desyrd, because it is beleeuid good, who can think an honest man, without rewarde? But of what? Of that that is fayrest & greatest. Remember this breefe[1] that a little afore I gaue you to be the cheefest, & so conclude: When the greatest good is blisfulnes, they must needes be happy that are good, because they are so. And they that be happy, must needes be lyke to God. Therfore good mens reward is such as neyther any day drawes away, nor powre minish, nor Ire[2] darken, but lyke to him they be. Which being true, no wise man may doute of the wicked mans inseparable payne. For where both good & yll, payne & reward be crosse one to an other, it followes that such reward as haps to goodnes, the same must needes be of contrary sorte, for payne of wicked. For as sinceritie to the

The honest are rewarded by their own sincerity, and the wicked are punished by their own vices.

honest is rewarde, so to the wicked their vnhappynes is their plage. So as who euer is punisht must needes be wicked.[3] Yf therfore they wold way well themselves, can they suppose them voyde of payne, whose wickdnes in all ylls not only touchith them, but greevously infectes? See on thother syde, such parte as is to the good contrary, what payne doth follow them. I haue taught you afore that all that is, must be one, and that the only good is one. Then it followes, to what so that is, that seemes to be good. Then whosoeuer faylith from that good, he leaves to be: so that, when euill they be, they leave to be that they were; but to prove that men they were, the forme of their humayne body shewith, but turned into malice, they haue left their humayne nature. And since that true pietie alone may lift vp a man, it followes, that whom wickednes hath throwen downe from state of man, hath cast him downe beneth the merit of man. So it haps, that whom transformed thou seest with vice, thou mayst not suppose him a man.

---

[1] The text is *corollarii*. Chaucer has: "corolarie."   [2] The text is *improbitas*.
[3] Meaning badly given of: *Iam uero quisquis afficitur poena, malo se affectum esse non dubitat.* Chaucer has: "þan who so þat euer is entecched and defouled wiþ yuel."

[MYT. III.] *DE CONSOLATIONE PHILOSOPHIÆ.*

The violent robber of others goode*s* is farvent in his robberyes, swellith in coueting,[1] & mayst call him woolflyke, feerce & contentious, exercises his tongue in bralles,[1] euin lyke a dog. The secret lurker joyes with fraude to catche,[1] And so is foxlyke, untemperate in ire he chafith,[1] & men beleeue him a lyar; but fearfull & flyeing, fearith & dredith that needes not,[1] And he to deere is compared. The sluggy & dullard languishith[1] & lyke an ass doth lyve. The light & vnconstant man changes his intente*s*, & differs so nought from the byrde*s*, And is plunged in filthy & vncleane luste*s*, And is kept in the delyte of his owne[2] lewdnes. And so it haps, that he that forsakyth honesty leaues to be a man; for not to be able to attayne a dyuine state, is tournid to the bestly.

The nature of the wicked man sinks to the level of the beasts.

III. MYTER.

Ulisses Captaines Sailes,
And Sailing Shippes in Sea
Eurus to Iland broght,
The Goddis fear Sitting   4
As borne of Φebus Line
To her newe Gestz
The Charmed Cup doth giue.
Wiche as in diuers Sortz   8
Herber rular gides her hand,
This man the bores Snout do couer,
Another the Marmican[3] *lion*
With Tuske and paw indueth.   12
This like to the wolfe nv borne,
Whan wepe he wold, he houles.

A description of Circe's enchantments.

[1] In all these places a question, and then follows the answer.
[2] The Queen has mistaken *suis* (swine) for "his own."
[3] The text has *Marmaricus*.

METRUM III.

Vela neritii ducis
Et uagas pelago rates
Eurus appulit insulae,
Pulchra qua residens dea   4
Solis edita semine
Miscet hospitibus nouis
Tacta carmine pocula.

Quos ut in uarios modos   8
Vertit herbipotens manus,
Hunc apri facies tegit,
Ille marmaricus leo
Dente crescit et unguibus.   12
Hic lupus super additus,
Flere dum parat, ullulat.

These enchantments had power only over the body and left the mind untouched.

Another as Indian tigar
Walkes in his house as mild.   16
Thogh from many euelz
The winged Arcadian God
Pitying the besiged Captaine
from gestz plague preserved,   20
Yet wicked Cup the Sailars
With mouthes supte vp,
And swin changed Ceres corne
for foode of Acorne chosen,   24
To lost men naught remained
Of body nor of voyce.
Only ther mynd stabel aboue
Whan the monstars suffar, wailes.   28
O hand to weke nor herbes of power,
Thogh Limmes to Change,
Hartz yet alter may not.

More dangerous is mental poison even when it does not injure the body.

Whithein bides man strengh   32
Hid in his towre.
Thos venoms with more fors
Man from himselfe withdrawes,[1]
Who thogh the body not   36
The Soule with woundz assailes.[2]

IV. Prose.

"I see," quoth I, "that vicious men haue no wrong, tho they be said by property of their mynde to beastes be transformd, tho in show they kepe the forme of humayn body. And yet I

---

[1] Line left out: "*Dira quae penitus meant.*"   [2] Or "assoiles".

Ille tigris ut indica
Tecta mitis obambulat.   16
Sed licet uariis malis
Numen Arcadis alitis
Obsitum miserans ducem
Peste soluerit hospitis,   20
Iam tamen mala remiges
Ore pocula traxerant,
Iam sues cerealia
Glande pabula uerterant   24
Et nihil manet integrum
Voce corpore praeditis.
Sola mens stabilis super
Monstra quae patitur gemit.   28
O leuem nimium manum
Nec potentia gramina,
Membra quae ualeant licet,
Corda uertere non ualent.   32
Intus est hominum uigor
Arce conditus abdita.
Haec uenena potentius
Detrahunt hominem sibi   36
Dira quae penitus meant
Nec nocentia corpori
Mentis ulcere saeuiunt.

4 wold not haue, that the cruell & wicked mynde should be *Wicked men may be considered*
sharpnid by the fall of good men." "Neyther is it," quoth *more fortunate when they fall*
she, "as in convenyent place I will showe. And yet if that *into the hands of justice, than*
were taken away from them that they are beleeued to haue, *when they re-*
8 the wickedst payne should be in greatest parte releeuid. For *main unpunished.*
that that may perchance seeme impossible, hit must needes be
that wicked men be vnhappyer, when they haue fulfild their
desyres, than if they could not get what they wish. For if a
12 wretched thing it be to wysh that is nough*t*, it is much more
wretched to doo it. Without which the desyre of a wretched
mynde wold fall. Wherfore when ech man hath his own
misery, it must needes be, that by tryple misfortune, they be
16 vexed, whom thou dost see haue a will to doo the worst." " I
graunte it," quoth I, " And yet that quickly they might want
this misfortune, I wish them depriued of possibilitie to doo mischeefe." " They shall want it," quoth she, " sooner perchaunce
20 than eyther thou woldest, or they themselues think they may.
For neyther is any thing so long in the short mesure of our
lyfe, that an immortall mynde may suppose to tarry to long :
whose greate hope & hye woork of mischefe oft is destroyde
24 by an vnlookt for & souden end, which settes an end to
their misery. For if iniquitie make men miserable, he must
be more wicked that longer lastes : whom most vnhappy I
should judge, if their last death might not end their woe.
28 For if we conclude the truth, of wickednes misfortune, infinite
must we suppose that misery that is euerlasting. Wonderfull
thinges," quoth I, " is this declaration & hard to be graunted,
but I know them to well agree to such thinges as before haue *It is quite er-*
32 bene exprest." " Rightly dost thou think," quoth she : " and *roneous to suppose that wicked*
who so thinkes a hard conclusion is made, it were reson he *people are happy.*
should showe, that ther hath bene som falshod in the pro-
position, or that the tyeng of their argument bootith not for a
36 necessary conclusion. Or els all the abouesaid graunted, ther is
no cause to cauill in the subsequent. For this that I saye,
not only seems not wonderfull, but, by such thinges as are
alledged, most necessary." "What ?" quoth I.[1] " I saye that
40 happyer be wicked men whan they suffer punishment, than

---

[1] Following sentence should begin with the transl. of "*Feliciores, inquit.*"

The wicked are happier when they suffer punishment, because their vices are thereby corrected.

those who*m* no payne of Justice touchith? Nether mynd I now to speake of that every man think*es*, That wicked con-ditions being corrected by revenge & brought to the right way by terro*ur* of their prison, to othe*r* men may serue for example to shun theyr fault*es*. But in other sorte I suppose the wicked vnhappy, tho ther were no cause of correctio*n* to make them vnpunished, nor no respecte of ensample." "What should this other way be?"[1] "Haue we not said afore, that good men be lucky & euill men miserable?" "So it is."[2] "Yf therfore[3] som goodnes chau*n*ce to misery, is it not much more happyer for him, than if his misery were alone by it self, wit*h*out any goodnes mixture?" "So it seemes," q*uoth* I. "But yf to that miserable man that want*es* all good thing*es*, that euill be added to him to be alone, is he not much more to be accompted vnhappy, whose mysfortune is showed him thorow the partici-pa*t*ion of som good?" "What els?"[4] "Therfore wicked men, when they are punisht, haue som good joyned wit*h* it, that is their punishme*n*t, w*h*ich for Justice sake is in it self good. And they whan they want their correctio*n*, ther is som thing besid*es* of euill, which is, want of punishment, w*h*ich deserue ably thy self hast co*n*fest is the greatest yll Iniquitie can haue.[5] More vnhappy therfore are wicked folk*es*, whan they want their pu*n*ishme*n*t, than when they receaue their iust reward. For greatest iniquitie is co*m*mitted, when Just men be vexed,

Every one must allow that all that is good, is just, and all that is evil, the contrary.

& wicked slip fro*m* their reward." "Who can this denye?" "Wherfore,[6] ech man must need*es* grau*n*te, that all that is good, must need*es* be iust, & yll that is the contrary."[7] "These be such thing*es* need*es* must follow the aboue co*n*-cluded. But I pray thè," quoth I, "shall there be no soules punishme*n*t after the dead body?" "Very greate," q*uoth* she, "of w*h*ich som be vsed by bitter payn*es*, other by a pacifieng[8] Clemency. But now my mynde is a little of these thing*es* to dispute. For this hitherto we haue don, that thou mightest knowe the vnworthy powre of euill men is none at all. Euin such as thou co*m*playnedst were voyde of punishme*n*t, that

44

48

52

56

60

64

68

72

---

[1] "*Et illa inquit*" left out. [2] *inquam* left out. [3] *inquit* left out.
[4] *inquam* left out. [5] "*Negare non possum*" left out.
[6] *Ait*, "she said," left out. [7] "*Respondi tum ego*" left out.
[8] The text is; "*purgatoria clementia*."

76 thou mightest see they neuer want the payne of their wickednes, And that the liberty which thou wisshest should be *Repetition:*
ended, thou mightest learne not to be long, And so much *wicked folks are more miserable*
more vnhappy, if longer, most vnlucky, yf eternall. And *when they escape punishment*
80 then I sayd that wicked folkes were more miserable, shun- *than when they are punished.*
ning their Just payne, than punisht with their right revenge.
So follows it true with my opinion, That then they are
greeuid with sorest punishmentes, whan they are supposd less
84 plagued." "Whan I consider thy reasons," said I, "I can
suppose nothing more true. But if I turne me to mans Judgement, who is he, to whom not only these thinges will not seeme
to be beleeuid but scar[c]ely to be herd?" "So it is," quoth
88 she. "For they can not, that haue vsed their eyes to darknes,
lyft them vp to the light of a cleere trowth, & lyke they *When the eyes*
be to such byrdes, whose sight the night dooth cleere, & day *are accustomed to darkness they*
darkens. For while they beholde not the order of thinges, *cannot discern anything in a*
92 but their own affections, they suppose the liberty and lack of *bright light.*
payne, for their faultes, the happiest. But now looke what
the euerlasting light makith. Yf to best thou doo apply thy
mynde, thou shalt neede no iudge to defer thy rewarde, Thou
96 thy self hast ioyned thè to the Excellency. Yf thou turn thy
indeuors to worsse, beyond thy selfe seeke no revenger. Thou
thy self to worst hast throwen thè, & lookest to heauen
& clayey earth by fittes, when all outward thinges fayles
100 thè, by thyne owne reason shalt perceaue, the difference
between Sky & Claye. But the vulgar cares not for this.
What tho? Shall we speake of such thinges now as shewes
men most lyke beastes? What yf a man losing his sight hath
104 forgotten that euer he had it, shall he suppose he lackes
nothing of a mans perfection? Shall we suppose these men, tho *Those who do*
they see, to be blynde? They will not leave so, But will with *wrong are more unhappy than*
certain grownd of reson know, that they are more vnhappy *those who are wronged.*
108 that do wrong, than those that suffer it." "I wold fayne know
these reasons," said I. "Thou dost not deny,[1] a wicked man is
wourthy of all payne?" "I deny it not." "You think to, they
are vnhappy that diuers wayes are wicked.[2] 'Such as are
112 worthy punishment, therfore no doute are miserable?" "It

---

[1] *Inquit* left out. [2] "*Ita, inquam*" left out.

agreeith well." "Yf therfore thou satest as a Judge,[1] on whom woldst thou inflict the payne? eyther on him that made or suffred the wrong?" "I doute not[2] but that I wold satisfy the sufferer by the punishment of the Actor." "Then wretcheder is the maker, than the Receauour." "It is reason."[2] "For this & many other causes all hangyng on one roote, hit appeers that synne of his owne nature, makes men wretched, And that injury is not the receauers misery but the giuers. But Orators doo otherwise.[1] They go about to moue commiseration of the iudges for them that haue commytted som greate & cruell thing, when rather a juster commiseration ought to be had of such as be not brought by irefull accusers, but by such as themselues beemones & takes compassion of, as tho they wold bring the sick to the phisician, & cut of the disease by the false punishment. By which eyther the endeuour of the defendors should coole, or if it should proffitt them, must be turned into the forme of the accusation. But wicked men, yf they see any but a small clift wher vertue is to be seene, where wicked vice they may put of, by paynes cruelty, vnder coulour of recompensing vertue, will not call this cruelty, but will refuse their defendors labour, & giue themselues wholly to the accusers & Judges. So as wise men haue no place left them for hate. For who but a very foole will malice a good man? And who but he that lackes reson, will not hate the yll?[3] For, as the bodyes sicknes, so is vice the myndes disease: euin as we suppose that sick men deserve not hate but commiseration, so ought they not be persecuted but pitied whose mynde than all sicknes bytterer, Iniquitie hath besieged."[4]

A judge must, therefore, punish the doer and not the receiver of wrong.

Sickness is a disease of the body and vice of the mind, therefore wicked men are to be pitied and not hated.

[4] M. of the iiijth booke.

IV. MYTER.

What boutes hit make so great strife
And with thy hand thy dethe procure?

---

[1] *Ait* left out. [2] *Inquam* left out. [3] No question in the text.
[4] Here follows a duplicate translation of the fourth Book, occupying twelve pages, ff. 58—63.

METRUM IV.

Quid tantos iuuat excitare motus
Et propria fatum sollicitare manu?

If dethe you seake, she draweth ny
   Agreyng, not abides the winged horse.   4
Whom Serpent, Lion, Tigar, beare, and bore
   With bite do seake, with blade your selues pursue :
That properties agre not but do difar,
   Ar they the Cause of wicked strife and war,   8
And perische wold with weapon diuers?
   No Just meane of Cruelty ynough.
Fit Mede woldest thou giue desartz?
   Of right the good do Loue the yl bemone.   12

It is foolish of mankind to wage war with one another, it would be wiser to love the righteous and pity the wicked.

V. PROSE.

Than I began: "I se," quoth I, "what felicitie or misery it is, that is sett in the desertes of honest & wicked men. But in common fortune I see, but little good or yll to be. For no
4 wise man wold rather choose to be exul, poore, dispisde, than riche, reuerenced, mighty, & florishing abide in his own Citie. For then more plainly & with better witnes, is the propertie of wisdom seene, when the happines of Rulers be as
8 it were skatterd among such peeple as be straungers, When cheefely geayle, lawe & other tormentes for due punishment rather pertayne to wicked Citizens, for whom they were first ordeynd. But when these be turnd in wry sorte, &
12 wickedest payne doo presse good men, & yll doo snatch reward from vertue, I wonder much what may seeme the reason of so vniust a confusion, & doo desyre of thé to know. For lest wold I maruell therat, if I beleeued all
16 thinges were mixt by chanceing luck. Now, God the guide, my doute increasith; which when oft tymes he giues to good, delytes, to euill hard haps, somtyme agayne he giues yll chance to good, & grauntes the yll their wish, without ther

The objection that the wicked are often prosperous and the righteous the reverse, is combated by a reference to God's providence.

God sometimes grants good men their desire, and sometimes the wicked.

   Si mortem petitis, propinquat ipsa
Sponte sua, uolucres nec remoratur equos.   4
   Quos serpens leo tigris ursus acri
Dente petunt, idem se tamen ense petunt.
   An distant quia dissidentque mores,
Iniustas acies et fera bella mouent   8
   Alternisque uolunt perire telis?
Non est iusta satis sacuitiae ratio.
   Vis aptam meritis uicem referre?
Dilige iure bonos et miseresce malis.   12

As God is the ruler of the world, we must not doubt that all things are therein rightly ordered.

could a cause be founde, what hit should be that makes a 20 difference from chaunceing haps." "It is no wonder," quoth she, "if any thing rash & confounded be beleuid when orders reason is vnknowen. But thou, allthough thou knowest not the cause of so greate an order, yet because a good guyder 24 the world tempers, doubte thou not all thinges rightly orderd be."

*5 Myter of the iiij*th *booke.*

V. MYTER.

Amazement and admiration are often excited by ignorance of the cause.

Yf man know not how stars
The Arcture next by hyest poles doo slyde,
Nor why Bootes slow glydes by ye wane
And sluggy flames in sea doo dip,   4
When her swift rysings to soone performs,
Of hyest heauens ye lawe will muse.
Of fulled Moone the hornes whitenid
Infected with ye bounds of darkest night,   8
And such as with her shyning face were shaded
Dymmed Pheba those stars discouer :
A common error folkes assayles

Examples of natural phenomena not understood by the ancients.

And brasen tymbrells stryke with many strokes.[1]   12
None musith that ye southest[2] wynde
With hurling waue astones ye shore,
Nor that ye hardnid snowy ball by cold
By feruent heate of sonne resolues.   16
For ready is the cause of y^{is}[3] be seene,
But hydden causes whyrls ye mynd.

[1] On the occasion of eclipses of the moon, it was a custom among the ancients to strike upon brazen vessels, in order, as they thought, to free the moon from enchantment.
[2] The Latin text is *corus*, north-west wind.
[3] Observe the use of the *th* symbol in other words besides "the."

METRUM V.

Si quis Arcturi sidera nescit
Propinqua summo cardine labi,
Cur legat tardus plaustra Bootes
Mergatque seras aequore flammas,   4
Cum nimis celeres explicet ortus,
Legem stupebit aetheris alti.
Palleant plenae cornua lunae
Infecta metis noctis opacae   8
Quaeque fulgenti texerat ore

Confusa Phoebe detegat astra :
Commouet gentes publicus error
Lassantque crebris pulsibus aera,   12
Nemo miratur flamina cori
Litus frementi tundere fluctu
Nec niuis duram frigore molem
Feruente Phoebi soluier aestu   16
Hic enim causas cernere promptum est,
Illic latentes pectora turbant.

Such as our Age scarce knowith lyke
And vulgar fleete,[1] *at souden gase.*
Let cloudy faultes of error giue his place
And wonders sure be seene shall ceasse.[2]

<small>Wonders cease when the cause of them is understood.</small>

VI. Prose.

"So it is," said I; " but since thy office it is to vnfold the cause of hidden maters, & expresse reasons hid vnder shade, I besech thè, to looke on this, & for that this miracle doth most vexe me, teache it me." Then she, smyling a little: " You call me to a matter that all men chefely seek, to whom scacely suffisith to taste alone. For it is such a mater that one dout cut of, inumerable others as Hydras heades increase; nether euer will ther be an end, vnles a lyuely fyre of the mynde doo bynde it. For in this mater, we inquire of the purenes of Prouidence, of the succession of Chaunce, of hapning Luckes, of the knowledge & predestination of God, & of our free will, which of how greate burden all these be, thy self canst waye. But because this is som portion of thy medecin to know these thinges, tho we be wrapt in a strayte lymite of tyme, yet we will stryue somwhat to determyne. For if thou delyte in a musicall song, thou must differ a little thy delyte, while I doo tune in order the Reasons knyt togither." " As please yo^u," said I. Then as begynning of an other theme, thus she disputed : " The creation of all thinges, & the disposing of mutable Natures, & what euer by any meane is mooued, getes the cause, order, & forme of Godes mynde, stabilitie. And this sett in the top of her Purenes, appoyntes a sondry manner for ech action : which order, when it is beheld in the very cleerenes of diuine vnderstanding, is named *Prouidence*. But when it is referd to those thinges that hit moouith & disposith, of the Aunciente*s* it is called *Desteny:* which easely shall appeer [to be][3] divers, yf a mans

<small>Explanation of the difference between Divine Providence and fate.</small>

<small>Further proofs to show that the prosperity of the wicked is unreal and only a wise disposition of providence.</small>

---

[1] Text is "*mobile vulgus*", inconstant crowd.
[2] This meter is in a secretary's hand.   [3] The MS. is damaged here.

Cuncta quae rara prouehit aetas
Stupetque subitis mobile uulgus.   20
Cedat inscitiae nubilus error,
Cessent profecto mira uideri.

mynde will see the efficacy of both. For Prouidence is Godes
pleasure, appoyntyd by him that all rulith & all disposith.
But Destiny is the disposing of causes joynd to remoouing
causes, by the which Prouidence knittith all thinges by her
orders. For Prouidence includith all, whither they be diuers
or infinite, but Desteny deuideth euery thing according to her
motion, distributing it to place, to forme, & tyme : that this
deuiding of temporall order joyned to the diuine pleasure may
be made¹ Prouidence, But that joyning, being seuerd &
deuided into tymes, that is Fate. Which tho they be sondry,
yet they depend one of an other. For fatall order proceedith
of Prouidence purenes. For as a craftes man, conceauing in
his mynde the forme of a woork, causith him to end, & that
which he hath plainly & presently foreseene, he ordrith by
tymes rule : so God by his Prouidence singularly & stable
disposith all thinges to be don. But by desteny so devided,
aboundantly & in his due season workes it. Whither Desteny be
exercised by familiar Spirites that serues for Godes Prouidence,
or whither the fatall work be knytt by the soule alone, or
Nature seruing in parte therto, or celestiall courses of the
heavens, or by Angelicall powers, or by sondry industry
of Spirites, or by som of these, or by all : This is most
playne, that the forme of all thinges vnmoueable & simple is
Prouidence. But Destiny is of such thinges as the Diuine
Cleerenes disposith to be don, & makith the mooving lynk
& orderly Rule. So followes it, that all that subiect be to
fate, be vnder Rule of Prouidence, vnder whom Fate it self
down layes. But som thinges there are by Prouidence appoynted that doo exceede Fates force. Those thinges they be
which fixed stably, next to diuinitie, exceede the Nature of
Fates mutabilitie. For as of all Circles the inmost that turnes
themselves about one rounde, coms neerest to the purenes of
the midst, and as a steddy stay of all that rolles about, doth
circuite the same, but the vttmost by wyder bredth rolled, the
more hit goes from the vndeuided midst of the poynte, so much
the more hit is spred by larger spaces, but whatsoeuer drawith
neere & accompanith the midst, & with his purenes is

The difference between Providence and Destiny.

God by His Providence disposeth how all things are to be done.

All who are subject to Fate are also under the rule of Providence, for Fate is subject to Providence.

---

¹ The Queen has read *fit* for *sit*.

ruled, ceassith to be stopt or ouerrun : with lyke reason, that
furdest goes from the first intent, is wrapt in straighter
knotes of Fate. And so much the freer is any man from the
68 same, as neerest he doth drawe to the orderers wheele. And
yf he stick to the euerduring eternall mynde, wanting change,
he goith aboue Destenyes necessitie. For as Reason is to
vnderstanding, & that that is made, to that that is, And
72 as tyme to Eternity, & Circle is to the middest poynte : So
is the order of fate changeable, compared to the stable purenes
of Prouidence. For desteny moouith heauen & skye,
tempers the elementes among themselues, & turnes them
76 thorow diuers changes : & such thinges as be bred & dye,
renewes such¹ by lyke generation of frutes & seedes. This
knittes actions, fortunes of men by an indissoluble lynk
of causes, which since they com all from the begynning of
80 an vnchanging Prouidence, it must needes be that otherwise
than so, they can not change. For so thinges be well ordred,
yf the euerlasting purenes of Godes mynde doth prescribe an
vnturning order of causes. But this Rule byndith in, thinges
84 mutable & rashly fleeting, by his owne steddynes. Wherby
altho to yo^u that can not consider the order of thinges they
seeme confuse, and rombled togither, yet he that is cause of all
good, directes all thing to hit. For ther is no man how
88 wicked soeuer, that for yll-sake, will doo ought so. Whom
tho as I haue told you afore, in seeking good, an yll errour
hath turnd, yet the order that coms from the roote of all good,
turns no man from his begynning. But what, thou wilt saye,
92 can be a greater confusion or a woorsse, than that aduersitie
& prosperitie happens to good men, & alyke to euill
doth hap, both wisht and hated? Doo men lyve of such
integritie of mynde, that it must needes be that they be
96 wicked or good, that be supposed so? For in this we see
diuers judgementes of men vary, whom som thinkes worthy
rewarde, other suppose deserue punishment. But let vs
graunte that one man may discerne the good & yll men :
100 Can he looke vpon the inward temper of the mynde, as well
as of the body? The wonder is not vnlyke to him that

As Reason is to understanding and Time to Eternity, etc., so is the order of Fate changeable when compared to the stable pureness of Prouidence.

Although the order of things may seem to vs confused, they are in reality kept in order by the Cause of all good.

We can only discern the bodies of men and not their inward thoughts.

---

¹ "such" is underlined, to be omitted.

knowes not, why to men of wholle bodyes, somtymes to these
sweet thing*es* please, som other delyte in sowre : why sick
men som be helpt by lenitiues, som other cured by corrosiues. 104
But this a phisician that knowes the meane of his helth &
sicknes togither with his tem*per*, nothing wonders at. What
other thing is the mynd*es* helth, than sincerity ? What the
sicknes, but vice ? Who other is eyther keep*er* of good, or 108
ouerthrower of yll, than the directo*ur* and phisician of o*ur*
mynde, God himself ? Who when he look*es* out of the glasse [1]
of his hye prouide*n*ce, knowith what for ech man is best.
And that he knowes is best, that he gyues him. And this is 112
the greate miracle of destenyes order, when it is treated by a
skyllfull p*er*son, at which the ignorant woonder. And that
I may somwhat touche what mans Reason may com*p*rehend
of God*es* depth, in that mater that thou supposest to be most 116
just, & keeps greatest equalitie, it seemes all be different
fro*m* him that knowith what Prouide*n*ce is. And as o*ur*
frend Lucan sayde, the wynners cause pleased God, the woonne
Cato. For in this world what so thou seest be done beyond 120
hope, is the rightest order of all, And p*er*uers is the co*n*fusio*n*
of opinio*n* her self. But if a man haue so much ma*n*ner,
that he will agree both of diuine judgeme*n*t & humayne,
yet is he of his mynd*es* strength so weake, as if any adue*r*sitie 124
hap him, he will leaue to prise ynnocency, by who*m* he could
not keepe fortune. For the wise giuer sparyth him who*m* he
knowes aduersity will him payre,[2] so as he will not suffer him
labour in payne, for ought behooues him not. An other 128
man ther is vniuersally vertuous, holy, & next to God.
This man the diuine Prouide*n*ce judgith a wicked thing wit*h*
aduersitie to afflict, so that he will not suffer him be vext
wit*h* bodely disease. For as an excellenter than my self 132
sayde : 'A good man, his v*er*tues doo inhabite him.'[3] So it
co*n*clud*es*, that good men haue all thing*es* to rule, that
abou*n*ding iniquitie might be ruyned. To other men he
distribut*es* certain mixtures, according to the qualitie of the 136

Side notes: The health of the mind is sincerity, and its sickness, vice. / Man's Reason is incapable of com-prehending God's Providence. / Quotation of a saying of Parmenidas.

---

[1] The Latin text has *specula*, a high tower ; the Queen has mistaken it for *speculo*, looking-glass. [2] So in MS.
[3] A saying of Parmenidas, which is now translated as follows :
  "The gods built the body of a good man."

mynd. Som men he stingith lest they should ouerflow into greate felicity. Others he tosses with aduersitie, that he may establish their myndes vertue, by patience, vse, & exercyse. *The Divine Providence metes out divers measures to divers men.*
140 Others som to much feare, that beare they might; som other to much despise that carry they can not. These men he leades by woe to know themselues. Som other deserue an honorable name with price of glorious death. Som other haue
144 shewed a sample to the rest, vnuincible of payne : And so doo shew to wicked men how vnwon vertue is. Which how rightly & in order & for their good to whom it hapt they haue bene don, ther is no doute. For euin that eyther sorowfull or
148 desyred haps to the wicked folkes, proceedes of like cause. And as for the wicked, no man wonders, for thinking them worthy all yll: whose punishment both feares other from faultes, & breedes their amendement on whom it is imposd: *The punishment of the wicked amends those on whom it is imposed and deters others from crime.*
152 Prosperous thinges serue for greate argument that they be good. But what ought men iudge of such felicitie ? when they see them the servantes of the wicked. In which mater somtyme they seeme to haue a dispensation, for that som mans
156 nature is so headstrong & rash, that neede of necessities cause may make him fall into a mischeefe, whom the prouiding of monny got, might serue for remedy. But when he lookes, his fyled conscience with faulte, & with himself
160 disputing of his fortune, perchance fearith that the losse should be sorowfull, of that the vse was delytefull. He will change therfore his condition, and whyle his luck feares to lose it, he will leave his wickednes. Vnworthy gotten felicitie throwes
164 downe som men to deseruid ruine; som men haue leave to punish, that they might invre good men, & punish the yll. For as no league ther is between the wicked & good, so can not the euill among them selves agree. What els, when ech *There is no league between the wicked and the good, and evil men cannot agree among themselves.*
168 man disagrees, their vices being sondry, & often doo such thinges, which they discerne they ought not doo, after don they be? So haps it oft, that Godes providence wourkith a miracle, that euill men make yll men good. For when they
172 see that they suffer harm themselves by euill men, abhorring such actors, retourne to vertues frute, while they study to be vnlyke such as they hate. For it is Godes only powre, to make of euill good, when vsing them as they ought, drawes

8 *

from them som effect of good. For order keeps ech thing, so as what so doth leave his assigned way of order, the self same tho it hap to an other, falles in rule, lest in Providences kingdom, Rashnes should prevayle. 'Hard for me it is these thinges that touche God, as all the rest, describe.'[1] For neyther doth it becom man to comprehend all shapes of his woorkes, or by tongue or wit expresse. Only this may suffise, that we perceaue that God the maker of all Nature, disposith so of all as directes it to the good. And while he hyes to kepe such thinges in order as he made, he dryves all euill out of the boundes of his kingdom, by the order of a fatall necessitie. So it followes, that such thinges as we beleeue the Earth to haue plenty, if we looke vpon the direction of Providence, we shall see ther is no yll at all. But now I see the burdned with waight of question, & wearyed with length of reasoning, to expecte the sweetnese of som verse. Take therfore a draught wherby refresht thou mayst trye strong furder to go."

We cannot comprehend the works of God, but it is sufficient for us to know that He is the maker and beneficent director of all Nature.

VI. MYTER.

Praise of Providence which regulates the dying and revivifying influence of the seasons, as well as all other periodical changes.

If wary alone of thundring God ye lawes thou wilt
With purest mynde beholde,
Of hyest heauen ye top doo vewe.
There Planets, with justest league of all,   4
Agreement old doo keepe.
The sonne styrd up by ruddy fyre
Phebas frosy axill tree ne letts,
Nor that Beare that on ye top of world   8
A running course doth bend,
That neuer other stars wet beholding

---

[1] A verse from the Iliad ; the Queen has not given a correct translation of it.

METRUM VI.

Si uis celsi iura tonantis
Pura sollers cernere mente,
Aspice summi culmina caeli.
Illic iusto foedere rerum   4
Veterem seruant sidera pacem.

Non sol rutilo concitus igne
Gelidum Phoebes impedit axem ;
Nec quae summo uertice mundi
Flectit rapidos ursa meatus,   8
Numquam occiduo lota profundo

MET. VI.] DE CONSOLATIONE PHILOSOPHIÆ.

Dround under western depth, is touched
And seketh not with flames the Sea to hit.[1]
Ever with equall turne of tyme
Hesperus showes ye later shades,
And Lucifer retourns ye fay[r]est day.
So Interlaced looue renewes
The eternall courses all,
So jarring warr from starry sky made outlaw.
[2] *the Elementz all accord tempars*
In equal Sort, that Striving
Moisteurs to droughts [by] turnes giue way,
That the Coldz kipe faithe with flames,
And hanging fire vpward bend.
And heuy erthe with waight bow downe.
by seluesame Cause in milddist springe
The flowring yere his Sauors yeldz,
hottist Sommer Corne dothe ripe,
And fruitful Autumne apples beares,
Dripping Showres Wintar moistz.
This temper feedes and brings fourth
What so lyfe in world doth brethe.
The same snatching makes & plucks away
By the last gasp ending Spring.
The maker hye meane while sitts
Ruling bends of all ye Raynes,
King & lord, spring and fyrst

12 Regularity of the movements of the heavenly bodies.

16

20 Succession of the seasons.

24

28

32 God sits on high, ruling and directing all things.

[1] These two lines are corrected by the Queen.
[2] The following eleven lines are in the Queen's own hand.

Cetera cernens sidera mergi,
Cupit oceano tinguere flammas. 12
Semper uicibus temporis aequis
Vesper seras nuntiat umbras,
Reuehitque diem Lucifer almum.
Sic aeternos reficit cursus 16
Alternus amor, sic astrigeris
Bellum discors exulat oris.
Haec concordia temperat aequis
Elementa modis, ut pugnantia 20
Vicibus cedant umida siccis,
Iungantque fidem frigora flammis,
Pendulus ignis surgat in altum,

Q. ELIZ.

Terraeque graues pondere sidant. 24
Isdem causis uere tepenti
Spirat florifer annus odores,
Aestas cererem feruida siccat,
Remeat pomis grauis autumnus, 28
Hiemem defluus inrigat imber.
Haec temperies alit ac profert
Quidquid uitam spirat in orbe.
Eadem rapiens condit et aufert 32
Obitu mergens orta supremo.
Sedet interea conditor altus
Rerumque regens flectit habenas
Rex et dominus, fons et origo, 36

H

>   Lawe, and wyse, of just y\^e Judge,   36
>   And such by styrring as he rayses,
>   Buckdrawing stayes, and wandring keeps.
>   For but returning rightest lynes
>   Again he bent to bowing wheels   40
>   The Order that now stable keeps
>   Disseuerd all from Spring wold faynte.
>   Such is y\^e common loue of all,
>   That with returne, for end of good be kept.   44
>   In other sorte endure they could not,
>   Unles agayne by loue returnd
>   Back to the cause them made bend.¹

All created things proceed from God and return to Him again.

VII. Prose.

Every position in life may be happy;

"Doo yo^u see now what all these thing*es* we haue told may get?" "What is that?" said L "That all fortune may be good."² "And how may that be?"³ "Attend," said she: "When euery fortune eyther plesing or hard be made eyther to 4 exercise & reward the good, or to punish & correcte the yll, it is euident that all is a good cause that eyther is manifest to be iust or proffitable." "I perceaue⁴ this reason to be most true, and if I consider eyther prouidence or fate, that yo^u haue 8 afore tolde, your opinion leanith I perceaue to steddyest ground. But let vs set her yf please yo^u, among such as we haue supposed to be out of men's opinio*n*s." "What is that?"

though this is not the opinion of the people.

said she. "For the common speche of men deceaues itself, & 12 oft supposith mens fortunes hard. Will ye⁵ haue me a little draw neere to the vulgarest opinions?"⁶ "As it please yo^u," said I. "Doo yo^u not suppose that to be good that avayles,⁷

---

¹ This metre is in several places incorrectly translated by the Queen, see Chaucer.
² *Inquit* omitted.   ³ *Inquam* omitted.
⁴ *Inquam* omitted.   ⁵ *Inquit* omitted.
⁶ Here is omitted transl. of "*ne nimium uelut ab humanitatis usu recessisse uideamur?*"
⁷ The answer of Boethius is omitted: *Ita est inquam.*

Lex et sapiens arbiter aequi,
Et quae motu concitat ire,
Sistit retrahens ac uaga firmat.
Nam nisi rectos reuocans itus   40
Flexos iterum cogat in orbes,
Quae nunc stabilis continet ordo

Dissaepta suo fonte fatiscant.
Hic est cunctis communis amor   44
Repetuntque boni fine teneri,
Quia non aliter durare queant,
Nisi conuerso rursus amore
Refluant causae, quae dedit esse.   48

16 and such thing as exercises or correct*es*, good therfore?"[1]
"What els?" "But these belong to those wh*i*ch eyther vertuous jarre against aduersitie, or strayeng from vice take*s* vertues waye." "I can not deny it." "May the common peeple 20 deny that the rewarde is not good that good men haue?"
"No. For it must neede*s* be the best." "And what of all the rest? Will the common sorte think that that is not best that, tho it be sharp, yet lymite*s* wicked men by iust 24 payne?" "Yea," q*uoth* I. "I think that to be the most misery of all. Let vs beware lest following the common opinion we doo somthing vnawares.[2] By this that we haue graunted we conclude that worsse is the state of the*m* 28 that be eyther in the possibilitie, or in the aduaunce or obtayning of vertue, and yet byde in their iniquitie."[3] "This is true," said I, "tho no ma*n* dare confesse it." "Wherfore," said she, "so ought not a wise man beare wit*h* 32 greefe, fortunes wrestell, as it becoms not a strong man to be mooued, when a battell begyns. For the hardnes is argument for bothe, eyther to inlarge his glory, or to co*n*firme his witt. Wherby we call it force that stycking to his owne strenght 36 is not won by wo. For yo*u* cam not to vs in the aduancement of vertue, to make vs ouerflow wit*h* delites, or drownd in pleas*u*re, but that we should make a sharp battell against all fortune, and that neyther the sowre oppresse yo*w*, nor 40 pleasant corrupt yo*u*; the middle waye wit*h* steddy force maynteyne yo*u*. For who so beneth this or beyond goes has but felicities contempte, no trauells rewarde. For in your hand it is what fortune yo*u* will frame you, for 44 what so seemith sharpest eyther invre*s*, correcte*s*, or punishith."

A wise man must not flee from the struggle with fate, for he thereby acquires virtue.

Nothing can be worse than the state of those who have the opportunity of becoming virtuous and yet abide in their iniquity.

We hold fortune in our own hands by the way in which we receive her corrections.

---

[1] Here "*Fateor, inquam.—Bona igitur*" is missing.
[2] Here "*Quid? inquam*" is missing.
[3] "*Ex his enim, ait, quae concessa sunt, evenit eorum quidem qui uel sunt uel in possessione uel in prouectu uel in adeptione uirtutis, omnem, quaecumque sit, bonam, in improbitate uero manentibus omnem uessimam esse fortunam.*" The meaning of this sentence is not well given.

VII. MYTER.[1]

7 My. of the fourth booke.

Exhortation to heroism, of which Hercules is pointed out as an example.

Twis fiue yeres wratheful Atride made
With Φrisians ruines war,
The vnchast bed of brother so revenged.
he while hoissing Sailes to Grecians ship he gaue,   4
With wische and bloud the windes apeced,
dispoiled of fathers Care the cruel priest
his daughtars throte of life deprived.
Vlysses waild his Lost peers,   8
Whom bloudy Poleφemus in his Large den
Gulped down unto his Cruel panche,
And furius yet with his yeles hed
his Joy repaid with woful teares his owne.   12
Hardy Labors his Hercules did grace.
He Centaures proude did tame,
Of skin the Lion flead,
With Certain shaftes the birdz did hit,   16
Snatched Aples from the Looking dragon;

Description of the labours of Hercules.

his Left hand peaced[2] with golden metal,
Cerberus with threfold Cheane doth drawe.
A victor he is said to set the Lord for meat   20
To Cruel forefoted bests.
Hidra killed by venom sered,
Achelous streame with firy Looke
drowned under the shore his Shamed face.   24
Anteus he strake undar Libeans Sandes,
Cacus Apesed Euanndars wrothe

---

[1] This meter is in the Queen's hand.   [2] Sic. transl. of *gravior*, perhaps *pesed* (weighed).

METRUM VII.

Bella bis quinis operatus annis,
Vltor Atrides Phrygiae ruinis
Fratris amissos thalamos piauit.
Ille dum graiae dare uela classi   4
Optat, et uentos redimit cruore,
Exuit patrem, miserumque tristis
Foederat natae iugulum sacerdos.
Fleuit-amissos Ithacus sodales   8
Quos ferus uasto recubans in antro
Mersit inmani Polyphemus aluo;
Sed tamen caeco furibundus ore
Gaudium maestis lacrimis rependit.   12
Herculem duri celebrant labores.
Ille Centauros domuit superbos,
Abstulit saeuo spolium leoni,
Fixit et certis uolucres sagittis,   16
Poma cernenti rapuit draconi,
Aureo lacuam grauior metallo,
Cerberum traxit triplici catena.
Victor immitem posuisse fertur   20
Pabulum sacuis dominum quadrigis.
Hydra combusto periit ueneno,
Fronte turpatus Achelous amnis
Ora demersit pudibunda ripis.   24
Strauit Antaeum libycis harenis,
Cacus Euandri satiauit iras

And Shuldars thos wiche by heauens shuld pres
The bore the Same with folme did marke.
The Last Labor heauen beareing with nek unboued   28 *The reward for earthly labours is the attainment of Heaven.*
The heauen decernes far Labors pane.
Forward go that Stronge be wher hiest way
Of graetest Sample bides.   32
Why, Sluggardz! baks do you tourne?
The erthe won the heauens he
        giues.

*This is the end of the
fourth booke.*

[*Endorsed.*]   The fourth booke.
These are written with the hand
of Queene Elizabeth.

---

*Quosque pressurus f ret altus orbis
Sa^tiger spumis umeros notauit.*   28
*Vltimus caelos labor inreflexo
Sustulit collo, pretiumque rursus
Vltimi caelum meruit laboris.*

Ite nunc fortes ubi celsa magni   32
*Ducit exempli uia. cur inertes
Terga nudatis? superata tellus
Sidera donat.*

THE FIFT BOOKE.

I. Prose.

<small>Philosophy takes up her parable.</small>

This spake she & tournd the course of talke to treate & dispatche certain other thinges. Then I told her: "Right was her exhortation, but worthyest of all her autoritie, but this I haue found by experience true, that lately yo^u told me of prouidence, how she was wrapt in diuers other matters. But I ask, whither ther be any at all, or whither chaunce be." Then she told me: "I hye to performe my dett, and shew thè the way to bring thè to thy Country. And tho these thinges for knowledge be most proffitable, yet be they somwhat strayeng from the path of our intent. And so must we use it,

<small>She gives a definition of chance according to Aristotle.</small>

lest wearyed by the bye crookes, thou mayst not be hable to endure the journey to right way." "I feare not that," said I. "For place of quiet I shall haue most, to know such thinges as most delyte me. And when all the manner of thy disputation hath bene playne of greatest assurance, no cause I haue to doute of the rest." "I will obey thy will," quoth she, & thus began: "Yf any man defynes chaunce to be a hap that lightes by rash motion & by no knot of causes, then I graunte ther is no chaunce. And see it [is] a vayne voyce that nought signifies. For what place can ther be left for rashnes, wher God in order all keepith? For it is a true sayeng, That of nought, nought is made, agaynst which none of the old wryters could gayne say, tho they did not suppose ther were any foundation layde by him that all made, but that all were subiect to som materiall cause, as tho the Nature of all reason

<small>Boethius asks Philosophy if there is nothing that may be called chance or luck.</small>

made it. But if ought ther be that springes of no cause, it must needes be, it is made of nothing. And if this can not be so, nether is it possible for any such chaunce to be, as we haue aboue reherst." "What then," quoth I, "Ys ther nothing that may be rightly calld chance or luck? Or is ther any such, tho vulgar peeple knowes not, to whom such name pertayns?" "Aristotle myne," quoth she, "in his Phisickes

hath defynd it in a neere reason to breefenes & trouth." "How so?" quoth I. "As oft," quoth she, "as any thing is don for any cause what euer that haps beside the intent of him that
36 did it, that is called Chaunce: as if a man digging vp his grounde for cause of tylling should fynde turnd vp a waight of golde. This is beleeuid euer to hap by chaunce: But it coms not of nought, for it hath his own proper occasion, of
40 which the happing & unlookt for luck, seems to haue wrought this hap. For if the plow man had not harrowd his ground, & yf the layer vp had not there hid his monny, gold there had not bene found. These be the causes of happing Chaunce,
44 because it coms of meeting & agreeing causes, not from the Doers Intent. For neyther did he that hid it, nor he that plowde it, mynde to haue found it there. But this agrees, that made him fynde it because the other hid it. Therfore it
48 is lawfull to defyne Chaunce to be a thing vnlookt for, & a hap growing of such thinges as for an other intent is don. But order it self that goes on with an vnshonning turne, that it is, that makith causes agree & meete, which comming from
52 the fountayne of prouidence, disposith all in their place & tyme."

Philosophy answers that Aristotle has defined it briefly and truly.

Chance may be defined as something unexpected and the result of an action done with some other intent.

I. MYTER.[1]

Neare the Craggs of Achemians rock wher turned to folowars
brestz the flying warior dartz doth throw,
from one springe Tigris ekce Euphrates arise
Strait by waters parted Soundred be.   4
Who met and in One Cours reclaimed,
The Streame that Eache depthe drew agries:
Let top Sailes meet and trunckis by currant drawen
and mixed waters fil the chaunging Cours,   8

The above definition of chance is exemplified by two rivers.

[1] In the Queen's own hand.

METRUM I.

Rupis achaemeniae scopulis ubi uersa sequentum
  Pectoribus figit spicula pugna fugax
Tigris et Euphrates uno se fonte resoluunt
  Et mox abiunctis dissociantur aquis.   4
Si coeant cursumque iterum reuocentur in unum,
  Confluat alterni quod trahit unda uadi:
Conuenient puppes et uulsi flumine trunci
  Mixtaque fortuitos implicet unda motus,   8

And Suche falz as bending erthe hath Skattered
A running Ordar of falling Gulfe ordars.
So what so Seame by Slakning ranes to slip
Chanchis bit yet indures and by a Law goes on. 12

II. Prose.

Of human liberty, of will and its misuse.

"I mark it," said I, "& as you say, so agree. But in this course of agreing causes, is ther any liberty in our will, or does a fatall chayne constrayne the motions of mens myndes?"
"Ther is one," said she: "for nether shold ther be a naturall 4 Reason,[1] but that there were an arbitrable liberty. For that that naturally can Reason rule, that hath Judgement, by which

A man desires what he wishes and shuns anything he does not wish.

all by hit self discernes. Then it knowes both what to shun & wish: He desyres that he wisshith, & shuns that he 8 thinkes meete to flye. wherfore to such as reason haue, a liberty of willing or denyeng is. But in all, I suppose not alyke. For to celestiall & divine substances ther is a playne iudgement & vncorrupted will, & a strong powre 12 ready to perform the desyred. And needes it must be that humayn soules be freer, when they keepe themselues in the contemplation of Godes will, & lesse when they slyde to bodyes Care, & lest of all, when they are lymed with earthly 16

Human souls are freer the more they devote themselves to the contemplation of God's will and the less they care for the body.

lyms. But it is the greatest bondage, when they, giuen to vice, hath fallen out of the possession of their own Reason. For when they throw theyr eyes from light of hyest truth to base & darkest maters, straight dymd by ignorance cloude, 20 are vext with slayeng affections, which increasing, & agreing vnto, they heape that bondage to themselues they bring, and are in a sorte captiued by their own libertie. Which he beholding that sees all from the first, & vewes the sight of 24 his own prouidence, all destenyes he desposith, agreing to their merit, 'all thinges beholdes & heares.'"[2]

[1] The text has "*rationalis natura*," "understanding being."
[2] The last five words of the text are in Greek, a quotation from Homer: ΠΑΝΤ 'ΕΦΟΡΩΝ ΚΑΙ ΠΑΝΤ 'ΕΠΑΚΟΥΩΝ.

Quos tamen ipsa uagos terrae decliuia casus
Gurgitis et lapsi defluus ordo regit.
Sic quae permissis fluitare uidetur habenis
Fors patitur frenos ipsaque lege meat. 12

II. Myter.

Cleere Phebus with purest light
The honnyed mouth of Homer sings.
Who yet ye deepe bowells of earth and sea
With weake Sight of beames pears not.[1]   4
Not So of the Great world the framar.
Gainst him that al from hy doth view
No waight of erthe may resist,
Not night with darkist Clouds Ganesays.   8
In moment stroke his mynd all Sees,
What wer, what be, what shal bifall :
Whom Sole alone for that he al espies,
Truly thé may Sole Call.   12

Comparison of God with the sun.

God views the whole earth from above.

III. Prose.

"Lest I shold be confounded with a harder doute, I pray yo^u tell me what this is?" "I do coniecture," quoth she, "what most troubles thè. Me thinkes[2] it a crosse mater & in it self disagreing, that God all knowes, & yet ther should be a free will. For if God all forsees, nor beguilde can neuer be, it must needes follow, that his prouidence hath seene, must be. Then yf from the begynning, not only mens deedes, but their counsells & wills he hath forknowen, no free will should be. For nether can any man doo, nor will, but that that his diuine neuer fayling prouidence knowes. For yf such thinges as be foreseene might be turned, then shold there not be an assured foresight of that shuld happen, but shold breede an vncertain opinion, which to beleeue of God, I iudge iniquitie. For nether do I allow that reason, by which som men beleeue, they can lose the knot of this question. For

Defence of free will against the so-called doctrine of predestination.

If from the beginning not only men's deeds but their counsels and wills be foreknown, there can be no free will.

---

[1] "Peers," or appears, incorrect transl. of *perrumpere*. This and the remaining lines are in the Queen's hand.   [2] *Inquam* left out.

Metrum II.

Puro clarum lumine Phoebum
Melliflui canit oris Homerus.
Qui tamen intima uiscera terrae
Non ualet aut pelagi radiorum   4
Infirma perrumpere luce.
Haut sic magni conditor orbis.
Huic ex alto cuncta tuenti
Nulla terrae mole resistunt,   8
Non nox atris nubibus obstat.
Quae sint, quae fuerint ueniantque
Vno mentis cernit in ictu :
Quem, quia respicit omnia solus,   12
Verum possis dicere solum.

they say, that that shall not hap only because God has
foreseene it, but contrariwise, because it was sure to hap,
therfore the diuine prouidence knew it, & therfore it is
necessary that this shold fall to the contrary parte, For, because they are foreseene, that makes not that they shall hap,
but because they must be, they are foreseene. As tho this
were the contention, whither the cause of ech thing be the
foreknowledge of necessitie that so it should be, or the fore-
prouidence of God that makes necessitie.[1] But we will
stryue to make it playne, how the order of causes is such,
that necessary must be the hap of that that chaunces, altho
we doo not see aforehand the neede of that haps. For if a
man sytt, of necessitie he must know that he syttes; and
contrarywise, whither the opinion be right that because he
sittes, therfore of necessitie he must sitt: In both ther is a
necessitie, in the one of sytting, in the other of truth. But
it followes not, that therfore he sittes, because the opinion
was true that he did so, but the opinion is rather true because
he sat afore. So when truth is on both sydes, ther is a
necessitie of both. The lyke we must reason of prouidence
& thinges to com. For altho they be foreseene, because
they shall hap, they hap not yet bicause they are foreseene.
Yet of necessitie, they must needes eyther hap foreseene by
God, or prouided for chaunce, which is ynough to kyll the
libertie of our will. But how out of reason is it, that the
hap of temporall thinges should be said the cause of eternall
foresight? For what is it els but to think that God therfore
foresees, that that is, because it should hap, than for to think
that such thinges should hap, the diuine prouidence to be the
cause? Besides, when I know any thing to be, it must needes
be that that was. So when I know what shall be, it must
needes be that so it shall be; & so it should follow, that
the chaunce of that that is foreseene can not be shund.
Lastly, yf any man think awry of that that is, not only that
is not a knoledge, but is a false opinion, furr different from
the trouth of knowledge. So as, yf any thing so shall hap,
that of hit ther is no certain nor necessary hapning, who can

Things do not happen because they are foreseen but because they must happen.

It is quite unreasonable to say that the chance of temporal things should be the cause of eternal foresight.

If any man think wrongly of anything that exists, that is no knowledge but a false opinion very different from the truth.

[1] Here the meaning of the text is very obscure: "*quasi uero quae cuius rei causa sit praescientiane futurorum necessitatis an futurorum necessitas prouidentiae laboretur.*"

know aforehand that that must needes hap? for as the knowledge it self is mixt¹ with falshed, so needes must be the same that of her is gatherde. For that is the cause, why 56 science wantes falshed, because it must needes be of necessitie, such thing as true knowledge must comprehend. What then? How doth God foreknow these vncertain thinges? For if he perceaue happing chaunces, that can not be shund, if it be 60 possible that such thinges happens, than is he deceaued: which not only is iniquitie to think but as yll to speake. But if he knowes that they shall be such as they shall, in eyther knowing they shall hap, or not chaunce, what a fore-64 knowledg is this, that comprehendes nothing sure nor certain? For what makes mater, or why should we esteeme this mocking prophcy of Tiresia? 'What I shall say, or shall be, or shall not.' Why should diuine prouidence excell humayn opinion, 68 if it judge vncertainties as men doo, Whose sequele is vncertain? And if with him, the surest founten of all thinges, no vncertaintie can abyde, sure is the hap of those thinges. that vndoutedly he knowith shall hap. Wherfore ther is 72 no liberty in mans counsells nor actes, which Godes mynd, that all foresees without falshodes errour, tyes & constrayns to one end. Which once concluded, what a fall shall hap then to humain cause, is playne. For in vayne rewardes to 76 good and payne to yll be sett, to whom no volentary & free motion of the mynde is due. And that should seeme most wicked of all other, that now is deemed justest: Eyther wicked men be punisht, or the good rewarded, whom no self 80 will turnes them to eyther, but a certain necessitie of hap compels them. So neyther should ther be vice nor vertue, but rather a mixte & vnseparable confusion of merite. Wherby (than which nothing can be wickedlyer imagyned,) 84 when all order of maters is led by prouidence, & nothing lawfull for mans determinations, hit concludes, that all our faultes be turnd to the Authour of all good. So should ther be no reason of hoping ought, or of intreating. For what 88 should any man hope or sue for, yf an vnturning necessitie constraynd all thinges that we wish? So should the conuers-

As knowledge is unmixed with falsehood, the same holds good of the result of knowledge.

Divine Providence would be no better than human opinion if it judged uncertainties as men do.

It would be in vain to reward good and punish evil if there were no free will.

---

¹ The text has *impermixta*, "unmixed."

Men would be deprived of all their comfort in God if all things were governed by necessity.

ation we haue among men, & comfort of God, be taken away: which is of hope & prayer. For if thorow price of true humilitie, we deserue the vnestimable inclination of Godes grace, being the only meane men seeme with God to speake, & joyn to his vnexpressable light by meane of our prayer, euin afore we obtayne yt: which, if we beleeue the necessitie of thinges to hap, shall seeme to haue no strenghth, wherby we may styck & cleaue to the Prince of all thinges? And so of necessitie, Mankynde, as a little afore thou hast told, shall consume disseuerd & disioynid from his own fountayne."

III. MYTER.[1]

A setting forth of the Platonic doctrine: that the principal part of our knowledge, is a recollection of what we knew in a previous existence.

What disagrijng Cause the bond of all things breakes?
What God suche wars twixt two trothes makes,
That what so coupled singly agree
The selfsame mixt must be disionyed?   4
but discord none among the truthes befals,
And Certain Sure vnto themselues do stik?
but mynd opprest by blindid Limmes
Can not by flame of overwhelmed Light
The smal knots of al things finde.   8
But why with suche desire doth true mynde seake
The hiden Cause of thinges serche Out?
Knowes he that gridely to knowe he wyls?   12

Men ardently desire to search out hidden causes.

Why strives he to knowe agane the had?
If ignorant he be, why blindid things seakes he?
for who that wischeth that knowes not what,
Or who foloweth that he wotz not?
Or may he finde, or found knowe   16

[1] In the Queen's own hand.

METRUM III.

Quaenam discors foedera rerum
Causa resoluit? quis tanta deus
Veris statuit bella duobus,
Vt quae carptim singula constent   4
Eadem nolint mixta iugari?
An discordia nulla est ueris
Semperque sibi certa cohaerent?
Sed mens caecis obruta membris   8
Nequit oppressi luminis igne

Rerum tenues noscere nexus.
Sed cur tanto flagrat amore
Veri tectas reperire notas?   12
Scitne quod appetit anxia nosse?
Sed quis nota scire laborat?
At si nescit, quid caeca petit?
Quis enim quidquam nescius optet,   16
Aut quis ualeat nescita sequi?
Quouc inueniat, quisue repertam

Suche forme of wiche he knowes not shape?
And whan he viewes the hyest mynd,
The Chief and al togither may he get?   20
but now the mynd hid in Limmes Cloudes
hathe not of al forgot his owne,
And, thogh the partz be lost, retaines the hed.
Who euer seakes the trueth to knowe,   24
Of nether Sort is rightly Called:
for nether al doth knowe nor ignorant of al:
but top of al retaining kipes by whos aduis,[1]
From hy the seen draweth, that bettar he may   28
The partz forgot the kept rejoingne.

Though the details of what was formerly known may be lost the whole is retained.

IV. PROSE.

"This is an old quarrell," quoth she, "of prouidence, vehemently handed by Tully, when he deuided destenty, & a thing by thé much & long sought, but yet not by any of yo^u sufficient nor certainly found out. Whose cause of darknes is, for that the motion of mans Resons can not attayne the purenes of Godes foreknowledge, which yf she might by any meanes imagine, no doute at all were left. Which yet I will attempte to expresse & make playne, if I had once dispatcht the thinges that first thou mouest. For I ask, why dost thou think the reason of men that wold expresse it, is not sufficyent? which for that hit supposith the prescience not to be the cause of necessitie to haps, therfore thinkes that free will is let thorow the foresight. For whence dost thou drawe thy argument of the necessitie of haps, but supposing they are foreknowen, they must needes hap? Yf therfore the foreknowledge doo ad no necessitie to that followes, as thou thy self confest, what cause is ther then that our volontary haps

Argument the same as in III. Prose, viz.— Defence of free will against the doctrine of predestination.

This argument is based on the conclusion that because a thing is foreknown it must of necessity happen.

---

[1] Sense obscure.

Queat ignarus noscere formam?
An cum mentem cerneret altam,   20
Pariter summam et singula norat?
Nunc membrorum condita nube
Non in totum est oblita sui,
Summamque tenet singula perdens. 24
Igitur quisquis ucra requirit,

Neutro est habitu: nam neque nouit
Nec penitus tamen omnia nescit:
Sed quam retinens meminit summam 28
Consulit alte uisa retractans,
Vt scruatis queat oblitas
  Addere partes.

should be compeld to the sure end of causes? For argumentes sake, mark what wold follow, Then should we agree ther were no prescience. Are they compelled to a necessitie, be- 20 cause they hap by our own free will?" "No." "Let vs reson that he haue free will, & yet that it makes no necessitie: then yt remaynes that our free will is wholle & sownde. But thou wilt saye, foresight, tho it bring no necessity that 24 thinges must hap, yet it is a token that such thinges may hap. And by this meanes, tho there were no foreknowledge, yet necessary end of thinges shold be. For every lyke showes what it is, but doth not make that it showes. Wherfore we 28 conclude that som¹ thinges hap of necessitie, so that the foreknowledge seemes to be a foretoken of the necessitie. Or els if it were no foreknowledge,² hit could not be the signe of that which is not. Now yo^u haue the conclusion euident 32 by a fyrme reson, which is not drawen out of signes & argumentes that be farr from the mater, but of conuenient & necessary causes. But how haps hit, that those thinges do not chaunce that be foreseene shall be? As tho we did 36 beleeue that such thinges should not hap, which the diuine prouidence hath foreknowen shall hap, but rather this doo we think, tho they doo chaunce, no necessitie of nature hath made them so to be; which heerby thou mayst easely see. 40 For we beholde many thinges while they be don, subiect to our sight: euin as such thinges we looke that car men shold doo in draweng & turning of those he guydes. and so of all other maters. But doth any necessitie compell this? No. 44 For in vayne should be the end of art, yf all thinges, compeld were mooued. Such thinges therfore when they are don, want a necessitie to compell them, the same afore they be don, without necessity must be. Wherfore some thinges there be 48 that haps, whose end is free from all necessitie. For I suppose no man will saye, that those thinges could neuer hap which he hath seene to be don. Therfore these thinges fore knowen haue their haps free. For as knowledge bringes no necessity 52 to doo so, foreknowledge compels nothing to be don. But

It is not necessary that because things are foreseen that they must happen, but it is a token that they may happen.

This conclusion is not deduced from reasons foreign to the subject, but from plain and evident ones.

No one will say that things which he hath seen done cannot happen.

---

¹ Text has a negation, "*Quare demonstrandum prius est nihil non ex necessitate contingere.*"

² The text has only *haec*, which refers to "necessity," not to "foreknowledge."

thou wilt saye, This is douted, whither ther can be any foreknowledge of that that necessarily must not hap. For that
seems to disagree. Dost thou think that necessitie must needes
follow such thinges as are foreseene?[1] Yf ther be no necessity,
it can not be foreknowen, & so nothing can be comprehended by knowledge but it must be certain. And yf we
beleeve uncertain haps to be none, but such as certain knowledge hath foreseene, it is playne that that is the darknes of
our opinion, not the trouth of our knowledge. For els otherwise than truth is, thou shouldest think, & haue a beleefe
awry from the integrytie of true knowledge. Of whose errour
this is cause, that men suppose all thinges that they knowe
to be deryued of the force & nature of the causes themselves, which wholly is contrary. For all that is knowen,
is comprehended, not according to his worth, but according to
the knowers powre. For as, by this short example, it is
playne, that the circuite of a body is knowen diuersly by
sight, & diuersly by touche; for when hit remayns aboue,
does from thence behold all with beames cast abrode: but
when kept in his own circle, & so bound in about the compasse
of his owne motion, he circles rowndnes with his owne partes
parceaveth; so Man himself is beheld in diuerse sortes, by
sense, imagination, reson, & understanding. For sense judgith
of the figure that is set in his materiall subject. Ymagination
lookes vpon her forme, without her matter. But Reason ouer-
passith this, & wayeth her show, which remaynes in all thinges
by an vniuersall consideration. But vnderstandinges eye
lookith hyer: for ascending to the largenes of the vniuersalitie,
lookes vpon her simple forme, with the pure myndes insight.
In which this is most to be considered: for the vppermost force
of vnderstanding, includith the inferiour, but the lower can
neuer ryse up to the hyar. For nether is sense ought worth
without his subiect, or ymagination behold vniuersall formes,
or Reson comprehend the simple forme; but vnderstanding
as looking from aboue, conceauing the right forme, judgith a
right of all thinges that be vnder, & in that sort comprehendes it as knowen to none other. For hit knowith the

Side notes: If there is no necessity a thing cannot be fore-known, and if we believe in no uncertain chances this results from the darkness of our opinion and not from the truth of our knowledge. All that is known is comprehended not according to its worth but according to the power of the knower. Sense judges of things in their material form, while the imagination looks upon the form without the matter.

---

[1] No question in the text. "*Dissonare etenim uidentur putasque, si praeuidcantur, consequi necessitatem.*"

vniuersality of Reason, the shape of ymagination, & senses matter, nor vsing reason, imagination, nor sense, but orderly by one twynkell of the mynde, all ouerlookith. Reson allso when hit beholdith all thinges, can not comprehend by ymagination, nor vsing sense, such thinges as be to be ymagened & to be felt. For this is hit that defynes the vniuersalitie of euery mans conceyte. A man is a resonable ij footed Creature: which tho it be an vniuersall knowledge, yet no man is ignorant but hit hath sense & imagination, which no man considerith by Imagination or sense, but by a reasonable conceyte. For tho Imagination tooke her begynning seing & forming figures, yet, tho sense were away, it respectith all sensible thinges, tho with a sensible and imaginary reason. Do you not see then, how in knowing all, they rather vse their own propertie than of thinges knowen? & that by reason: for when all Judgement remaynes in the acte of the Juger, it must needes follow that euery man performs his worke, not by others powre, but his own."

[Sidenotes: When reason beholds all things it cannot comprehend by imagination such things as are to be imagined and felt. When judgment remains in the act of the judger, it follows that every man performs his work by his own power and not by that of others.]

IV. MYTER.

[Sidenote: Explanation of the manner in which our perceptions arise.]

Ons in the porche¹ wer broght in men
Of obscure line,² and old thé wer,
Who Sens and Image out of lest notes³
In mens myndz ingrauen beliue,
As oft haps the running stile
In seayng⁴ paper leue,

[Sidenote: Boethius endorses the opinion of the Stoics that our minds are quite passive in the reception of perceptions.]

Some printid Lettars stik,
That marke haue none at all.
But if the mynd by her owne raigning
Expris by motions naught,
Saue only patient lies

---

¹ Hall of the Stoics.   ² Difficult to understand.
³ "Notes" must be a scribe's error. Trans. of *corporibus*.   ⁴ Sic. Trans. of *aequore*.

METRUM IV.

Quondam porticus attulit
Obscuros nimium senes
Qui sensus et imagines
E corporibus extimis
Credant mentibus imprimi,
Vt quondam celeri stilo

Mos est aequore paginae,
Quae nullas habeat notas,
Pressas figere litteras.
Sed mens si propriis uigens
Nihil motibus explicat,
Sed tantum patiens iacet

Subjiect to bodies markes	12 Our minds are active first in creation of logical ideas, secondly in the formation of opinions, and thirdly in other logical operations: syllogisms, deductions, and inductions.
And vain the fourmes	
Glaslike of all doth make.	
Whenche this that in our mynd raignes	
Knowelege of al discernes?	16
What power al beholdz,	
Who the knowen deuides?[1]	
And knowing[2] eache way	
Now lifts on hie the hed,	20
Than falz to Lowest thinges,	
Than gathering in hit selfe	
With truethe fals rebukes?	
This is the making Cause	24
Wiche muche more mightiar is	
Than suche as only material markes	
Receaues with her owne prints.	
But yet a passion doth begin and sturs	28
The myndz fors while body liues,	Some external cause must give the impetus to this activity of the mind.
Whan ether Light the yees doth hit,	
Or Sound in ear doth strike.	
Than sturred strengh of mynd	32
What figures within hit holds	
Joigned like he Cals,	
Applies them to the outward knowen,	
And fancies mixe to formes	36
That hiden rest within.	

[1] Transl. of "*Quae diuisa recolligit?*" is missing.
[2] "Taking" is a better transl. of *legere* than "knowing."

Notis subdita corporum
Cassasque in speculi uicem
Rerum reddit imagines,
Vnde haec sic animis uiget   16
Cernens omnia notio?
Quae uis singula perspicit
Aut quae cognita diuidit?
Quae diuisa recolligit   20
Alternumque legens iter
Nunc summis caput inserit,
Nunc decedit in infima,
Tum sese referens sibi   24
Veris falsa redarguit?
Haec est efficiens magis

Longe causa potentior
Quam quae materiae modo   28
Inpressas patitur notas.
Praecedit tamen excitans
Ac uires animi mouens
Viuo in corpore passio,   32
Cum uel lux oculos ferit
Vel uox auribus instrepit.
Tum mentis uigor excitus
Quas intus species tenet   36
Ad motus similes uocans
Notis applicat exteris
Introrsumque reconditis
Formis miscet imagines.   40

V. Prose.

Explanation of the distinction between the various degrees of intelligence,

"For yf, in feeling bodyes,[1] the motions that be made outwardly affecte the senses properties, & that the bodyes passion doth go afore the strenghth of the doers mynde, which provokes the myndes action, & styrrith in meane while the 4 quiet fansyes that inward remaynes: yf in sensible bodyes,[2] I saye, the mynde is not afflicted [3]with passion, but by violence shewith the same that the body makes, how much more those thinges which are most voyde of bodyes affections,[3] 8 in discerning, follow not outwardly they cast afore them, but doth performe the action of the mynde? By this reson, many knowledges haue giuen place[4] to diuers & differing substances. For only sense deprived of all other knowledge, 12

the highest of which is to be found in the Divine, and the lowest in that of the immovable molluscs.

wantes to lyving thinges that haue no motion, as the sea shells, & such other as by cleaving to rockes, be nourished. But Imagination seems only an affection in creatures that moue & haue desire to shon or seek. But mans reson is 16 only proper to himself, as vnderstanding to God: so as that knowledge exceedes all other, that by her own nature not only her own, but knoweth the rest of knowledges subiect[5] to her.

Here the great disputed question of the Scholastics is touched upon: Whether there be so-called universalia.

But what if sense be taken from reson, & Imagination lost:[6] 20 shall we saye ther is no thing vniuersall that generally Reson hath to looke vnto? For that that is sensible & imaginary, that can not be vniuersall, for eyther true is the Resons iudgement, & sense. to be nothing worth, or because it knowes 24 that many thinges be subiect[7] to sense & Imagination, therfore vayne shold the conceyte of Reson be, which,[8] because it is sensible & singuler, considers yet an vniuersalitie aboue it. Besydes, yf Reson, gaynesaying, aunswers, that she sees 28

---

[1] "*Quod si in corporibus sentiendis.*" The Queen appears to have mistaken *sentiendis* for *sentientibus*.

[2] The same error as in note 1; here Chaucer has also "sensible bodies."

[3]–[3] In this sentence the Queen appears to have taken the common, instead of the philosophical meaning of the words, and thereby the true meaning is lost.

[4] Incorrect transl. of *cessere*, "fallen to the lot of."

[5] The expression *subjecte* of the text must be taken in the philosophical sense.

[6] This sentence is quite otherwise in the original. "*Quid igitur, si ratiocinationi sensus imaginatioque refragentur, nihil esse illud uniuersale dicentes quod sese intueri ratio putet?*"

[7] The same misunderstanding as in note 5.

[8] From here to the end of the sentence the real meaning is lost.

what is sensible, what imaginary, in the reson of all that comprehendes, yet she can not aspire to the knoledge of that only, for that her science can not exceede the bodyes shape.
32 But we must beleeue of the knoledge of all thinges with[1] a steddyer & perfeter Judgement. In this controuersy therfor, we that haue both powre of resoning, imagining, & feeling, shall not we more allow the cause of reson? It is
36 euin lyke as mans Reson doth not think how it may looke vpon Godes vnderstanding of outward thinges without it self doo know it. For thus yo^u dispute: Yf such thinges as seeme not to haue certen & necessary sequels, the same can
40 neuer be foreknowen surely to hap, therfore ther is no prescience of such thinges; which if we beleeue to be, then should ther nothing hap of necessitie. Yf therfore, as we be partakers of reson, so we had the iudgement of Godes will,
44 as we iudge that imagination & sense ought to giue place to Reson, so shold we deeme it most just that humayne reson should submit hit self to Godes mynde. Let vs therfore lyft vp our selves into the Top of his vnderstanding: for there
48 reson shall beholde that in hit self it can not see, that is, how those thinges that haue not certen & sure endes, yet shall shewe them assured, & a determynd foreknoledge. And that is not opinion, but an included purenes of the hyest
52 knoledge that is shut in no lymites."

Boethius answers this question in the affirmative.

The measure of Divine prescience is explained by contrasting it with the imperfection of human knowledge.

An exhortation to trust in Divine wisdom whenever we find our own unavailing.

V. MYTER.

In how many shapes pas beastes on ground:
Of wiche of bodies Long the dust some turnes
Withe fors of brest contin[u]ed trace doth trail:
Some whos swiftnis wings the windz do part   4
And strait the bredhth of largist skie doth pas:

Man alone of all living creatures walks upright;

---

[1] This "with" destroys the sense of the original.

METRUM V.

Quam uariis terras animalia permeant figuris:
Namque alia extento sunt corpore, puluremque uerrunt,
Continuumque trahunt ui pectoris incitata sulcum:
Sunt quibus alarum leuitas uaga, uerberetque uentos,   4
Et liquido longi spatia aetheris enatet uolatu:

which fact should be a constant reminder to him to turn his mind to higher aspirations.

Some on ground ther steps to print reiois,
Or griny fildz to pas, or woodz to haunt.
Whos formes thogh thou see difur far,   8
Yet downe face thers ther dullid sencis.
Mankind alone his hed vpward bendz,
At eas doth stand with body Clad and erthe Lookes on.
This figure warns, but for the Clays deceat,   12
that thou with liftid Looke that heauen aspiring upcast thy he[d],
On hy thy mynd shuldst raise, Lest overwaid
Thy body made aloft thy mynd shuld Lowar sit.

VI. PROSE.

An attempt is made to explain the Divine substance.

"For that therfore, as a litle afore 1 showed, all that is knowen, not of her own, but of the nature of such thinges as are comprehended is knowen,[1] Let vs look now as much as becoms us, what is the state of the diuine substance, that we may the better know, what is the knoledge therof. It is the common judgement of all that lyve by Resons Rule, that God is euerlasting. Let vs consider what is eternitie. For this

God is eternal. What is eternity?

shall show us both Godes nature, & his knoledge. Eternitie is therfore an vnending, wholle & perfet possession of lyfe, which more cleerly appeers by the comparison of temporall thinges. For what so lives in tyme, that present from past, goos on to the following, And nothing is ther appoynted in tyme, that altogither can comprehend the whole compasse of his lyfe. For if he knows[2] not the morrow, & the yestarday hath lost, & in this present lyfe none otherwise ye lyve than in that changing & transytory moment; Then that that suffers change of tyme, altho it were as Aristotle

4

8

12

16

---

[1] "is knowen" was probably intended to be omitted.
[2] The text has *adprehendit*, "reached."

Haec pressisse solo uestigia gressibusque gaudent.
Vel uirides campos transmittere, uel subire siluas,
Quae uariis uideas licet omnia discrepare formis,
Prona tamen facies hebetes ualet ingrauare sensus.   8
Vnica gens hominum celsum leuat altius cacumen,
Atque leuis recto stat corpore despicitque terras.
Haec, nisi terrenus male desipis, ammonet figura,
Qui recto caelum uultu petis exserisque frontem,   12
In sublime feras animum quoque, ne grauata pessum
Inferior sidat mens, corpore celsius leuato.

thinkes of the wourld, that neuer hit began nor euer shall end, Boethius answers, something that has no present, no past, and no future.
& that the lyf therof shold stretch to the endlesnes of tyme,
20 yet could yt not be such, that rightly euerlasting may be
judged. For albeit he could at once comprehend wel the
whole compasse of our lyfe,[1] yet that that shall & hath not yet
chaunced, can he neuer attayne. Then it follows, that what-
24 soeuer comprehendes & possesses the wholle fulness of endles
lyfe, to whom nether any thing comming is absent, nor any
thing past is gon, [that] rightly eternall is showed; & must
needes be that present with himself, wholly his own may euer
28 stand, & hath in his presence the infinitenes of the wavering
tyme. Wherfoore they haue not rightly don, who, when they Error of those who interpret Plato to say that he holds the world to be as ancient as God.
hard that Plato thought this world neuer to haue had begyn-
ning, nor euer to receaue end, suppose that by this meane the
32 world should be made eternall, lyke him that is eternall. For
it is an other thing that Plato meanes to attribute to the
world, meaning of a lyfe that might guide him to be eternall.[2]
An other thing it is that our wholle lyfe present should com-
36 prehend the presence of the vnending lyfe, which is manifest
to be the property of Godes mynde. For he himself ought
not to be iudged auncienter for quantytie of tyme, than that
he made, but rather for the property of his owne pure nature.
40 For the infinite motion of temporall thinges doth but counter- Eternity may be designated as a never-ending present.
fet the present state of the vntourning. And when it can not
nether picture it nor equall it, abydes vnremoued by his constancy, & by the wekenes of that is present, doth weaken
44 it self into the infinite quantity of that shall be & was. And
when he can not possess the whole fulnes of his own lyfe, in
that parte that he neuer leavith to be, he seems to counterfet
that that he can nether fulfyll nor expresse, bynding himself
48 to any kinde of representation of this that is small, slyding,
& momentary : which, because hit bearith som ymage of the
euerlasting presence, to whom soeuer it haps, this good it does,
that he seems so to be. But because hit can not last, hath
52 taken an endles journey of tyme, and so he makes, that by

---

[1] "*Infinitae licet*" left out.
[2] "*Aliud est enim per interminabilem duci uitam, quod mundo Plato tribuit.*" The true meaning of this sentence is not well given. Chaucer has: "For oþer þing is it to ben yladd by lif interminable as plato graunted to þe worlde."

going he contynues lyfe, whose fulnes he can not comprehend in byding. So therfore yf we wold gyve right names to matter, following P[latos] Rule,¹ we should name God Eternall, & the world perpetuall. Because therfore all judgement com- 56 prehendith according to the nature of such thinges to which he is subiecte, to God therfore all is eternall, and a lyke is euer his state : his science ouerpassing all motion of tyme remaynith in the purenes of his owne presence comprehending the infinite 60 space of that is past and shall,² And all considerith in his own pure knoledge, as don now they were. Wherfore, if thou woldest way his foreknoledge by which he all vnderstandith, thou woltst judge that he hath not aforeknowledge of thinges 64 to com alone, but rightlyer a science of neuer worn contynuance.³ Wherfore we must not call it foresight, but prouidence, which being set ouer all thinges, yea in the meanest, vews them all as out of the very top & spring of all. Why 68 dost thou ask therfore, why necessaryly thinges must needes be, that by Godes light be ouerlookt? When not men themselves make all thinges they see thinges necessary, because they see them. For does thy looking on make any necessity 72 for such thinges to be, as thou dost beholde? No. And if we durst compare togither diuine & humayne presence, euin as yoᵘ see certain thinges at this instant, so he eternally all beholdes. Wherfore this diuine foreknoledge changith not 76 the naturall property of thinges, but lookes of such thinges as are present that they shall hap in tyme. Nether does he confound the judgementes of causes, but only with the vew of his mynde, knowith what needes must be, & what shall 80 not hap. As yoᵘ, whan yoᵘ see a man walke vpon the ground, & does behold the sonne aryse in skye, tho at once both ye vewe, yet yoᵘ see that the one is volontary, & the other yoᵘ judge necessary. So therfore Godes looke beholding ech 84 thing, doth not perturbe their propertyes, tho present to himself they be all, yet by tymes distance they are to com. So hit concludes, that this is not opinion, but rather a knoledge sticking to truthe ; when he knowes⁴ any thing that shall be, 88 then he is sure that of necessitie it must be. Heere, yf yoᵘ

Sidenotes:
From the eternity of God Boethius concludes that He foreknows and foresees all things.

Why the prescience of God would be better named Providence.

The question of Predestination is treated in a negative sense. Divine wisdom foreknows all things, but exercises no compulsion.

Divine knowledge has no influence upon events.

---

¹ Defaced, the text has "Plato" but not "rule." ² "and shall" underlined.
³ The text has *instantiae* (present). ⁴ A negation is missing here.

say that God seith that that shall happe, it can not be then
but it must hap, & that that can not chose but to chaunce,
that must fall out of necessitie, And so wold yo^u bynde me
to needes name, I must confesse that it is a mater of soundest
troth, but such one as no man can attayne to, but must haue
an Insight of diuinity. Therfore I will answere, that one
thing, if it be referd to Godes knoledge, is of necessyty ; yf it
be wayde in his owne nature, is free & absolute. Therfore
there are ij necessities, the one playne, as that it must needes
be that men be mortall, the other is conditionall, as, if thou
knoest a man doth walke, it must needes follow that he goes.
For it can be no otherwise, but that that a man knowith is
playne. But this 'yf' drawes not of consequence the other that
is playne & simple. For such a necessity our own proper
nature makes not, but the joyning of that 'yf'; for no necessitie compels a man to go, but willingly he walkes, tho
when he steps he must go. So, yf prouidence sees any thing
present, that must needes be, tho it haue no necessyty of
nature so to be. And God as present beholdith all such
thinges as following shall happ to proceede of free will. All
these thinges referd to the diuine sight be necessary for the
state of Godes knoledge, but considerd by themselues, they
differ nothing from the absolute liberty of nature her self.
All things therfore doutles be made, which God himself
foreknowes shall be, but som of these proceedes of free will;
which, tho by being they hap, yet they lose not their owne
nature, for afore they hapt, they might haue fortuned not to
hap. What yf they be not necessary, when they hap necessarily by the state of Godes science? This is the difference,
that euin as these thinges that I propounded afore, the son
rysing & the man going, which whyle they are a doing, can
not but be don ; yet the one, afore it hapt, was of necessity, the
other not so. So those thinges that, present, God beholdes,
are in lyke sorte, but of them som haps by causes necessity,
the other by the powre of the doar. Wherfore we haue not
saide amisse, that som be necessary in respecte of Godes
knoledge, other if they be by themselues considered, be
vnlosed from necessityes knot : for euin as all that is playne
to our senses, yf ye refer it to Reson, it is vniuersall, if to hit

The same event is necessary with regard to God's knowledge of it and uncertain with regard to its own nature.

Some events although foreknown to God occur from the exercise of our own free will.

Examples of occurrences which involve a necessity.

Argument against Divine prescience and answer to it.

self that is don, it is singuler. But thou woldst saye, yf in my powre it be set to change my purpose, I will make voyde prouidence, when perchance I shall change that she foreknew. I will answere thè, I graunte that thou mayst change thy purpose, but because the euer present troth of prouidence beholdith that eyther thou may doo, or whither mayst tho .. ¹ .. ust, ... whithersoever thou turnst thè, ... shalt thou neuer shun his diuine foreknoledge, as thou canst not fly the sight of his present eye, tho thou be turnd by thy free will to sondry actions. What? woldst thou say shall diuine scyence be changed by my disposition, that whan I will this or that, she shall seeme to chaunge the turns of her knoledge? O no; for Godes looke forerunnith all that shall be, and wryes to the presence of his own knoledge, & back callith, not alterith, as thou supposest, the varyeties of his knoledge, now this, now that, but in a moment steddy he preventes & compre-

A second argument against the Divine prescience.

hendes thy sondry changes : which presence that all comprehendes & sees, he hath not got of the hap of such thinges as shall chance, but is proceeded out of his purenes. Wheron is concluded that yᵘ hast told afore, how vnwourthy it were, that the cause of Godes science shold performe haps. For the force of his knoledge, by a present vnderstanding, comprehendith all, appoyntes to all a meane, & owes nothing to the comning. Which being true, ther remaynes a sure liberty of will to mortall folkes. For neyther lawes be wicked, that doo propounde rewarde & payne, yf our wills were freed from

From the whole of the preceding discussion the inference is drawn, that God sees our actions, hears our prayers, and rewards the righteous.

all necessity. There lastith also a vewar of vs all, the foreknowing God, whose euer present eternitie of sight agreith with the following property of our actions, And so dispensith to good reward, to yll their desartes. Neyther in vayne doo we put trust in God, nether of small price our prayers, which being truly made, can neuer fall in vayne. Avoyde vice, therfore, prise vertue, your myndes lift vp to true hopes, & settle your humble prayers in hyest place. For yoᵘ . . . .¹ necessitie, yf you will not your self beguyle, when yoᵘ doo plead afore the eyes of that iudge that all discernes."

Fift Booke.

¹ MS. decayed here.

II.

𝔓lutarch.

DE CURIOSITATE.[1]

CHAPTER I.

p*er*chanche hit might be best to Shun at aL that home;   *If an unhealthy*
  wher throughout the wind passage no*n*e ca*n* get,   *house cannot be*
Or dimmed darke, or subiect to the Cold and windz,   *done away w.th*
  Or elz to siknis thral that bredeth helth decay   4   *altogether, it ought at least to be rendered more sanitary.*
but if So one deLight by Costom in suche place
  the Lights may changed be, or staiers alter Case,
Or dores some for[2] the passage, some other shutted be,
  wiche fayrar muche may frame hit Cleare wit*h* bettar helth.
And Some haue served ther Cities turne by altering suche;[3]
  A Sample may my Country[4] make as said hit is   *Example of*
that bending to Zephyrus wynde, & fro*m* Parnasus taking[5]   *cities which have been altered on*
  sone   *account of their unhealthiness.*
  that to y*e* west his course did turn by Cherons help,   12
hit wryed was to east, the sons arising place.
Empedocles Eke the knower weL of natures cours
Is Said to stop the gaping deap[6] of hil and the Rok,
  wiche grevous was and siknys ful the place.   16
for that the Northen[7] wind did beat on neagbours filds,
  and thus the plage Out chast fro*m* regions grou*n*d.

---

[1] This translation of Plutarch is all in the Queen's handwriting.
[2] "for" written over "ware" (?) struck out. "for the passage" ἀνοίξαντα (opened).
[3] πόλεις τινὲς οὕτω μεταθέντες ὠφέλησαν, some cities have been thus improved.
[4] The Greek word is πατρίδα (fatherland).
[5] "taking" written over "receauing" struck out.
[6] "deap of hil and the Rok" written over "whirlpole mountain," struck out. ὄρους τινὰ διασφάγα βαρὺν.   [7] The text has νότος (south wind).

Therfor if plagy wilz¹ ther be that noyfuL ar vnsound
  Arising tempest great and dimly darks the mynd,   20
best shal hit be giue them repuls and down throw flat to ground,
  So to our selues we bride an air clear a Ligh and brethe ful
    pur.
And if this may not be, yet Let our Labor at lest be this,
  that by al menes that possible make we may   24
Tourning from us and changing aL [that] brideth vs offence,
  we make them serue Our tourne and helpe us the beste.
A sample Let us make of Curius nideles Care,
  Whose study is naugh els but other homes to knowe² 28
diseas, that nether void of enuy nor pure from wickedn[is].
Why than, O man, with enuye fuL an others yls,
  Sharpist sight dost set, and in thyn owin stil³
Inward drawe thy science study, and so hit apply,   32
  that thy busy Care⁴ be tourned from outward to thyn
    own?
And if thou fancy haue to enter storyes⁵ yvels,
  thou hast ynough at home that ydel thou ne be,

    As great a streame as waters floud doth bring to bay,⁶ 36
  Or Circled Oke by fawLing Leves from tre,
So great a store of faültes in thy Life shalt find;
  A hepe eake of yl desiars fraught in thy mynd,
No Les neglect of that thou shuld by office yeld.   40
  for as the writ of Senoφon telz⁷ the ordar how good frugal
    men
do part aside suche Laid vp stuf as Sacrifice nides,
  and do deuide from banquetz cost; in sort that some
do Serue the plowshares turne, in other place the war; 44
  Euen so do thou deuide thy ivels part that enuy bridz,
A part let Ielosy'haue, some for Cowardz frute do leue,
  for sparing some, reserue all thè do Count and know;⁸

Definition of Curiosity, which word is not a correct translation of the Greek, rather tell-tale, busybody.

Let people turn their attention to themselves, where they may find abundant material for study.

---

¹ Unhealthy passions, πάθη νοσώση.   ² Transl. of κακων omitted.
³ τὸ δ'ἴδιον παραβλέπεις (dost not observe thine own).
⁴ The Queen here translates πολυπραγμοσυνην (curiosity) with "busy care."
⁵ The text has ἱστοριαν, which, as in Herodotus, means "searching out."
⁶ "bay" or "say" (sea)? the Greek word is a doubtful one, ἁλιζόνος.
⁷ "telz" written over "writes" struck out.
⁸ ταῦτ' ἔπελθε, ταῦτ' ἀναθεώρεσον· (turn thy attention to that and observe it).

Suche windowes as to neghbours hous giues the vewe, 48   *Curiosity should be debarred from entering our neighbours' houses, and be confined to our own.*
  And Curius foote steps make a way to patent,[1]
But other wayes Open thou must, truly fit and sound,
  Suche as to Seruantz romes in thy hous thé bring,
Somtime into thy womens Closetz, and wher thy slaues abide;
  thes be suche thing as axing study and busy care do nide,
Wher never profitLes businis nor wicked work hath rome,
  but ful of weLth and holesum Councel giues thè,
Whan eache man telz himself this tale and this accompt; 56
  Whens Slide I? what don haue I? what ther vndon shuld not?[2]

CHAPTER II.

but now[3] as fables teL that Lamia at home doth blindedly,   *Comparison of curiosity with Lamia of the fable, who is blind at home and only sees when abroad.*
  her yees she putz in vesselz Store til furthe she go,
that in her hed thé go, and Open bendz her Lookes;
  So eache man abrode in others matters with hate, 4
Into his thoght a Curius regard into his hed as yee he putz;
  from faultz Our owne and wicked actz by ignorance Led we slip,
On thes nor Rolling yees nor Light of them receue.
The Curius more profit yeldz his foes than good vnto himself;   *Curiosity only injures itself and is advantageous to its victims.*
  that telleth them ther Lacks, and wher thé do, and
that bettar thé may ware the warnid to correct;
  neglectz at home the dedes that nide wer to regard,
So stoned[4] is his Care for that most other touche. 12
Vlisses eke no word wold giue to mother his,   *Ulysses is instanced as an example of how curiosity is to be overcome.*
  Til of the proφet axed he had the cause, why to hel he went;
And after he to dame returned and wemen rather axed,[5]
  What wenche Tiro was, wher faire Cloris bid, 16
And what bred Cause for murthering Epicastes life.
  Whan woful knot of Corde she knitz to hiest beame.[6]

---

[1] "patent" is written over "nideles" struck out; neither word makes sense; the Greek is ἐμφραξον (close).   [2] The last four words are doubtful.
[3] After "now," "adays" is struck out.
[4] Perhaps "astonied"; the Greek word is πτόησιν (absorbed).
[5] πρός τε ταύτην ἔτρεψεν αὐτόν, καὶ τὰς ἄλλας γυναῖκας ἀνέκρινε (he turned to her and asked about the other women).   [6] Odyss. xi. 278.

but we ouer secure[1] and knowing naugh that most vs touche,
Inquires of others liues, as why Our neghbors Sire 20

Several examples of curious questions often heard.
A Sirian was, and grand dame[2] why a Thresia*n* borne;
And suche ma*n* Owes talentz thre, nor Vsery hath paid.
Yea, and somtime suche things discours, whens suche a wife leaue home,[3]
Why he and he haue in a Corner talkt togither. 24

Socrates and Aristippus are given as instances of praiseworthy curiosity.
but Socrates romed vp and downe with doute ful great,
what wordz what Spiche Pitagoras vsid to brid belife;
And Aristippus in Olimpias meting Ischomachus axed;
Why Socrates in his disputes, so wyn could yonge men; 28
Who whan he picked had some sedes and sa*m*ples of his wordz,
So moued was, that skant he stedy cold his pas,
And grew throughout bothe pale and Lene; untiL
thirsty and inflamed to Athenes he hoissed vp his sailes, 32
And bothe the man his wordz and φιλοφιε[4] he lerned,
Wiche did Contain in so*m*me to all Co*n*clude in short,
That al men shuld an audit make of al ther iuels,
and So the*m* bettar knowe to make the*m* shun the more. 36

CHAPTER III.

Some people do not desire to examine themselves because they are full of evil.
An other sort ther is that broke can not a Louk
On Life ther owne, but demes hit as a yrcksome shewe,
Nor reasons Lustar beare thé can, reflectio*n*s hers thé Shun;
but ther mynd filld all with eache mans iueL al shaking dreads. 4
What dwels wi*th*in abrod hit goes and Gasith round about,
And others sins do vew, bothe nurs and crame ther vice.
For as the he*n* oft in the house wha*n* food[5] is broght,
Runs to a Cornar strait, and ground doth skrape wi*th* claw,
That some wher in the dounge on grain at lest may find.

---

[1] "over secure," ἐμελήσαντες.
[2] granddam. The Greek wordis τήθη (nurse).
[3] The Greek is ἐπανηρχετο (comes home).
[4] *Sic.*   [5] "food" written over "met" struck out.

So fareth hit with Curius¹ mans vice who passing ouer,
   institutes Lessons, and skaunted matter in Retorik give,²
And other caus³ suche as no man grives is axed,   12
   In hepes thé throw⁴ the housis secret iuelz and hid.
Righ weL applied is that the Egiptian⁵ said to him that axed,   *Witty answer of an Egyptian.*
   What hid was that he had? that made hit hid, quoth he.
Nor is hit the fasion to enter others house with out he afor knoke;   16
   though now the portars add to for harmerLing,⁶ and rings did hange
Vntouchet with out, served for the eare from him that enter wold,⁷   *The inquisitive man chooses the worst households for his prying and avoids the better ones.*
   Lest stranger migh the huswife in⁸ her house surprise,
beting of her maid,⁹ or chastening her man,   20
   Or shirLes might heare that maiden gaue for Skourge;
The prying man to alL this wyL sliLy make his one,
   Suche one as hedes not to behold a Chast and wel ruuld hous,
No thogh a man in treating sort wold cal him to that sight;
   but suche as kay requires, a Clog or sparred dore,
Vncouver List, and to the vulgar sort abrode hit migt,
   Of all the wyndz thé greue us most and troble bride.
Ariston telz, whos turne back strawes vs anoy;¹⁰   28
   but Curius man no neghbors cloak, nor clothes estimes,
but wales he brekes, and opens dores, even to Sily maidz,
In sort euen suche as wind that perceth in and enters rome,   *In this way he makes himself hated.*
   wher bacchus feasts, roundz and daunce, he may behold; 32
Euen suche as in the night to dianes temple dedicate were,
   with hedy yea espies what faultz he may find ther.

---

¹ Some illegible letters before "mans."
² So fareth hit, etc. παραπλησίως οἱ πολυπράγμονες, ὑπερβάντες τοὺς ἐν μέσῳ λόγους καὶ ἱστορίας (so it is with the curious; they pass over the discourses and histories which lie before them).   ³ "Caus" written over "matter" struck out.
⁴ The Greek word is ἐκλέγουσι (gather).
⁵ "Egiptian" written over "Ethiopian" struck out.
⁶ *Sic*, "hammered" erased.
⁷ ἀλλὰ νῦν μὲν εἰσὶ θυρωροί, πάλαι δὲ ῥόπτρα κρουόμενα πρὸς ταῖς θύραις αἴσθησιν παρεῖχεν (now there are porters, and formerly there were knockers on every door which announced the approach of a stranger).   ⁸ "in" written over "amid" struck out.
⁹ ἵνα μὴ τὴν οἰκοδέσποιναν ἐν μέσῳ καταλάβῃ ὁ ἀλλότριος ἢ τὴν παρθένον, ἢ κολαζόμενον οἰκέτην, ἢ κεκραγυίας τὰς θεραπαινίδας (surprise the mistress or her daughter, or a slave being punished, or the maids shrieking).
¹⁰ The Greek has ὅσοι τὰς περιβολὰς ἀναστέλλουσιν ἡμῶν: "which blows open our cloaks."

CHAPTER IV.

<small>Curiosity desires to know everything, and especially about the great, but this is very dangerous.</small>

besides as Cleon sais whom Comedie old reproved :
"His mynd in Clopis was, his handz in Etole hid." [1]
So mynd of Curius ma*n* at onis in riche mans hous doth make abode,
and in self time the Cotage poor doth haunt, and Court of king.
And at a wedding Latly made to prie the businis of eache man,
bothe of the gestz that biddid be and of the Chifest alL ;
And so as not of periL void he ventur makes therof ;
but Like to him that henban tast with Curius fault,   8
that gridy is to knowe afor he fele is reued of his Like ; [2]
so who so serche the mightiars ylz first dy or vnderstand,
for who disdains to Looke on Sun beames Large and windo,[3]
and nides wiL star on bodies Sun hit selfe to bold that striue
The Light from him to turne, ar bliuded starke for here.

<small>Wise answer of Philippides to Lisimachus.</small>

Righly sayd Φilippides the poete, to Lisimachus who axed,
"What of myne shal I imparte as of my gift to thè ?"
"What so thou wylt," q*uoth* he, "so secret none thou giue me."
For what so kingdome [4] hathe of pleasur and of Ioy   17
Outward set furthe be, banquetz, riches, solemne, liberaL shewes ;
but if hid aught ther be, nor hit assist ne Ons hit touche !
Nor Coverd be a kingly Ioy whan prosperous hap arrives,

<small>Anything which lies concealed is often bad, beware therefore of bringing it to light.</small>

Nor scorne make at his sportz nor whom with bringeth kindly gifts.[5]
What hidden is fearful, woful, Sower, and vnknowen,[6]
the tresor of an Ouerflowing, wasting Ire,
Or rather habit deape in mynd to rolle revenge,   24
Or Zelozie of wife, or Sons suspect, or dout of frind,
Fly thou this darke and thikky mysty folded Cloude ;
A flasche and thou*n*dar shal burst out whan hidden shewes.

---

[1] Quotation from "The Knights" of Aristophanes.
[2] φθάσει τῆς αἰσθήσεως προανελὼν τὸ αἰσθανόμενον: "He will lose his consciousness before he has made his examination."
[3] οἱ τοῦ ἡλίου τὴν ἀφθονόν γε ταύτην καὶ κατακεχυμένην ἅπασιν ἀκτῖνα παρορῶντες (Those, who instead of looking at the sunbeams which are spread out over all).
[4] "kingdom." The text has βασιλέων (kings).
[5] οὐδὲ γέλως παίζοντος οὐδὲ φιλανθρωπίας παρασκευὴ καὶ χάριτος (nor the laughter of a joker, or his endeavours to amuse others).
[6] "woful, Sower, and vnknowen." The Greek is ἀγέλαστον, δυσπρόσιτον (not laughable, dangerous to approach).

CHAPTER V.

What way therfor for fligt or shuning of the same ?   *We should turn our curiosity*
If strait thou do as said is [of] yore to spare thy busy care,   *from bad things to good and*
but best if mynd thou turne [to] helpz and delites ;[1]   *pleasant ones.*
O busy man cherche what the heauen, erthe, air and sea
    afourdz ;   4
wither doth delite thè most the smal or great to knowe ;[2]
If great, than Care wheus son arise, and wher she doth couche,
    Aske why the mone at times, as man, so changeth she,
Whence so great Light she tooke, and whens she Lost repairs,
        " Whan Left she hathe us semed how may hit be   *For instance, to astronomy, and*
        that strait her new face faire to vs aperes   *observe the wonders of the*
        Slily to the Circles fuL increasing makes   *heavens.*
        Again whan beauty hers hathe shone unto the top
        Than waning eldar growes tiL none be she[wn]."
for thes thingz be natures secret inward workes,
    nor dothe disdaine suche Science to the Lerned folke.
but great thinges thou despice and dost not reke serche ?   16
    be Curius than for things of Les regarde ;
Aske thou than of that wiche erthe brings furthe,
    why some do florisshe stil and grine remaine,
In euery season grine thé be as she that bosts herself,   20
    some other sort in some what Like to thes thé shew,
Some other kind be bared Left and Lea,[3] Like husbandman
    that thrift neglects at ons that al his goodz hathe spent ;   *Or botany and the growth of*
    for nether iust, honist, nor plesing wer suche shewe.[4]   *plants.*
Than why do diuers grondz[5] brede frute of sondry sortz,
    bothe Long, Cornard, halfe round and rounded alL ;
perchance of this thou carest not muche, for yL, non is.
    If nides thou sekest in ivels a Curius Care,   28
Iven Serpent Like that fed and nourist is in poisund wood,   *Or the history of the world, where*
    Let us suche curivs man bringe to stories read,[6]   *evils enough are related, the*
And gather ther suche stuf as doth include and teL   *consideration of*
    A plenty great of al mishaps, aboundance of all iveL,   32   *which will do no one any harm.*

---

[1] Doubtful.   [2] "knowe" written over "vewe" struck out.
[3] "Lea" probably lay.
[4] This line is written on the back of the leaf, by itself. It is not in the Greek text.
[5] "grondz." The text has καρπους, "plants," not "grounds."
[6] "Stories read" written over "the stories study" struck out.

for ther do ly the ruine of men, the wast of Goodz,
   the wifes dishonor, the sarvautz baitz,[1] the frindz slander,
The venom prepared, enuies, ZeLosies, wrak of frindz,[2]
   The treasons huge of kings from kingdoms thrown ;   36
Fil thou with thes thy Curius nice[3] desiars,
   pleasure taken this that bride Can no wo,
nor dolor, to such folke as thou dost dwell with alle.

CHAPTER VI.

Curiosity is eager for news, but not good or pleasant news.

but as hit semes the Curius man Cared not for old pane,
Nott Suche as wonted wer but sly and unfond harme he vews,
   that willingly may tragidies new made[4] behold,
He rekes not for to felowe Comiche Caus nor mery matter. 4
   Than if he mit with one that talk of mariage makes,
Or sacrifice telz, or brides retourne,[5] hideles and Lasy
   the Curius man hit heares, and tels how oft that he hard,
And wilz the tellar be brief in short or pas hit ouer ;   8

Favourite subjects for curiosity.

but if a Sittar by do teL a tale of a dishonestid maid,
Or wife that wedLok brake, or Cartel sent, or brothers debat,
   heare he sLipith not nor siuseth[6] makes for Laisur,
but sekes for more mens tongz, and Listen makes his eares.
   How rightLy said is this : " that easilar il than good to
      mortal men arrives," [7]

Comparison of curiosity with a cupping instrument, and with certain back doors in towns.

And rightly said is this of Curius natured man.
   for as the boxing Glas the worst from flesche do draw,
So eares of noysy folkes the wor[8] . . . he draweth out,   16
And bettar for to say, as Cities haue some[9] gates
   VnLucky and void of noys of multitude the great,
by wiche condemned men to dy ar oft Conveied,
   and throw wiche thé throw that filthy is and fowL,   20
And naugh by them ther goes that pure or hoLy is ;
   So by the eares of Curius man naugh Good or faire doth pas,

---

[1] " baitz " ? The Greek word is ἐπιθέσεις (persecutions).
[2] " frindz." The text has οἴκων (family).
[3] " Nice " written after " fondLy " struck out.
[4] " made " written over " fond out " struck out.
[5] " brides retourne " : the Greek word is προπομπήν (funeral).   [6] *Sic*; senses ?
[7] " οἴμοι τὸ κακὸν τῆς εὐτυχίας ὡς μᾶλλον ἐς οὓς φέρεται θνητῶν." Alas! that sorrow should much more easily penetrate into the human ear than joy.
[8] MS. torn.   [9] " suche " written after " some," and struck out.

but Slaughtar talk in to ther eares has passage sure,
    and ther abides wiche wicked Cursed tales them brings. 24
  " Euer chanting teares within my hous do dweL"
This is the muse for Curius man and Siren his alone, *A more exact definition of curiosity.*
  Nor aught than this may Joy them best or please.
for Curius folke have gridy wyl to heare[1] that secret is and hid.
  No suche Opens Yea to aught if good thé haue at aL;[2]
And some whiL thé do faine suche good as ther is none.
  And so the nisy man that gridy is to know the ivel,
Is subiect to disiase that Joyes at others harmes,   32
  the bretherne true of spite and enuious folkes.   *Definition of envy.*
For envy Sorow is for good that others Joys;
  A gladsomnis of iveL the Joy conciued of others wicked actz;[3]
And bothe procides of malice humour, beastLike and mad. 36

CHAPTER VII.

but yrksome So vnto eache man the Opening is of his iveLs, *Curiosity causes hatred, because no one likes to see his own failings brought to light;*
That may chuse to dy befor his Secret disease the doctor prove[4]
What if Heroφilus, Erasistratus, or Esculapius, choys men therfor,
Carying the Cures instrumentz, if standing without dores,   4
  Wher axed wiche[5] fistula in the thigh[6] suche man hathe had,
Or wither a wife a Cancer hathe in secret hiden place?
  ALbeit the heltheful Care be nidfuL of suche art;
Yet no ma[n]ar,[7] I belive, but Cast of wold suche on as hit
    wolde axe,   8
Whom no unLouked for nid uncald wold sike Out others
    harme.
The busy man sikes out aL thes and many wors,   *and an inquisitive person*
  that with no mynd to Cure, but Clattar out the same;
Wherfor no inknowne[8] thé shal giue that names the cuyrous
    folk.   12

---

[1] "heare" written over "serche for" struck out.
[2] οὐδεὶς δἀγαθὸν ἀποκρύπτει κεκτημένος, ὅπου καὶ τὰ μὴ ὄντα προσποιοῦνται (no one conceals anything good which he possesses, but oftener claims the possession of good which he has not).   [3] wicked acts, κακοῖς (misfortunes).   [4] "prove" doubtful.
[5] "wiche" written over "wither" struck out.
[6] The Greek word is δακτύλιον (finger).
[7] Sic. ἀλλὰ πᾶς ἄν τις, οἶμαι, τὸν τοιοῦτον ἀπήλασεν.
[8] "inknowne" looks more like "nikurne"; but qu.

for serchers we disdain and hardly brooke we can,[1]
Not wha*n* thé find that openly is broght to vew of all,
but suche as hiden be in vesselz and in packz;

neglects his own interests while he is spying into other people's business. And yet the Law hit bidz, and for negLect shuld smart. 16
in other sort the nice [2] men Lose ther owne for others serche,
Nor dweL thé chuse in Country soiLe, for quiet fildz no care;
but yet if after Longed time thé to the Contry Goe,

The curious townsman, when in the country, only asks about the folk's losses, and then goes back to town. The rather vewe ther neigbors fild,[3] and pas ther owne; 20
and axis, how many Oxen he hathe Loste in nu*m*bar alL,
And how much Sowcred wine he Cast away wi*th* Los;
And furnist this, he quikLy to the Citie retournes.

but he that is a plowma*n* right,[4] receue ful sLowly wyL suche newes 24
as of fre wyl is fro*m* the Citie spred abrod;
"And sais, tha*n* wyl fal out my diggar shaL tel me tales,
On what barganes strifes haue ther ende in plea;
for even now [5] Curivs of suche matter this wicked wreche doth walke."[6] 28

CHAPTER VIII.

Inquisitive persons dislike a country life, and prefer that of a town, where they can gratify their love of news. but busy man the Cloiny [7] life doth hate as empty cold,
That nurs [8] no tragicke part woful, nor wicked Cause,
but go thé wyl to Jugis seates, to markets and to portz;
Vsing this vois, "have you no newes today, wer ye in fair? 4
"What than? do you beliue the Cities reuolt in thre hours time?"
And if suche tale he hathe, from his horse he Lights,

---

[1] ὅθεν μισοῦνται δικαίως καὶ γὰρ τοὺς τελώνας βαρυνόμεθα καὶ δυσχεραίνομενον: "They are therefore justly hated. For we also complain of, and are angry with the tax-gatherers." [2] "nice" translation of πολυπράγμονες.
[3] "fild" translation of ἀμπέλοις (vineyard).
[4] "plowman" written over "husbandman" struck out.
[5] "iven now" written over "at this hour" struck out.
[6] Quotation from Aristophanes:
"εἶτά μοι σκάπτων ἐρεῖ,
ἐφ' οἷς γεγόνασιν αἱ διαλύσεις 'ταῦτα γὰρ,
πολυπραγμονῶν νῦν ὁ κατάρατος περιπατεῖ."
"He shall relate to me while digging, on what conditions peace was concluded for even now," etc.
[7] *Sic.* perhaps "clowny"? See also p. 139. [8] "nurs" perhaps "has."

taking ha*n*dz, imbrasis the man, and listing sits him by.
If met he do a man that tel can naugh, "What sais thou? 8
Wert thou in pleading place?[1] didst thou not pas the hal?[2]
Nor hast not faLn in passangers suche as Last from Italye
  come?"
praised be therfor the Locre*n*s law who did forbid   *The Locrian law fined all home-*
A questio*n* ons at his ret[urn], (MS. *torn*) . . . any newes 12 *comers who askt for news.*
and promist was . . . (MS. *torn*).
for as to Coukes ful welcome is the nu*m*bar great of shipe,
to fisshar eke spaum[3] fuL thik of fische find,
So Curius men wische plenty of iveL, and businis make, 16 *Curious folk want trouble and*
new and strange eue*n*t, wiche euer thé hu*n*t and kil.   *changes to tattle about.*
Yea hideLy[4] do the Thurian Lawes, that charge no Citizen
  think,
in Comedie be vsed; but to the murdring[5] or Curius me*n*.
for adultry desiar of other pleasur, inquiry and serch also 20 *Adultery is the fruit of curiosity.*
Of matter suche as hid is hardly to be knowe*n*;
for Curiositie a palssy is, co*n*sumptio*n*[6] eke that shews what
  shuld Couet
Wiche makes the chatting vice to foLow Care of knowing
  muche.

CHAPTER IX.

And so can not be shuned but sLandar felowes the busy Care, *Loquacity and*
Wiche made Pithagoras teche fiue yeres Sile*n*ce to young *scandal go hand in hand with curiosity,*
  men,
Wiche Cal he did Ἐχεμυθια; the suafes[7] thing that Silence
  doth expres,
Yea hit Can not be but wicked tong doth Curiositie fere. 4
for what thé gladly heare, thé willinly readely teL,
And what wit*h* hide[8] from some, thé yet to others tel delite, *consequently people are very*
Wherfor this disease besides more Iuels, brings this to bote, *reticent in the presence of the*
that Let it dothe to haue that most thé seke to get; 8 *inquisitive.*

---

[1] "pleading place" translation of ἀγοράν (market-place).
[2] Translation of στρατήγιον (general's house).   [3] "spaum"? perhaps spawn.
[4] "hideLy," heedfully.
[5] The first three letters are doubtful. Greek word is μοιχους (adulterers.)
[6] "palssy is consumption," παράλυσίς ἐστι καὶ φθορά: is an "illicit opening, a laying bare."   [7] Doubtful; qu. suavest.   [8] hide (heed) σπουσῆ.

for al men hides them wel and hides them from suche feloship,
Nor wyl do aught, or say in Curius sight or Eare,
but Councel defers, and businis Care for other time appointz,
Vntil suche man away him get from Companie thers ; 12
And if perchance a busy man Come in, wher Secret tale

Comparison of the curious with a cat.

Or earnist aught be don, no nother wise than as the Cat
In running hides his meat so sknatz¹ from hand that ready was.²
So that oft that other here or Se may to suche, 16
Nor vewe nor eare may Serue ther turnes.

A curious man is never trusted.

In fine, a Curius man Lacks al confidence or trust,
for rather to sLaues and strangers charge³ our Lettars we commit, 19
Or trust (MS. *torn*) . . . ler than to Curius knowen⁴ frindes.
but bellerefon not Lettars born⁵ against himself did open,
but hand restrained from kingly writ with tempar suche,
As he woLd do with Continenci from his wife.

The curious and adulterous are foolish too: they pass by the easy for the hard and ugly.

to be a Curivs man, Lackz tempar nowhit⁶ Less 24
Than if adulteres part he plaid as faut no Les.
To this distempar⁷ this is worst that foli madnis hathe,
for in negLect of most and Commen womens haunt,
To the shut and Glorius One, perhaps to the deformd,⁸ 28
be Caried to : what madnis more, or brain siknis may be.

They give up gay sights to whisper to slaves and maids.

So fareth hit with Curius folk, who, passing by the fairest shews,
Lectors studies⁹ and disputes, others Lettars breakith vp,
with eares CLose to neghbors wales, and whisperars adz, 32
wher seruantz and women bide, yet not void of ding,¹⁰
but Sure euer of Slandars mark and infamy.

---

¹ *Sic.* snatched ?
² καθάπερ ὄψον γαλῆς παραδραμούσης αἴρουσιν ἐκ μέσου καὶ ἀποκρύπτουσιν, "we put away everything likely to excite his curiosity, as we hide meat when a cat comes by."
³ "charge" written over "trust" struck out.
⁴ "knowen" written over "familiar" struck out.
⁵ "born" written over "Caried" struck out. ⁶ "no" struck out.
⁷ "distempar" written over "incontinence" struck out.
⁸ "by chance" written over, and struck out.
⁹ "Lectors studies", "ἀκούσματα καὶ σχολάς." Feasts for the ears, and studies.
¹⁰ "ding," ἀκινδύνως (danger).

CHAPTER X.

Yea, nideful for suche Curius Ons to shake of ther disease, *A good antidote against this passion is to consider how little advantage or pleasure it has ever brought us.*
Remembar what ther gaines haue bene, or what ther Los.
for if, as Simonides said, whan sometime he Opened had his deskes,[1]
One fild with rewardz ful he found, but empty that of thankes,
So if man sometime shaL serche and open the Curius mans bages,
ful of unnideful, vaine, and stufd with aL vnplesing thingz;
Perchanche the first sight wyL him offend whan by al menes he shal make plain how undeliteful, vaine and skornful al thé be.   8
Now go on, If any entring in to ancient boukes, and takes out *If you took out of Homer all headless lines, and all Archilochus's railings against women, you ought to be curst.*
the worst from them, and bouke he haue so invented,
As out of Homeres vers that hedles named be,
Or out of tragical Solosismz, or out of suche vers   12
as ArchiLochus againe women Lewdely and ful sawsy made,
In maner suche him selfe betraing and deciuing;
Worthy do you not think him of tragical curs and ban?
"Ivel may thé betid, the Sercher out of humain woes!"[2] 16
Yea, hit shal not nide tragicaL curs, for of hit self unsemely and fruteles sleing the storming of others sin;[3] *Your book would be like Philip's Rogue-Town.*
such Citi as that was wiche Φilip of wikedz wretched men first bilt, named therfor Πονηροπολις[4] as fild ful of yL. 20
Curius men therfor, while round about thé gather and hepe,
Not fault of Vers or Poesy, but Crimes of other Life ther faultz and incongruety and about them each,
a most unplesing vngraceful tables of other iuels,   24
wiche ther owne memory fittest instrument maks. *In Rome, some folk despise art and care only for monsters,*
for [5] as at Rome some picturs, and yea in dide, formes bold of boyes, of women thé dispise, about thé go,
and bide in market place wher monstars sold be,   28

---

[1] "deskes," κιβωτούς (chests).   [2] Qaotation from a lost tragedy.
[3] sleing the storming, etc. ὁ θησαυρὸς αὐτοῦ γέμων αλλοτρίων ἁμαρτημάτων· (such a collection of other peoples' faults).   [4] English and Greek letters mixed in MS.
[5] Correct translation: "As in Rome many people do not regard the pictures, the statues, or even the beauty of the boys and girls exposed for sale, but wander round the monstrosities exhibited in the market-place."

	Vewing and axing for foteles me*n* that armes haue lik Cat;[1]
but they soon get disgusted with them.	Or thre yead me*n*,[2] or Suche whos nek is like to[3] Camel torne,[4]

Or if ther any be of kind that " mixture hathe of Like
Or yueL shapd untimely birth;"[5] but if dayly thé be broght
To suche a sight, short wiL ther Liking be, and some wyl hit

Let spiers into other folks' sins remember how little good they've got from it. abhor;
So suche as Curius be of others Liues and Liuing birth,
About the rabeL and Sins that haue befalne in others hous,[6]
Suche as afor thé pried on Comes to ther mynd,   36
Remembar thé do how of the hede of others yuels
thé gather haue no Credit nor profit any.

CHAPTER XI.

The best way to cure ourselves of curiosity is purposely to abstain from observing what passes around us as we walk through the streets.

Hit muche may therfor avaiL suche maladie to driue,
If first from dede may hap alof with vse our self inure,
And so may Lerne in this motio*n* to tempar giue our self,
for disease increase hathe growe*n* by Customs use;[7]   4
wiche els wold turne to wors, if hit had further gone;
but how hit may be do*n* of Custome Let vs speke.

What hardship is it, not to read epitaphs on graves or inscriptions on walls?

beginningz first be made of easy things sone[8] do*n*,
And suche as Comen haps and vulgar peple vse.   8
for what mad[9] matter passing by monumentz old
to neglect[10] to read verse or writ that graffin be,
or what hard thing wer hit to pas by suche skrapings,
As walz in writings receue and not to read?   12
In Silence warning vs that nothing ther is writte*n*
That profit or delite may bride vs or to giue vs;
but doth remember a writing good: "be best frind of ours,"

They're poor stuff.

And other Like to this ful vain and fild with toys;   16
wiche in the*m* selves semes not to hurt in reading,
but SliLy thé annoy for briding Care to knowe vnnideles thing,
And as the huntars rates ther houndz that usith change,
And with ther Lyans[11] them pluk back and with drawe, 20

---

[1] τοὺς ἀκνήμους καὶ τοὺς γαλεάγκωνας (without calves to their legs and with crooked arms). [2] Three-eyed men. [3] "is like to" written over "resembles" struck out. [4] "Camel torne" translation of στρουθοκεφάλους (sparrows' heads). [5] Verse from Homer. [6] These two lines are not well translated. [7] After "use" is struck out "wiche sLowLy makes us profit and good." [8] "sone" written over "quickly" struck out. [9] "mad," χαλεπόν (hard). [10] "disdain" written over "neglect", neither word struck out. [11] *Sic.* lines.

and kipes ther Sente bothe pure and hole in right chase,
That egerLar¹ thé firme ther pace and folowe firme,
"and winding with ther sent the steps² of the^r game;"³
So aught hit fare with Curius man that runs to euery gase 24
In striuing for to see or Lift his eare al to hire,
bak kipe him and withdrawe, him selfe reserue for profyt more.
for as the Lions walke with couuer Clawes, and Eglis eke ther talon,
Lest sharpnis thers, and fiersnes, to muche thé duL; 28
So mynding how al Curius Care haue sharpist sight,
And narowly Lookes on knoweLege of sondry sortz,
Let us not hit Consume, nor blunt in worsar thing.

Prowling eagles and lions sheathe their claws to keep them sharp, so let us keep curiosity for learning, and not blunt it on evil.

CHAPTER XII.

In Secund place, Let us invre if by an others hous we go
  not to Louk in, nor rolle our yees to that wiche is within,
In vsing Curius serche in stede of other handz,
  but ready haue Zenocrates saw, that did deny, 4
"That differens any wer whither fite or hand⁴ the hous did enter;"
for Guest it is a shame an inner ivel to vewe.⁵
For thes be suche in hous most, potz that Lies on ground,
Or maidens sitting stiL, but nothing naugh worth, or graue.
Yet a shame⁶ hit is with glanche on suche to bend our yees,
And hither turne⁷ our witz sharpnis and pliing mynd;
for to suche thinges a Custom make is wicked.⁸
Diogines ons whan saw he did dioχsipon⁹ in Olimpia race
In Charet Caried, not hable with drawe his Yea from woman fair,
but bak wrying and turning nek in casting on her Looke;

Another good plan is to pass our neighbours' doors without looking in, and to occupy our minds with something better worth thinking about.

In houses you see but pots and lolling maids: a shame to look at.

Diogenes ridiculed Dioxippus, when driving, for turning round to ogle a girL

---

¹ *Sic.*   ² "steps" written over "vewe" struck out.   ³ erse from Homer.
⁴ "hand," ὀφθαλμούς (eyes).   ⁵ "vewe" written over "abide" struck out.
⁶ "shame" written over "fowle" struck out.
⁷ "turne" written over "bend" struck out.
⁸ "yL" written over wicked; neither word struck out.
⁹ Greek word Διώξιππον, a proper name.

"behold," quoth he, "a wrestLar stout with wry nek by
   maid is won!"¹
The busy men you may behold to eche shew ther hed thé
   tur[n] about,   16
whan Custom and Care hathe made them ready to vewe eche
   thing.

No man ought to let his senses rove about,
but I suppos, that no man Ought permit his sence abrode to
   range,
Lik maiden that no bringing vp hathe had, suche as wer
   meet.

but make them attend to their work, and abide by reason.
but whan from myndz Care Sence² is sent to businis wark,
   Attend suche thingz and quicLy teL thy message answer;
And than againe in thy selfe with reasone make abodd
   and ther abide not strayinge out of office charg.

As Sophocles told how the Aenianian's horses bolted (Electra, 724-5),
but now hapz that wiche SoφocLes wont is teL;   24
   "And so as freed hors the bit
         that Careles³ hand of holdar
             did neglect /"⁴

so do the senses, and drug reason with them.
So Sence (as we have told) void of a guide or vse,   28
   furthe thé go and often drawe the mynd to that and more,
At Lengh hurLes him downe to breke his nek.⁵
Wiche makes that falsly said and brakd⁶ is of democratus
That of purpos he pluckt Out his yees, holding them to fired
   glas,   32
   and from the same reflection tooke, Lest that thé shuld
his mynd kepe shut and oft cal back to owtward Caus,
   not sufering that thé shud him Let, Left them at home;
That he migh bide in vnderstandings good, as shutting she[we]
   from windowes that to hie wais bend ther Light.

Those who use the mind most, are least acted upon by the senses.
but most tru hit is, that rarely thé do file what do thé shuld,
   that vexeth oft ther mynd with busy Carefull thoglt.⁷

---

¹ "τὸν ἀθλητὴν ὑπὸ παιδισκαρίου τραχηλιζόμενον:" Correct translation: "How a stout wrestler had his head turned by a tender maiden."
² The Queen has personified "sense."
³ "Careles" written over "sliper" struck out.
⁴ Greek text: "ἔπειτα δ'Αἰνιᾶνος ἀνδρὸς ἄπτομοι
            πῶλοι βίᾳ φοροῦσιν."
⁵ "to breke his nek," καταβάλλουσι τὴν διάνοιαν (on unnecessary things).
⁶ Bragged.
⁷ Meaning not well given of these two lines: τοῦτο μέντοι παντὸς μᾶλλον ἀληϵές ἐστιν, ὅτι τὴν αἴσθησιν ὀλίγα κινοῦσι οἱ πλεῖστα τῇ διανοίᾳ χρώμενοι.

yea Musis[1] dipe thé fur from towne did place,   40
And night as firmest frind to knoweLege great,
Thé titeld with Euphponen[2] name, supposing that suche vse
and ease, whom no other Care did Let or hindar,
Shuld haue great helpe to such things as seke thé did.   44

CHAPTER XIII.

yea, and that is not hard nor Cumber hathe therin,   *A third method is to avoid all places where assemblies of inquisitive people are to be found.*
As oft as men ban thé or Cursing wordes aforde,
No eare to giue therto, but as a defe man hard them;
Or whan great pres is in the pLace, to sit thè stil;   4
And if thou Cans not rule thè so, arise and go thi way.
For if thou feLowe Curius folke, no good therof thou getz;
but profit great shal thè bifal, if curius part thou shun,
with violence great, thou vse and vse hit may reason Lore.[3]
And profit taking from this grounwork and earnestar Custom,
Right wel shalt do if theatur thou do pas wher pleasant augh is plaid,   *Don't go to the theatre, or other noisy resorts.*
and if thy frindz do thè intreat to Comedie or game, deny.
Or if comen shutz about the ringe, witsafe not.[4]   12
for as Socrates did weL warne us to take hede and beware
Of suche meat as did prouoke the unhungrie man,
Alike he saide of draughtz suche without thrust to take;   *Shun alluring shows.*
So must we shun suche shewes and tales as intise and allure
Whan nide of them we haue not at all, but ar to muche.   *Cyrus would not look at the lovely Panthea.*
Yea Cirus wold not Panthea behold nor vewe,
And whan Araspus told him how she worthy was be seen;
"That is the Cause," quoth he, "why more I wold refrain her;

---

[1] μουσεῖα, museums. No equivalent to "dipe" in the Greek text.
[2] *Sic.* for εὐφρόνη, *i. e.* "Night."
[3] "thou vse," etc.: ὑπακούειν τῷ λογισμῷ συνεθιζόμενον (accustomest thyself to listen to reason).
[4] βοῆς ἐν σταδίῳ γενομένης ἢ ἱπποδρόμῳ μὴ ἐπιστραφῆναι. Probably "witness not." "Witsafe not" written over "turn not" erased.

" Yea, if I shuld thy CounseL folowe and go to her,
" Perhaps she woLd perswade me againe retourne again,[1]
" Euen whan my Laisur aught not be[2] to sit by her and Louke,

He had more serious work. Nor would Alexander see Darius's beautiful wife. But we peep into women's litters for bad ends.

" In leauing of more Serius hideful matters. "   24
In maner suche[3] nor Alexander wold darius wife behold[4]
Whan fame she had of beauty great and praised her muche ;
but meting mother hers, a woman old, the maiden fair denied.
We while ful sLiLy Looke in chamber of the wife,   28
thogh pentische Like the windowe built, we think no harm,[5]
The curius Care our owne we suffar Slip, to curious aL.[6]

CHAPTER XIV.

It is also a wholesome discipline not to look too closely into things which do concern us, in order that we may all the more easily accustom ourselves to ignore those which do not.

hit profitz also sometime that iustice may be don to pas ouer suche ded,
That thou mast more accustume thè to flie from that as wrong,
and that thou mast the bettar invre in continent sort,
Sometime forbeare the Lawful Companie of thi owne wif,   4
Lest another time thou be inticed to other mens.
briding this Custom in curiositie, prove sometime that thè doth touche, neglect ;
nor suffer ons thy eare to give therto a hede

Don't listen to folk's gossip about your own house.

And if a man wold tel thè aught don at thy home, diffar,   8
and from thy eares fur set what wordz of thè be said.
Edidpus busy serche did wrap him in most harmes ;
for whan of him selfe he axed as he no Corinthe wez,
but Guest, he met with Laius, who after kild he had,   12
and mother his owne in mariage tok, with whom he got kingdom,
with dowary hers, whan than happy he thoght he was,

---

[1] *Sic.* "again" written over "to her" struck out.
[2] "be" written over "permit" struck out.
[3] "In maner suche" written over "After this sort" struck out.
[4] Translation of "εἰς ὄψιν ἦλθε."
[5] Correct translation of these two lines is : "We think it no harm to cast an eye into the litter of the women and to hang on the windows." The Queen has translated φορείοις (litter) with "pentische," pent house.
[6] οὕτως ὀλισθηρὰν καὶ ῥευστὴν εἰς ἅπαντα τὴν πολυπραγμοσύνην ποιοῦντες, while in this way we only whet our curiosity, and increase our desire to satisfy it.

PLUTARCH'S DE CURIOSITATE.

Againe he questioned who he was,[1] wiche whan his w[ife][2] *See what trouble came of Oedipus asking questions, finding that he'd married his own mother.*
   wold Let
more earnest he, the old man as gilty he wer rebukd ; 16
Omitting no good menes to make bewrayd al that was hid.[3]
   Than whan suspect herof his mynd had moche distract
And old man had skrigd out, "O worthi me[4] whom nide to
   spike constrains ; "
yeat[5] kindeLed and vexed with Curiositis stinge made answer,
   "Compeld to heare, yeat heare I must."
So swet a Sowre hit is nor may be withstode Curiosities *So bitter-sweet is the itch of curiosity.*
   motion,
As wound that bloudies hit self while hit is Launged.
but who is freed from this disease and is Of mildy spirit, 24
   Nor gilty is of any iueL, shal thus begin to say,
      "O Goddis, how wise art thou, that dost forget *How wise is he who forgets ills!*
      the yl."[6]

CHAPTER XV.

Wher for against al this a Custoum must be made, *When we receive a letter we must not be in too great a hurry to open it.*
   that strait a Lettar broght may not be broken vp ;
As many do, wiche whan thé think ther handz to sLow thé
   ad to ther tithe ;
Whenseuer post do Come, mete him not, nor Let us change
   our pla[ce].[7]   4
If so hit hap a frind ariue, and say that some what he wyl *If a friend offers you news, ask for something useful.*
   tel him ;
yea, rather, if aught thou brings of profit and of help.
Whan ons in Rome dispute I made, a Cloin,[8] that Domitian
   after kild,
   Who envied muche the princis [Clown's] Glory, listening
      to my Lectur,   8

---

[1] "who he was" written over "more of himself" struck out.
[2] MS. torn ; transl. of γυναικος.
[3] "The old man," etc. ἔτι μᾶλλον ἤλεγχε τὸν συνειδότα γέροντα, πᾶσαν προσφέρων ἀνάγκην· (he pressed the old man still harder, and even severely threatened him).
[4] Translation of οἴμοι ; perhaps error for "woe to me:" "οἴμοι πρὸς αὐτῷ γ' εἰμὶ τῷ δεινῷ λέγειν."   [5] Œdipus.
[6] Line from Euripides, "Orestes"—"ὦ πότνια λήθη τῶν κακῶν, ὡς εἶ σοφή."
[7] ἐξαναστῆναι.   [8] Clown. In the text is *Rusticus*, a proper name.

<small>At a lecture of mine, the Emperor's letter came to one of my hearers: I stopt: but he wouldn't open the letter till I'd finisht.</small>

And in the while a Soldiar comming, Ceasars pistel gaue him,
A silence made, whom none wold Let to reade the sent,[1]
Refuse[d] hit, nor wold hit open tiL endid was my reading,
and that I had dismist my hearars and scolars ;   12
Wherin eache man did admire the grauitie of this man.
but whan by aL menes and ways he nurris shaL

<small>But if a man indulges his curiosity, it leads him to open friends' letters and do unfit acts.</small>

Curiosities maladie, and so shaL make hit stronge and
       violent,
than easy hit is not hit refrain and rule,   16
for that by vse hit thrown is [and] born to things vnLawful.
  Yea, the Lettars teare vp, and frindz secretz discover,
And sacred things behold whom no mans vewe aught se,
and steps setz in place unfit, and kingly wordz and dedes
    do serche.   20

CHAPTER XVI.

<small>Examples of the great hate aroused by those who make a business of curiosity.</small>

And tirans to, who ought aL knowe, ar made most odius
  by thos men who eares[2] thers and flatterars be called.
    Therfor youngar Darius the first some hirars he had,
      αυτοκυστας[3] cald,
himself mistrusting, douting others moe and fearing ;   4
but dionisians mixed amonge the Siracutions suche flering folk
  Whom in changest state, whan Siracusians found, distroied.[4]

<small>Informers are of the same breed as curibus folk.</small>

for flatterars[5] ar of kind and stoke of Curius line.
And Senthars[6] two inquire, what ivel another or ment or
    did ;   8
Yea, busy men iven wretched haps of neighbors thers do
  serche,
Euen suche as fals vnto ther share though fur vnloukt for wer,

<small>Impious people first get from curiosity their name: 'listeners to mills grinding.'</small>

And to the Vulgar folke hit teL abrode suche newes thé [seke?].
And said hit is that wrongged folkes[7] beare suche newes of
    curius vice ;   12

---

[1] ὅπως ἀναγνῷ τὴν ἐπιστολήν (in order that he might read the letter).
[2] Spies (and informers).   [3] Greek word ὠτακουστάς (listeners).
[4] Correct translation of these two lines is : "The two Dionysinses sent these informers to Syracuse, but when a revolution broke out there, the people seized them and beat them to death."
[5] The Greek word is "sycophant."   [6] Probably "censors" is meant.
[7] The Queen has translated ἀλιτήριον (wrongged folkes).   Correct transl. : wicked.

CH. XVI.]   *PLUTARCH'S DE CURIOSITATE.*   141

for (as Like hit was that famine had athenes plaged, nor
 ownars wold ther corn vttar,
but in night and secret sort Grinde thé did ther store)?
Thes walking about did note and marke ther milles noys,
 to Wiche ther names wer giue*n* alitern, propar for suche.
Of Like Cause thé say wer Sicoφantz cald and so surnamed; So Sycophants
for wha*n* by Law hit was forbid that no man shuld figues were called 'Fig.-informers.'
 gather,
Suche as the*m* found and broght to Light bar Sicoφa*n*tz name.
Yea that wer not unfit for Curius folke to shame the*m*
 ther[with],   20
If thé knowe them gilty of suche and Like andeuor as thé hold, Let the curious
Wiche hated most and Griuous ar to aL thé haunt. be ashamed of likeness to the hated informers.

[*End of the 16th Essay of Plutarch's " Morals."*]

[*This translation is labelled on back as follows, the dated entry being in the Clerk's hand,*]

Plutarks Curioscity translated in to English by queene Elizabeth: this beeing the originall and all writt with her one hand.[1]

her M*a*^{ties} translation of a treatise of Curiositie written by Plutark. & putt into English miter. begon the iij*de* of this Nouember, & ended the ixth of the same monith, & copied out by her M*a*^{ties} order to me the xiij*to* of No.

3 3.° Nouember. 1598
a°. xl°.

[1] This is in a more modern hand.

III.

Horace.

DE ARTE POETICA.

TRANSLATED BY QUEEN ELIZABETH.

If a painter put a black fish's tail to a beautiful woman, you'd laugh.	IF to mans hed a pantar wold
	   a horsis neck Conjoine,
	And Coulored fethers ad therto
	   With Limmes togither set, 4
	That face aboue of woman faire,
	   The rest fowle Like the moudy¹ fische,
	For suche a hap, my frindz,
	   Could you your Laughtar kipe? 8

Like this, is a book, whose beginning and end don't agree.	Beliue me, Pisons, euen to this tablet
	   That my book be Like,
	Whose vane shapis shalbe faned,
	   As sik mans dreames be wont, 12
	So as nor fote ne hed in one agrie.

Poets and painters take liberties; but they mustn't couple lambs with tigers.	"An Iniud power bold the poet and pantar had."
	We knowe this Lein, axe and giue the same ;
	   Not so the wild and tame do pere,² 16
	Nor of the birdz that Serpentz bride,
	   Nor Lambes fal from the Tigres tetes.
	Oft to beginnings graue and shewes of great is sowed
	   A purple pace, one or more for vewe,³ 20
	Whan wood or aultar Dians aught be drawen,
	   Or of running Streames in fairest fildz,
	Than pant the Riuer Rene, or rainbow seak,⁴
	   But for al thes hire is no place ! 24

---

¹ For "ougly" struck out, perhaps "muddy."   ² "pair," Latin *coëant*.
³ "Oft to" etc. *Inceptis gravibus plerumque et magna professis purpureus, late qui splendeat, unus et alter assuitur pannus,*
⁴ "seak," probably "arch," transl. of *arcus.*

HORACE'S 'DE ARTE POETICA.'

You Can perchance the Cipers trie present
    What botes to pant for gayne a foteles[1] man[2]
From broken kile to swim to shore.
    A pot ful Large was ment be maid ;   28
How hapned than the while a pipkin framed?
    In time let be what so thou wilst,   *Let everything have simplicity and unity.*
So that hit plain and One remain.
Of poetes greatist part, O father, and youthes worthy[3] your
    Sire,   32
    All be begiled by shewe alone of good.   *Most poets are deceived by appearances.*
While brife to be I Striue, skars understode I am ;
    And treting maters slite, I feale my Strengh decay ;
Professing Causis dipe,[4] my shalowe mynd astons, 36
    And Criping Low on ground, to safe yet fearing flawe :
Who so One thing expres in to to many sortes,   *The desirer of variety paints a dolphin on trees.*
    A dolφin on the tries[5] doth hange, and bore in streame.
So flight from fault fals into Lack from want of art. 40
    A Sely Smithe in Emilius Stage play, in bras,[6]
Wil nailes and silky heare with his pensel shape ;
    Vnhappy man in Chifist part of worke,
For wanting of skil to pictur all he cannot.   44
    Self same am I, if aught I striue Compound,
No more I wische than wondar of iuel formed nose,
    Or vew of blackist yee, with here of Likist hue.[7]
Take you that write a matter suche as equalz best your skil ; *You writers choose a subject that suits you ; reflect on it : and you'll not want copiousness nor clear arrangement.*
    And Long do pause on what your shuldars doe refuse,
Or what thé beare may best : who that he chuse[8] best
    understands,
Nor Eloquence shal he want, nor ordar cleare.
For Grace and Vertu shal he place, or forbeare ;[9] 52

---

[1] The Queen has read *exspes* (hopeless) for *expes* (footless).
[2] The Latin text is : "*acre dato qui pingitur*" (for pay gets himself painted).
[3] Or "worthe" : *digni*.
[4] The Queen here does not give literal rendering of the Latin text, viz., "*Professus grandia turget*" (He who promises great things becomes bombastic).
[5] "tries" substituted for "woode" : *silvis*.
[6] "A Sely," etc. *Aemilium circa ludum faber unus et unguis exprimet, et molles imitabitur aere capillos.*
[7] "No more," etc. *non magis esse velim. quam naso vivere pravo spectandum nigris oculis nigroque capillo.*
[8] "chuse" sub. for "reades" : *lecta eris*.
[9] "For Grace," etc. *Ordinis haec virtus erit et venus, aut ego fallor.*

So as what now be said, or what hirafter after shal
Muche he defars, and for the present time Omitz.
This Loue he doth; this skorne of promised vers the skribe.¹

<small>You'll succeed if you can make a known word new.</small> In placing wordz, if thou be skant and wary bothe,   56
The spiche shal florische wel and be estimed.
Yea, if new word for old wel sodered thou do place,
Yea, and nide be, with new shewe, the hiden yore expound;
To frame may hap some wordz that girdled Lethes² lack.   60

<small>New-coind from Greek words will be accepted.</small> A Licence thou with shamfast leue mast take
The new made wordes and faned Like Credit beares,
If from the Grikis spring thé softly be withdrawen.
But romane what to Plauto and Cicilius shal he giue,   64
If Varios Loue or Virgil hit be Caught?³

<small>Why am I envied if I make a few new words, when Cato and Ennius made many?</small> Why, if I litel get,⁴ nide enuid I to be,
Whan Caton and Ennius toung inriched ther weany (?)⁵ spiche,
And new names to ther matters gaue?   68
Hit Lawful is, and euer shal, a word assigne by mark to know.⁶
As primar Leues of wood first faule and chaunge to nirest yere;

<small>Old words die; new ones flourish like young men.</small> So eldred age of wordz turnes so to ther decay,
And youngmen Like the borne first florische and increas.⁷   72
To dethe we owe Ourselves and all we haue;
Whether Neptune by erthe be receued,
and sayinth in by northern winde the sailing ships,⁸
Wiche is a worke and act for kinge;   76

---

¹ "This Loue," etc. *hoc amet, hoc spernat promissi carminis autor.*
² Horace has "Cethegi."
³ "But romane," etc.   *quid autem*
        Caecilio Plautoque dabit Romanus, ademtum
        Virgilio Varioque?
⁴ The Latin text is: "*Ego cur, acquirere pauca si possum, invideor?*"
⁵ "ther Countries" and "ther mater" struck out: *sermonem patrium.*
⁶ This verse ends in the middle of a page: the next begins a fresh leaf. *Licuit, semperque licebit, signatum praesente nota procudere nomen.*
⁷ Here the Queen has mistaken the meaning, which is: "the words flourish and grow strong like youths."
⁸ "Whether Neptune," etc.   *sive receptus*
        terra Neptunus, classes aquilonibus arcet.

Or wither a coustumed marische fit for orcs,
Fede the Cities nire and makes them feale [1] the plowes waight.
Or streame change the Cours, the fo to frutes;
By Learning bettar way. All mortal dede shal end : 80 Men's works end, so do words;
Ne shal Our wordz knowe honor augh, nor liveliste grace. tho' some shall live anew.
Muche shal renue that haue bine falle*n*, and tha*n* decay
Suche wordz as haue bine reuerenst wel, if vse hit grant,
On whose beck bothe fors and fourme of spiche [2] depe*n*dz. 84
How Kingz and Chiftanes actz, and eke ther doleful woe, Homer has shown how Kings' deeds should be related.
In verse how thé in nu*m*bar be exprest Homere hath told.
With onjvend [3] [*impariter*] ? linked vers at first a mone thé
   make,
But after winning wische ther verdit thé haue won.[4] 88
What author yet wil Simple Eglogs Leue
The Gra*m*mars mastars striue, yet iuge the verdit kipes.[5]
Rage withe his owne stile ArChilocas hath used (?).[6]
This ma*n*ner vers the Comidantz and tragike bothe begun 92
WeL fitting wordz for bothe,[7] exciding vulgar Shoutes,
And mitist for the greatist, waightist Cause.[8]
Our muse Comitz to stringe,[9] bothe body and ther race Harp-strings should sing of Gods, Athletes, and Horse-races.
The winning WrastLar, and hors the first at stop [9] 96
And telz the Youngemens Cares, and frechat wines.[10]
Thes changes to obserue and Coulors shewed of work,[11]
If I knowe not nor Care, why Poete am I called?
By Sely shame chuse not to knowe than sike vs lerne 100
A mery play wold not admit a tragik vers ; Thyestes' supper must not be told in common verse.
Thiestes scene disdaines that wordiest vers decerns,
Be told in menar verse by pourist Comidant.
Let all things be as sorteth best ther place. 104

---

[1] "them" refers to "marische" and not to "cities."
[2] *norma loquendi*.   [3] unjoined.
[4] "But after," etc. *post etiam inclusa est voti sententia compos :*
[5] Translation not exact : "The learned contend, and so far the question is not decided :" *adhuc sub judice bis est.*
[6] "Rage," etc. *Archilocho proprio rabies armavit iambo.*
[7] The Queen has not understood "*alternis sermonibus*" (dialogue).
[8] Correct translation : "And born for action." *et natum rebus agendis.*
[9] ? MS. strange.   [10] *libera vina.*
[11] "Our muse," etc. "*Musa dedit fidibus divos, puerosque deorum, et pugilem victorem, et equum certamine primum, et juvenum curas, et libera vina referre. Descriptas servare vices operumque colores.*

Q. ELIZ.   L

Q. ELIZABETH'S ENGLISHING OF

  Yet Comedie sometime Lifts vp the voice,
 And wrotheful Cremes with puffed face [1] fights;
  And tragicke often moues in slavy gise

Poor exiles do not word complaints in foot-and-a-half long words.
 TeLeφus, eke Pelius, wh[en] [2] poore and exul bothe,   108
  Away throw thé, thes windblowen vase [3]
 And halved-quartered vers, do Care,
  If Care thé do with mone the Loukars-on to move.
 Versis faire do not Suffice, Let them be swite   112
  And suche as wher thé wyl may turne the hirars Eare!
 As mery man thé please, So wailing man Contentz

If you want me to weep, first wail yourself.
  The milddy Lookes: [4] if teares myne thou procure
 Thyselfe must waile, so shal thy misfortune yerk me.   116
  Ivel if you do your biddings place
 Teleφus or Peleus, or I shal slipe or Laughtar make.

A writer must take into consideration the position, temperament and nationality of the person who is speaking.
  For sory wordes fitz best a moning face;
 The furius thretful; seuere the dalear [5] wanton the graue, [6]
  For nature first us fourmed within ful fit,
 For the bent of eche fortune helpes or throwes to er[the?],
  In yrking drawes vs downe with wo opprest:
 Strait motions of the minde exaltz by toung exprest.   124
  If speakars wordz vnfit ther fate,
 The army all with skorne wil thé deride;

And be careful to preserve the historical conception of him.
  For muche hit doth auaill whir Dauus or Eros; [7]
 Or ripid Age or firs youthe in Growing yeres;   128
  Or ruling Dame, or Careful Nurse;
 Wayfaring marchant, Or plower of the griny fild;
  In Colchis or Assiria bred; in Thebes or Argus town(?)
 Or hiresay folowe, Or Writar, make thy matter fit for thé

Examples of Achilles, Medea, etc.
 Laudid Achilles do thou prais, hevy, [8] Ireful, graue, lerne
  shipp (?) [9]
 Lawes he denies euer made for him, naugh must gainsay thy
  armes fors. [10]

---

[1] "puffed face" *tumido ore* (pompous words).   [2] MS. why, *quum*.
[3] *ampullas* (swellings) *et sesquipedalia verba.*
[4] "As mery," etc. *Ut ridentibus adrident, ita flentibus adflent humani vultus.*
[5] dallyer.
[6] The furius, etc. "*iratum plena minarum ludentem lasciva, severum seria dictu.*"
[7] *Herus*, not Eros or Cupid.   [8] "hevy" or "hedy" subst. for "busy."
[9] Or hiresay, etc. "*Aut famam sequere, aut sibi convenientia finge. Scriptor honoratum si forte reponis Achillen impiger, iracundus, inexorabilis, acer.*"
[10] The last six words are interlined.

Medea Let be woode vnwon, Ino ful of teares,
Faithles Ixion, wandringe Io, mourning Orestes.   136
   If ignorant[1] thou aught to the scene committ,   *Characters which you have yourself conceived must be consistent from beginning to end.*
And darest new actors place perfourme,
Suche as thou first began, Louke to the end thou kipe.[2]
Ful hard hit in private sort the comme things declare;[3]   140
   And Rightliar shuldst thou Homers vers expres,
Than as first man the vntouch[4] and vntold to tel.
   GeneraL mattar shal be made thy private part,   *An old subject may be made original by the way it is treated.*
If thou stik not to Curius about the base and commen
        lines,   144
   Nor word by other like Glosar sure shalt thou vse,
Nor skolar like shalt thou sample thyself in act,
Whence shone forbidz thy foote eke Lawe of work,[5]
Nor So begin as Ciclicus writar Ons: 148 *A poet must not begin by promising too much.*
   "The Luk of Priam shal I sing and worthy war."
What fitting so wiede Chawes hathe promis now perfourmed?
The hilz ther frute do yeld, a skorned mouse is born.[6]
How righLar he, that fondly naught doth vndertake?   152 *The opening lines of the Odyssey are given as example.*
   "Shewe[7] me, my muse, a man in after tims of taken Troy
The manars of many a man that saw togither with their
        towns."
Who miss not smoke of flame, but Light from smoke to
        giue,
That thens he may shewe wondars great,   156
   Antiøaton, Silla, and with Ciclop, Caribid.[8]   *A poet must not go too far back with his subject.*
Nor Diomedz returne from MeLeagris Ruine,
   Nor Trojans war from his Granfathers shel[9] wil tel;
Euer to the end he hies, and to best[10] menes: 160

---

[1] ignorant transl. of *inexpertum*.
[2] This line *is* substituted for "Suche as thou first hast famed til end kipe stil." Here the MS. breaks off in the middle of a page, the next line beginning a fresh leaf.
[3] Ful hard, etc. "*Difficile est proprie communia dicere.*"
[4] *Sic.*; at first "vnknowen."
[5] Nor word, etc. "*nec verbum verbo curabis reddere fidus interpres, nec desilies imitator in arctum unde pedem referre pudor vetet, aut operis lex.*"
[6] The hilz, etc. "*Parturiunt montes, nascetur ridiculus mus.*"
[7] Beginning of the Odyssey. "*Dic mihi, musa, virum,*" etc.
[8] Charybdis.
[9] The Queen has mistaken *ovo* (egg) for *avo* (grandfather); for "shel" there is no equivalent in the Latin text, "*nec gemino bellum Trojanum orditur ab ovo;*"
[10] The Queen appears to have mistaken "*medius*" for "*melius.*"

Like as by notes the Listenars eares he drawes,[1]
That he despaires, intreting grace, he leues;
And So begiles as falz wit*h* tru doth mixe,

If applause is desired he must be careful to keep in mind the age of his characters.

That midst to first and Last wit*h* midst agrie.   164
Thou what I and people to desire, do here;
If nide you do a praisar, to the end suche as wil bide
Til Singar do afourd your Clapping ha*n*ds to work;[2]
Tha*n* must thou maike the manars of Eche age,   168
   And graunted must be Grace to Natures Changed yeare.

Description of the propensities of a boy;

The boy that Can pronounce his wordz,
And stedy his ground with sure pace,
Lips[3] for Joy to felow his Like,   172
Sturs vp his Color. Lets hit Light[l]y faL,
And changis oft in many a houre.

of a young man;

The berdLes youthe, at Last mastar Cast of,
Joys in horsis, dogges, and gras of open fild;   176
WaxLike rolled to Vice, to teachar Currt,
Late forsear of good, of his pence to Lavische,

of a middle-aged man;

Hauty, Glorivs, swift winged to leue that he Loved.
But eldar age, turning his Cours wit*h* myn*d* ma*n*like,   180
Riches sikes, frindz, to honor himself ingrafing,[4]
Well warning to do that strait to change he strives.[5]

of an old man.

Cu*m*bars many a one besige the aged man;
Or that he sikes thogh found as wretche he forbears,   184
And dares not ventur the vse therof:
Or that in feare or Yoy sort al things he vndertakz

All these different ages must not be confused one with another.

SLowghful a hoper, ydel, and gridy of change.[6]
Crabbid, whining, the praisar of passid time   188
Whan boy he was, a Juge and beatar of his youngar.
Growing yeres great auailes do bringe;
And passed gone as many do deprive.
Lest therfor agid part be giuen vnto the young,   192

---

[1] Like as, etc. *non secus ac notas* (Just as if they were known to him).
[2] If nide, etc. "*Si plausoris eges aulcae manentis et usque sessuri donec cantor ' vos, plaudite!' dicat.*"   [3] leaps.
[4] "ingrafting" incorrect trans. of "*inservit*" (devoting himself to).
[5] Well warning, etc. *commisisse cavet quod mox mutare laboret.*
[6] Or that, etc. "*vel quod res omnes timide gelideque ministrat dilator, spe longus, iners, avidusque futuri.*"

And mans estate bequived to the boy,
Let vs abide in suche as best agre and in ther time.

[*Endorsed:*] Her Maties translation of a peece of Horace *de arte poëtica* written with her own hand, and copied by me for her Matie the iiij^th of November 1598. and at that day I delyuered it vnto her own handes.[1]

Then follow some characters in cipher.

---

[1] The transcript here alluded to has not been discovered. The text is taken from the Queen's own rough draft.

APPENDIX.

SIR THOMAS CHALLONER'S TRANSLATION OF SOME OF THE METRES OF BOETHIUS, FROM A MS. IN THE PUBLIC RECORD OFFICE.

[STATE PAPERS, DOMESTIC, ELIZABETH, ADDENDA, VOL. 11, No. 121.]

TRANSLATED OWTE OF BOETIUS DE CONSOLATIONE PHILOSOPHIE.

The firste Metre of ye firste Booke. [*In Couplets.*]

I, THAT whilome with plesant witt cowlde jolye ditties make,
  Muste now, alas! with hevy harte but sadde verse vndertake:
For, lo! my Muses, all to rente, non otherwise endite.
How can we choose, with weeping eyes, but waylling metre wryte?   4
Yet, theis at least (as faithfull freendes) no terrour coulde affraye
  To be (for all my banishment) companyons of my waye.
Theis, of my happie lyksome yougthe ye glorye long ago,
  In withred yeeres & evell happe, do comforte now my wo.   8
For Elde with evells on his necke commes creeping wondres faste;
  And sorow hath his propre age when gladsomme yowth is past.
Vntymely horenes of my hedde doth stowping age resemble;
  My skynne do sagg in wrinkles slacke, my fflaggy lymbes do tremble. 12
O happie death, that makes no haste while welthy yeres abyde,
  And at a call to wofull men cowlde then espy her tyde;
But aye to carefull men, alas! how deaff she is to those!
  And cruelly she deyneth not the weeping eyes to close.   16
While Fortune with her trustles goodes did make me fleering cheer,
  Thou, wellcomme hower of my death, had whelmed me wellneere;
But now that fortune turned hath her fikle face to lowre,
  Vnthankfull lyf withholdeth me, and driveth of ye howre.   20
Whie did you boaste me (o my Freendes) a happie man soe ofte?
  He that is fallen from his state, stoode never sure alofte.

The seconde Metre of ye firste Booke. [*In* 10 *Fours,* abab.]

(1)

Alas ! the mynde yplonged in worldlye thoughte,
    How duske it is !
And lykes the darke, and settes the lighte at nowghte
    Her propre blisse :   4

(2)

So ofte as her ye blustring wyndes do throwe
    Which erthly are ;
And seeth no shifte, needes muste her truble growe
    Of worldly care.   8

(3)

This man, whilome that freely coulde discowrse
    All Heven at large ;
How Sonne and Moone and Starres eche in their cowrse
    Observe their charge :   12

(4)

And lyke a Maister cowlde their ordre laye
    How euerychone
Keeps in their moving sondrie tyme & waye
    By power of one :   16

(5)

Eke whence the wyndes with stormy blastes can reise
    The waves so hye :
What Sprite or powre this worldes steddy peise
    Dothe torne & guye :[1]   20

(6)

Or whie the welkyn riseth still to fall
    From Este to Weste :
What gladdes the Erthe in Spryngtyme over all
    With ffloweres dreste :   24

---

[1] guide.

152 APPENDIX. SIR THOS. CHALLONER'S TRANSLATION.

(7)

What gives that in the hotter tyme of yere
    The ffrutes be ripe :
And Grapes in Harvest for the belly cheere
    Do ffill the pipe :   28

(8)

Of all theis thing*es* the hidden cawses he
    Was wonte to serche ;
And yelde what mowghte the secrete reason be
    Of Natures werche.[1]   32

(9)

Now lyeth he dusked of his inwarde eyen
    As in a dompe ;
And in his necke the carefull cheynes so lyen
    Of worldlye lompe ;   36

(10)

That for the weighte w*hi*ch doth him grovelyng holde,
    He hath no myghte
To rise, but aye the foolishe Erthe beholde
    W*i*th dasled sighte.   40

[In this place sholde comme the thirde metre, w*hi*ch foloweth after.[2]]

The fowrthe Metre of the first Booke [*In* 5 *Sevens*, abcbcba.]

(1)

Whoso hath him sett
  A quyett lyf to lede ;
    And destenye
  Liste vnder foote to treade
    W*i*th harte so hye
  That neyther hope ne dreadd
His order lett :   7

---

[1] work.   [2] In margin in MS.; see next page.

(2)

 Not ones the threattes
  Of raging Neptunes yre
   With whelmyng waves;
  Ne therthquake, when ye ffyre
   Of Ætna Caves
  Vp to the Starres & hyer
 His balkyng ffettes; 14

(3)

 Nor ffyrye fflighte,
  That smytes the Towres with thonder,
   Maye him affraye.
  Why, ffooles, of Tyrantes wondre?
   Nys but a playe;
  Whose Rage wolde putt men vnder,
 And have no myghte. 21

(4)

 For ffeare thow noughte;
  Nor hope thow owghte; and then
   Disarmed is
   he spyte of angrye men.
   But fearing this,
  Or wisshing that; as when
 Thy waueringe thowghte 28

(5)

 Is not thyn awne:
  Thou hast throwne away thy Shylde;
   And cowardlye,
  As chaced owte of ffylde,
   Thyself doste tye
  The cheyne wherwith yhilde
 Thow mayste be drawne. 35

The thirde Metre of the firste Booke. [*In* 5 *Threes, same* aab.]

 Then sodeynlye me left the myrknes of the nyghte,
  And therwith gan my weakned sighte
   His former force recover. 3

154 APPENDIX. SIR THOS. CHALLONER'S TRANSLATION.

As when the rayny wynde that whourling Corus highte
 Hath made the Skye by stormye myghte
  All thicke of Clowdes to hover ;   6
The mistye Showres alofte do barre the Sonne his lighte :
 And er the twynklyng Starrs be brighte,
  Darke nyghte the Erthe doth cover.   9
If Boreas from his Cave be letten owte to ffighte,
 And putting all those Clowdes to fflighte,
  The hydden day discover :   12
All sodeynly the Sonne smytes with his beames arighte
 The wondring eyes of euery wighte,
  And sheens the worlde over.   15

[Here sholde come in, the 4th metre, which is alredye afore.[1]]

Th v[th] Metre of y[e] firste Booke. [*In* 11 *Sixes*, aba cbc.]

(1)

O maker of the starry Skye,
That sitting on thy steddy seate above ;
  Incessantlye   3
 Doste swiftlye welde the Heven rounde :
And makste the Starres that by a lawe they move
  To order bounde :   6

(2)

That now all rounde & full of lighte
The farther from her brother, dame *Diane*
  Doth dymme the sighte   9
Of all the lesser Starres abowte :
But nygh to *Phoebus*, aye more pale & wane,
  Her lighte goth owte /   12

(3)

And thilke that dothe begynne the nyghte
Tofore the Starres when *Phoebus* is to Weste ;
  And Hesper highte ;   15
Highte *Lucifer* an other tyme.
Behynde the Starrs arising in the Este
  Tofore the pryme /   18

[1] In margin in MS. ; see page 152.

(4)
Thow while the chilly wynter blaste
Hath spoillde the Trees, doste make ye drowsy daye
  The shorter laste /   21
And thow when Sommer hath begonne
His pleasant warmthe, hast bidd the nyghte away
  The swifter ronne /   24

(5)
Thy myghte doth { varye aye / allwaye chaunge¹ } the yere /
As when the leves while Boreas hath them clongen
  Have lost their cheere :   27
Sweete *Zephir* hem revives agayne.
And what in wynter was but seede, is sprongen
  To sommeres grayne /   30

(6)
So nothing brekes thy statutes olde,
But in the werke thow hast them tasked to,
  Their order holde /   33
Thus ruling all to certen ende,
Save only men ; thow lettest what they do
  Vnbridled wende /   36

(7)
For whie hath Fortune thus her will
In turnyng thinges now vp, now downe, so ofte
  Withowten skill ?   39
The payne that for offence besittes,
The Gilltless have : and wickednes alofte
  In honour sittes /   42

(8)
And harmeles ffolke with moste vnrighte
Ar of the Giltie troden vnder foote,
  & vertue brighte   45
Is hoodwynkte vnder darknes halte /
And laide is on the Juste, withowten boote,
  The wyckeddes ffalte /   48

¹ These two words in italics were intended to be omitted.

(9)
Noughte harmeth them their Crafte & guyle,
Nor periurye with goodlye lyes to paynte /
  But other while,   51
When Fortune listes her powre to showe,
The greatest kynges on Erthe, her tryces quaynte
  Can overthrowe /   54

(10)
O! now the wrecched Erthe beholde,
What ere thow be that thinges ylynked hast
  In league so olde :   57
No meane parte of thy workmanship,
We men, with Fortunes waves ar tosste & cast
  In steerles Shipp /   60

(11)
Be Steersman, and theis fflruddes alaye :
And as thow guydest all the Heven wyde
  In suche a staye :   63
Vouchesauf into that leage to tye
This Erthe alowe, that here may order byde
  With certentie.   66

The vjth Metre of ye firste Booke. [*In 5 Sixes*, abc abc.]

(1)
When *Phoebus* in the Crabb on hye
  Doth make the landes to reeke
    With parching heatt :   3
Then he that soweth the fforowes drye
  Must for his harvest seeke
    To Akorne meate.   6

(2)
Seeke never to ye pleasant wood
  The violettes to gether
    Of purple hewe ;   9
When wynter wyndes have waxen, woodd
  And ffildes with frosen wether
    Ar hore besnewe.   12

(3)

Nor seeke to croppe with greedy haste,
   For grapes in Springingtyde,
      The budding vyne: 15
For he that will of *Baccus* taste,
   He must till harvest byde,
      That rypes the wyne.   18

(4)

The tymes hath God himself so bounde
   To kepe their season due,
      By turne assignde,   21
Nor suffreth them their course confounde,
   Or shifte their turnes anewe
      Agaynst their kynde.   24

(5)

Whateuer makes to hastie waye,
   Doth owte of order ronne,
      And hedlong wende.   27
For (broken ones the sett araye)
   What Rasshnes hath begonne
      Forthinkes the Ende.   30

*The vijth & last Metre of y^e firste Booke,
which is made for this mesure*:

$$. \cup — —.$$
$$. \cup — \cup \cup — \cup — \cup —.$$
$$. — \cup \cup — \cup —.$$
$$. \quad \cup — \cup —.$$

[*In* 7 *Fours*, abba.]

(1)

The Starres brighte;
When cluddered thicke the colye Clowdes
Vnder a Cloke hem shrowdes:
   Can showe no lighte.   4

(2)

 The Seas calme ;
When sutherly wynde with his turmoille
 Sturres fro the myrie soylle
  The waves to walme :   8

(3)

 That erst myghte
Compare with yᵉ Skye for glassie green ;
 Mixte with yᵉ mudde vncleen,
  Withstandes the sighte.   12

(4)

 The smoothe course
Of Brookes fro the hills ; when Rocke or staye
 Falleth athwarte their waye :
  Will bounde & sourse.   16

(5)

 So Truth to,
If thow with a cleere eye wilt beholde ;
 Willing a pathe to holde,
  That leades therto :   20

(6)

 All Joye shonne :
Drive sorowe away ; wan hope forbere.
 Banyshe yᵉ Cowarde ffere.
  Ells art thow wonne   24

(7)

 To thoughtes vayne.
For clowdye & bridled is the mynde,
 Ledd with afection blynde ;
  Where theis do raigne.   28

APPENDIX. SIR THOS. CHALLONER'S TRANSLATION.

The firste Metre of ye seconde Booke.

[2 *Nines*, abca cdbdc ; *and* 1 *Seven*, abca cab.]

(1)

This skornefull dame,
As she apon a pryde
Liste turne the state of thinges
    To showe her game :   4
Her wheele abowte it fflynges
  Lyke Ewripus the ffludde,
  That shiftes so ofte his tyde.
    So that with ffurye woodd
Now overturnes she kynges   9

(2)

  So dradde before.   10
An otheres humble fface,
  (Full false) she liftes on hye,
That lay forlore.   13
She harkneth not ye Crie
  Of wretches wo begone ;
  Ne recketh of their case,
    But lagheth of their mone
Long of her self so slye.   18

(3)

  Thus playeth she.   19
  Thus listes she prove her powre :
To showe her ffolke a sighte
  Full straunge to see ;   22
One broughte in wrecched plighte
  And happie also be
Togetheres in an howre.   25

APPENDIX. SIR THOS. CHALLONER'S TRANSLATION.

The seconde Metre of y͏ͤ seconde Booke.   [3 *Eights,* abcd cbad.]

(1)

If asmoche as by raging blast
   The sea turnes vp of sande;
Or in the welkyn rounde abowte
   Ar Starrs that shyne by nyghte;   4
Of Good*es* somoche ypowred owte,
   W*i*th never stayed hande,
Thilke mesur full were allwaye cast
   That Horne of plenty highte: 8

(2)

Not yett for that lyke wrecches stille
   Wolde men leve of their playnyng.
Thoughe God all prodigall of golde,
   Their vowes streyte herde & gave   12
And heapte them hono*u*rs as they wolde:
   That had is, seemes no gaynyng:
But greedy of their glutting ffille,
   Aye galpe they more to have.   16

(3)

What Brake or bridell then may serve
   W*i*th steddy hande to staye
Of Avarice the prone desire?
   When drynking vp y͏ͤ fludde   20
Of Good*es,* sett*es* more the thurste on ffyre.
   He lives not riche for aye,
That, sighing still for feare to sterve,
   Beleeves he lacketh good.   24

Ther is no more of this yet done, my busynes otherwise occupieng my hedd & all my leys*u*re, by reason cheefly of myn office,[1] & p*a*rtlye for seeking how to lyve, being w*i*th y͏ͤ office further charged then releved ; but I hope er long to be vnladen therof, & more at leysure. And if you exhort me, I will go throughe w*i*th his metres all. I here that he is well translated late, all in prose.

---

[1] Sir Thos. Challoner was Ambassador to the Low Countries in 1559-60, and to Spain in 1561-5. The Calendar of State Papers assigns this translation, conjecturally, to the year 1563. Perhaps he alludes to his own "banishment" in the sixth line of the first metre.

GLOSSARY.

Accompt, *vb.* account, accompted, 86/54.
Accompt, *sb.* account, 123/56.
Ad, *vb.* add, 45/32, adz, 132/32.
Affraie, *vb.* scorch; affraies, 36/13.
Afore, *adv.* before, 6/15, afor, 66/5.
Afourd, *vb.* afford, 19/4, 73/25.
Agry, *vb.* agree; agrying, 61/15; agre, 149/194.
Aligh, *adv.* alike; aLigh, 122/22.
Allow, *vb.* approve, 21/6, 55/14.
Amase, *vb.* amaze; amasde, 23/45; amasid, 73/30.
Apeace, *vb.* appease, 14/44; apeced, 100/5.
Ar, are, present of to be, 122/19.
As, *conj.* used instead of that, 59/48.
Astone, *vb.* astonish, stun; astond, 43/1; astones, 90/14.
At lest, *adv.* at least, 1/5.
Augh, *sb.* aught, 137/10.
Auailes, *sb.* advantages, 148/190.
Aulter, *sb.* altar, 142/21.
Awry, *adv.* different from, 106/49, 111/64.
Axe, *vb.* ask, 129/8; axed, 123/14; axis, 129/21.
Ayre, *sb.* air, 67/66.

Baitz, *sb.* ? strivings, strife, 128/33.
Bakbyter, *sb.* backbiter, 9/45.
Balkyng, *sb.* 153/14.
Ban, *vb.* censure, 133/15.
Bancke, *vb.* bank, confine, 41/11.
Bedsfite, *sb.* foot of bed, 3/40.
Behoofuller, *adj.* more needful, 20/20.
Besnewe, *pp.* oversnowd, 156/12.
Bewray, *vb.* betray, discover; bewrayd, 139/17.
Bisetz, *vb.* besets, 61/18.
Bitte, *sb.* bite; bittes, 51/14; byt, 35/17.
Blatter, *vb.* prate, 129/11.
Blesse, *sb.* bliss, 59/57, 63/53.
Q. ELIZ.

Blissidnes, *sb.* blessedness, 64/79.
Blist, *adj.* and *pp.* blessed, 72/1.
Blotted, *adj.* degenerate, 28/38.
Blyndnes, *sb.* blindness, 28/64.
Boot, *vb.* to be efficacious; bootes, 10/82; bootith, 85/33; boutes, 88/1; botes, 143/26.
Bore, *sb.* boar, 101/28.
Bouke, *sb.* book, 133/9.
Boustius, *adj.* boisterous, 19/6.
Bow, *sb.* bough, 47/16.
Brall, *sb.* brawl; bralles, 83/52.
Brid, bride, *vb.* breed, 122/22, 124/26.
Bygnes, *sb.* bignes, 45/30.
Byte, *vb.* bite, 59/48.

Cach, *vb.* catch; cacht, 43/10.
Carke, *sb.* labour, 57/20.
Cartel, *sb.* challenge, 128/10.
Case, *sb.* stair case (separated), 121/6.
Cause, *conj.* because, 43/19.
Chatting, *adj.* 131/23.
Chaw, *sb.* jaw; chawes, 24/14, 147/150.
Cherche, *vb.* seek, 127/4; cerche, 57/17.
Chire, *sb.* countenance, 7/4.
Choys, *vb.* choose, 129/3.
Clift, *sb.* cleft, L. *rimula*, 88/130.
Cluddered, *pp.* gathered, 157/2.
Color, *sb.* choler, 148/173.
Conceite, *sb.* conception, 44, II/2.
Coniuration, *sb.* conspiracy, 10/87.
Conserve, *vb.* preserve, 71/47.
Convince, *vb.* convict, convinced, 11/121.
Couche, *vb.* set (of the sun), 127/6.
Coustum, *vb.* accustom; coustumed, 145/77.
Coyne, *sb.* coin, 48/30.
Craftes man, *sb.* artisan, 92/39.
Crake, *vb.* crack, boast, 39/7, 54/13.
Crooke, *sb.* bend; crookes, 102/11.
Currish, *adj.* stern, inimical, 40/16, 41/18.

M

GLOSSARY.

Dalear, dallyer, *sb.* 146/120.
Dalyance, *sb.* dalliance, 23/32.
Debat, *sb.* dispute, 128/10.
Decerne, *vb.* discern, 65/16.
Delyte, *sb.* delight, 45/23.
Delite, *vb.* delight, 65/12.
Deuide, *vb.* divide; deuided, 92/43.
Dew, *sb.* due, 14/30.
Difar, *vb.* differ, 116/8.
Differ, *vb.* defer, 91/16; diffar, 138/8.
Disagrein, *sb.* contrary; disagreins, 35/36.
Dolar, *sb.* giuer, 24/10.
Domar, *sb.* judge, 36/7.
Doulce, *vb.* soften; doulced, 16/40; dulce, 73/27.
Doulcenes, *sb.* sweetness, 43/2.
Doum, *adj.* dumb, 5/7; dum, 5/9.
Dusked, *pp.* darkend, 152/33.

Eake, *conj.* also 122/39; eke, 135/27.
Ech, *adj.* each, 10/93.
Egar, *adj.* eager, 24/13.
Eld, *adj.* old; eldred, old; eldar, older, 127/13.
Element, *sb.* letter, 3/18.
Elz, *adv.* else, 60/3.
Ensample, *sb.* example, 86/47.
Est, *sb.* east, 47/32.
Euin, *adv.* even, 9/49, 88/138.
Expulse, *vb.* expel, 49/3, 53/12.
Exul, *sb.* exile, 15/16, 89/4; exule, 15/4.

Fal, *vb.* fall; falz, 113/21.
Fals, *adj.* false, 14/36, 113/23; falz, 57/20.
Fame, *vb.* repute; famed, 25/18.
Fane, *vb.* feign; faned, 142/11.
Farvent, *adj.* fervent, eager, 83/50.
Faut, *sb.* fault, 132/25.
Felowe, *vb.* follow, share; accompany, 76/12; felowing, 6/10.
Felowe, *sb.* 1/6.
Fiar, *sb.* fire, 76/7.
Fiers, *adj.* fierce, 7/12; firs, 146/128.
Figue, *sb.* fig, 141/18.
Fil, *vb.* fill; fild, 49/45; fild, 49/44.
Fild, *sb.* field, 44/1; fildz, 49, III/4; fildes, 156/11.
Fittes (by), by turns, 87/99.
Flaggy, *adj.* bending, wavering, 150/12.
Flawe, *sb.* gust of wind; flawes, 4/3, 24/1.
Flea, *vb.* flay, flead, 100/15.

Fliinge, *adj.* flying, swift, 76/3.
Fliting, *adj.* fleeting, 49, III/6.
Fly, *vb.* flee, fleet; flyeing, 83/55.
Foli, *sb.* folly, 132/26.
Folme, *sb.* foam, 101/28.
Footeman, *sb.* pedestrian, 79/67.
Forbear, *vb.* forbear, 148/184.
Foren, *adj.* foreign, 50/34.
Forlore, *pp.* lost, forlorn, 159/13.
Forrowe, *sb.* furrow, 16/4, 21/55.
Fors, *vb.* force; forst, 60/4.
Fors, *sb.* force, 84/34.
Forsear, *sb.* foreseer, 148/178.
Forsles, *adj.* forceless, 7/12.
Forthinke, *vb.* repent, 157/30.
Fote, *sb.* foot, 7/2.
Fowle, *adj.* foul, 53/1.
Frie, *vb.* free; fried, 44/2; fries, 3/29.
Frosy, *adj.* frosty, 96/7.
Funeralz, *sb.* funeral, 72/6.
Fur, *adj.* far, 33/14; furr, 17/11, 38/33.
Furder, *adv.* further, 44/5 (prose); furdest, 36/9.
Furthe, *adv.* forth, 41/5.
Fyle, *vb.* defile; fyled, 95/159.

Gat, *vb.* got, 58/42.
Gayne say, *vb.* gainsay, 102/23.
Geayle, *sb.* gaol, 89/9; gial, 39/72.
Gesse, *vb.* guess, 64/99.
Gest, *sb.* guest; gestz, 83/6, 126/6.
Gives, *sb.* fetters, 81/10.
Glaiue, *sb.* sword, 52/25.
Glanche, *adj.* glance, 135/9.
Glorius, *adj.* boastful, 148/179.
Glosar, *sb.* glosser, 147/145.
Glutting, *adj.* 160/15.
Golfe, *sb.* gulf, 49, III/1.
Gote, *sb.* goat, 56/7.
Graffin, *vb.* graven, 134/10.
Gridy, *adj.* greedy, 126/9.
Griny, *adj.* greeny; verdant, 1/7, 146/130.
Grounting, *adj.* murmuring, gloomy; in Bavarian dialect, *grantig*; 1/8.
Guifte, *sb.* gift, 27/16, 35/40.
Guye, *vb.* guide, 151/20.
Guyle, *sb.* guile, 48/31.

Hability, *sb.* ability, 59/50.
Hap, *sb.* chance, 33/88; happ, 119/109; happe, 119/90.
Hap, *vb.* happen, 28/52, 111/55; happing, 26/44; happning, 91/11.

GLOSSARY. 163

Hard, *vb.* heard, 71/57.
Harte, *sb.* heart, 55/6.
Hast, *vb.* haste, 45/19.
Haver, *sb.* possessor, 33/3; havers, 52/30.
Hedles, *adj.* headless, 133/11.
Heede, *sb.* attention; hide, 131/6.
Heedely, *adv.* carefully, 70/37; hidely, 131/18.
Here, *sb.* hair, 143/47; heares, 2/11.
Hest, *sb.* behest, 57/19.
Hie, *adj.* high; hiar, 2/9; hie, 7/10; hye, 7/39; hy, 14/31, 105/6; hyar, 17/15.
Hie, *vb.* hasten; hied, 2/9; hyes, 55/9.
Hiim payre, *vb.* impair, 94/127.
Hit, *pro.* it, 3/30, 36/1, 63/47.
Hoiss, *vb.* hoist; hoissed, 124/32; hoissing, 100/4.
Hole, *adj.* whole, 42/12.
Holesum, *adj.* wholesome, 123/55.
Holy, *adj.* hollow, 7/7.
Holyly, *adj.* holy, 62/34.
Hoodwynkte, *pp.* 155/46.
Hors, *sb.* horse, 44/8.
Humain, *adj.* human; humayne, 8/9, 45/25.

Il, *adv.* ill, 128/13.
Indeuor, *vb.* endeavour, 11/120, 87/97.
Indew, *vb.* endue; endewed, 12/136.
In dide, *adv.* indeed, 133/26.
Ingraff, *vb.* engraft, 49/3; ingraffed, 25/8; ingrafing, 148/181.
Iniury, *sb.* injury, 9/35.
In sort that, so that, 122/43.
Invay, *vb.* inveigh; invayed, 16/31.
Invre, *vb.* inure, 135/1; Invres, 3/28.

Juge, *sb.* judge, 74/40, 76/22.
Juger, *sb.* judger, 112/107.

Kepar, *sb.* keeper; kepar, kipar, 46/9.
Kile, *sb.* keel, 143/27.

Lacks, *sb.* failings, 123/9.
Ladarwise, *adv.* ladderwise, 3/17.
Laude, praise, 53/7.
Launged, *pp.* lanced, 139/23.
Lawde, 53/68.
Lawes father, *sb.* father in law, 12/131.
Lest, *adj.* least, 1/5, 40/14, 49/46.
Lett, *vb.* hinder, 35/33; letted, 10/69.
Leue, *vb.* leave, 6/11.

Leue, *sb.* leaf, 13/19.
Lip, *vb.* leap, 148/172.
Lokar, *sb.* looker, 5/10.
Louse, *vb.* loose 33/5; loused, 13/23; lovsed, 30/11.
Lyk, *adv.* like, 12/131.
Lyksome, *adj.* pleasant, 150/7.
Lym, *sb.* limb, 64/87; lymmes, 31/40; limmes, 61/15.

Magnific, *adj.* magnificent; magnifick, 37/21.
Malice, *vb.* hate, 88/135.
Marish, *sb.* marsh, 37/17; marische, 145/77.
Meane, *sb.* measure, means, 25/14.
Ment, *vb.* observed, meant, 2/2, 6/19.
Middist, *adj.* most central, 93/71.
Minish, *vb.* diminish, 82/27.
Mold, *sb.* mould, heavy mass, 60/8; molde, 42/12.
Mone, *sb.* moon, 41/6, 54/6, 127/7; moan, 15/2, 53/11.
Monny, *sb.* money, 48/34; monnyes, 45/24.
Moude, *sb.* mud, 19/11.
Moudy, *adj.* ugly (Latin *atrum*), 142/6.
Mynde, *vb.* wish, 103/46; myndes, 20/7.
Myse, *sb.* mice, 35/1.

Naugh, *sb.* nought, 7/13, 122/28.
Ne, *conj.* nor, 126/19; not, 17/18.
Needly, *adv.* necessarily, 58/13.
Nether, *conj.* neither, 49/47.
Nide, *sb.* need, 148/166.
Nippingly, *adv.* sarcastically, 39/64.
Nire, *adv.* near, 65/8; nirest, 144/70.
Noyfull, *adj.* noxious, 31/38.
Nourris, *vb.* nourish, 3/26.
Nurris, *sb.* nurse, 140/14; nurs, 6/4.
Nurs, *vb.* nurse, 124/6.
Ny, *adv.* nigh, 89/3; nye, 79/57.

Of, *prep.* off, 11/118.
Ofspring, *sb.* offspring, 55/14.
On, *adj.* one, 124/9.
One, *adj.* own, 125/22.
Onely, *adv.* only, entirely, 44/9.
Ons, *adv.* once, 1/1, 19/8, 51/5, 135/12; onis, 125/3.
Orison, *sb.* horizon, 36/10.
Othe, *sb.* oath, 14/36.
Ought, *adv.* aught, 59/70.

GLOSSARY.

Pace, *sb.* piece, 142/20.
Pact, *sb.* compact, 42/22.
Palled, *vb.* paled, 13/12.
Pane, *sb.* pain, penalty, 10/30 ; payne, 94/128.
Parfaict, *adj.* perfect, 3/2 ; parfet, 62/18 ; perfaict, 69/9; perfett, 62/11; perfet, 59/75.
Partage, *sb.* union, 31/21.
Pas, *sb.* step, 124/30.
Paste, *adj.* past, 8/15.
Peaced, *vb.* loaded, French *peser*, 100/18.
Pears, *vb.* pierce, 105/4.
Pentische, *sb.* pentice ; pent-house, 138/29.
Perce, *vb.* pierce; pearce, 25/12 ; perced, 43/2.
Pistel, *sb.* epistle, 140/9.
Plage, *sb.* plague, 121/18.
Plies, *vb.* bends, 47/2.
Pliing, *adj.* bending, pliant, 135/10.
Plise, *vb.* please, 73/13.
Post, *sb.* messenger, 139/4.
Pray, *sb.* prey, 6/20.
Preestes, *sb.* priests, 11/113.
Preuayle, *vb.* prevail, 7/37.
Prevent, *vb.* anticipate, 120/16.
Prise, *vb.* praise, 94/123.
Prising, *sb.* estimation, 32/72, 57/5.
Profit, *sb.* prophet, 72/5.

Quarrell, *sb.* lawsuit (Italian *querele* has still this signification), 9/40.
Quyett, *adj.* quiet, 21/37.

Rabel, *sb.* crowd, rabble, uproar, 3/35, 134/35.
Rachelous, *adj.* reckless, 17/20.
Raine, *sb.* rein ; raines, 46/1 ; raynes, 15/12.
Rampar, ramper, *sb.* rampart, 17/20, 30/20.
Rauyne, *vb.* ravin, 7/38.
Ravins, *sb.* robberies, 9/36.
Raygnes, *sb.* reigns, 46/58.
Receites, *sb.* recipes, 16/39.
Reddys, *adj.* reddist, 57/10.
Reddy, *adj.* ruddy, 4/13, 26/1, 57/11.
Reke, *vb.* reck, 127/16.
Righter, *sb.* guider (Latin *rector*), 75/9.
Rive, *sb.* cleft, 57/6.
Rok, *sb.* rock, 121/15.
Rombled. *vb.* rumpled, 93/86.

Rome, *sb.* room, 8/8, 123/54.
Rondell, *sb.* roundel ; circle, 71/70.
Rowte, *sb.* multitude, 25/31.

Sacietie, *sb.* satiety, 54, VII/2.
Sagge, *vb.* 150/12.
Saw, *sb.* saying, 135/4.
Sawsy, *adj.* saucy, 133/13.
Scrapte, *pp.* scraped, 25/25.
Seld, *adv.* seldom, 35/36.
Sely, *adj.* silly, 4/22, 145/100.
Sent, *sb.* scent, 135/23 ; sente, 135/21.
Serenes, *sb.* sirens, 3/33.
Shamfastnes, *sb.* shamefacedness, 27/16.
Sheens, *vb.* shine, 154/15.
Shipe, *sb.* sheep, 131/14.
Shirles, *sb.* shrieks, 125/21.
Shirllest, *adj.* shrillest, 46/5.
Shop, *sb.* place, room, library, 8/7, 12/150, 15/19.
Sithe, *sb.* scythe, 44/3.
Sithing, *adj.* seething, 36/13.
Skant, *vb.* diminish, 18/56, 52/10 ; skanten, 27/19 ; skanted, 2/7, 51/10.
Skant, *adv.* scarcely, 124/30.
Skars, *adj.* scarce, 40/6.
Skaunted, *vb.* debated 125/11.
Sknatz, *pp.* snatcht ?, 132/15.
Skorned, *adj.* contemptible, 147/151.
Skrigd, *vb.* screeched, shrieked, 139/19.
Slake, *adj.* slack, loosened, dissolved, 42/15 ; slaked, 19/18.
Slipar, slippar, *adj.* frail, fleeting, 14/28, 26/15.
Slipe, *vb.* sleep, 146/118.
Slowe, *sb.* filth (Latin *cœnum*), 81/1.
Some, *sb.* sum, chief thing ; somme, 56/28.
Son, *sb.* sun, 5, III/5, 13/9 ; sone, 121/11 ; sonne, 118/30.
Sonne, *sb.* son, 28/44.
Sore, *vb.* soar, 76/1.
Sorte, *vb.* join, sort, 6/15 ; sorteth, 76/10, 145/104.
Sorte, *sb.* manner, 89/11 ; sortz, 83/8.
Souden, *adj.* sudden, 26/41 ; soudeyn, soudain, 56/20.
Sowered, sour, 130/22.
Sowernes, *sb.* sourness, 8/5.
Sowth, *sb.* south, 19/6 ; sowthe, 26/7.
Sparred, *vb.* barred, 125/25.
Stabel, *vb.* steady, 84/27.

GLOSSARY. 165

Starke, *adv.* strongly, completely, 126/13.
Steerles, *adj.* rudderless, 156/60.
Stile, *sb.* pencil, 2/2, 112/5.
Strait, *adv.* straight, 2/8; straict, 42/17.
Strait way, straight way, 59/61.
Strayned, *vb.* constrained, 25/35.
Sturd, *vb.* stirred, 19/12; stured, 24/2; sturred, 113/32.
Styrre, *sb.* stir, 64/107.

Tales, *vb.* tells, 69/15.
Tercian, tertian fever, 56/27.
Than, *conj.* then, 5/2, 6/3, 44, II/1.
Thé, *pro.* they, 3/20, 55/4.
Thè, *pro.* thee, 5/6, 23/43.
Thikky, *adj.* heavy, 126/26.
Thorow, *prep.* through, 12/154, 50/22; throw, 56/22.
Thralz, *vb.* enthralls, 22/10.
Thrides, *sb.* threads, 3/11.
Tijng, *vb.* tying, 46/4.
To, *adv.* too, 6/7, 18/45, 45/21.
Tothe, *sb.* tooth, 47/14; tithe, teeth, 139/3.
Trade, *sb.* kind, method (Latin *modum, ratione*), 8/12, 37/25.
Trouth, *sb.* truth, 53/9, 103/33; trothe, 69/11.
Trustles, *adj.* trustless, 150/17.
Twynkell (of the mind), flash (Latin *ictu*), 112/93.

Uniust, *adj.* unjust, 14/32.
Unshonning, *adj.* inevitable, 103/50.
Unwon, *vb.* inexhausted, unconquered, 2/5; unwoune, 7/4.

Vading, *vb.* eluding, evading, 2/17.
Valure, *sb.* value 50/40.
Venim, *sb.* poison, 6/27.
Verdit, *sb.* verdict, 145/88.
Vewar, *sb.* spectator, 56/25, 120/27.
Vnbounde, *adj.* boundless, 38/53.
Vniustely, *adv.* unjustly, 6/17.
Vnles, unless, *adv.* 54/18.
Vulousing, *vb.* unloosing, 46/4.
Vnsaciable, *adj.* insatiable, 23/26, 36/46.
Vois, *sb.* report, voice, 47/25, 130/4.
Vsde, *vb.* used, 10/83.
Vttar, *sb.* give out, 141/13.

Waight, *sb.* weight, 52/28.
Walz, *sb.* walls, 134/12.
Wan, *vb.* imp. of win, 9/42.
Wane, *sb.* wain, 90/3.
Wanhope, *sb.* despair, 158/22.
Ware, *vb.* beware, 123/10.
Way, *vb.* weigh, 82/35; wayde, 119/8: wayeth, 111/79; wayen, 26/36.
Wayle, *vb.* bewail, 55/13.
Weke, *adj.* weak, 9/30, 83/29.
Weldar, *sb.* wielder, guider, 14/44.
Wether, *sb.* weather, 67/54.
Whens, *adv.* whence, 127/8.
While, *vb.* wheel, 60/3.
Whither. *adv.* whether, 48/6.
Wides, *sb.* clothes, 3/11.
Wind, *vb.* scent, 135/23.
Won, *adj.* one, 74/56.
Wonder. *vb.* admire (German *bewundern*), 56/17.
Wons, *adv.* once, 4/4, 72/5.
Wontz, *sb.* customs, 3/29.
Wood, *vb.* would; wold, 82/35.
Wood. *adj.* mad (Latin *ferox*), 7/7, 147/135.
Wracke, *sb.* wreck, rack, injury; wrak, 11/96; wrack, 15/30.
Wracke, *vb.* wreck, 42/18; wrackt, 9/36.
Writ, *sb.* writing, 122/41.
Wry, *vb.* turn aside; wries, 2/15; wryed, 121/13; wrying, 135/14.
Wry sorte, Latin *vice versâ*, 89/11.

Ydel, *adj.* idle, 122/35.
Yea, *sb.* eye, 129/29.
Yead, *vb.* eyed, 134/30.
Yee, *sb.* eye, 2/16, 135/2, 143/47.
Yeles, *adj.* eyeless, 100/11.
Yeld, *vb.* yield, render, 54/7.
Yerk, *vb.* irk, 146/116; yrking, 146/123.
Yl, *sb.* ill, 122/30.
Ylynked, *pp.* linkt, 156/56.
Yplonged, *pp.* plunged, 151/1.
Ypowred, *pp.* pourd, 160/6.
Yre, *sb.* ire, 81/6.
Ys, *vb.* is, 102/29.
Yt, *pro.* it, 58/26.
Yuory, *sb.* ivory, 15/20.
Yvel, *sb.* evil, 122/45.

Zelozie, *sb.* jealousy, 126/25.

---

i=e words glost: *brid*, breed; *fild*, field; *gridy*, greedy; *griny*, greeny; *hide*, heed; *hidely*, heedfully; *in-dide*, indeed; *kile*, keel; *lip*, leap; *nire*, *nirest*, near, nearest; *plise*, please; *shipe*, sheep; *slipe*, sleep; *tithe*, teeth.—F.

The manufacturer's authorised representative in the EU for product safety is
Oxford University Press España S.A. of el Parque Empresarial San Fernando de
Henares, Avenida de Castilla, 2 – 28830 Madrid (www.oup.es/en or product.
safety@oup.com). OUP España S.A. also acts as importer into Spain of products
made by the manufacturer.

www.ingramcontent.com/pod-product-compliance
Ingram Content Group UK Ltd.
Pitfield, Milton Keynes, MK11 3LW, UK
UKHW041902230426
12049UKWH00001B/2